LIFELONG LEARNING AT ITS BEST

LIFELONG LEARNING AT ITS BEST

Innovative Practices in Adult Credit Programs

William H. Maehl

•

Foreword by

Morton Bahr

Jossey-Bass Publishers
San Francisco

Jossey-Bass books and products are available through most bookstores. To contact Jossey-Bass directly, call (888) 378-2537, fax to (800) 605-2665, or visit our website at www.josseybass.com.

Substantial discounts on bulk quantities of Jossey-Bass books are available to corporations, professional associations, and other organizations. For details and discount information, contact the special sales department at Jossey-Bass.

Manufactured in the United States of America on Lyons Falls
TCF Turin Book. This paper is acid-free and 100 percent totally chlorine-free.

Library of Congress Cataloging-in-Publication Data

Maehl, William H., date.
  Lifelong learning at its best : innovative practices in adult credit programs / William H. Maehl.—1st ed.
    p.   cm.—(A publication in the higher and adult education series)
  Includes bibliographical references (p.   ) and index.
  ISBN 0-7879-4603-6 (perm. paper)
  1. Continuing education—United States. 2. Adult education—United States. 3. Adult learning—United States.
I. Title. II. Series.
  LC5251 .M27 1999
  374'.973—dc21   99-6469

FIRST EDITION

HB Printing 10 9 8 7 6 5 4 3 2 1

The Jossey-Bass
Higher and Adult Education Series

CONTENTS

FOREWORD

OUR NATION IS IN the midst of an economic restructuring that is as historic as the shift in work from the plow to the factory in the past century. We are embarking on a new age, some call it a new economy, marked by advanced technologies, driven by computers at the speed of thought, and where knowledge is power.

In the old economy, workers were expected to leave their brains at home and follow the direction of management. Work was performed by rote or repetitive tasks. Unions concentrated on taking care of the bread-and-butter issues that affected their members. Management managed business. Workers were trained in the specifics of their jobs, and a high school degree was considered sufficient to provide a good life for one's family.

But all the old rules have changed. Nearly every job, from doing police work to delivering packages to changing oil, requires some level of computer skills. Employers now expect workers to exercise judgment on the job, work together in teams, and develop communications skills to clearly express their thoughts to coworkers and management.

Many workers and their families have found themselves caught in the middle of this transformation. They came into the job market under one set of rules, which then dramatically changed as an entirely new set of expectations was thrust upon them. Skills that had once served well for years became outdated. Today, we are told, a worker may hold six or seven different jobs with different employers over his lifetime.

But I reject that prediction. Provided with the appropriate opportunities, a worker may indeed have six or seven different jobs, but they can be with the same employer. Unfortunately, our society has not responded to the new pressures workers face for lifelong education and skills upgrading. In fact many workers themselves have yet to accept their need for lifelong learning. Government, business, higher education, labor, and the philanthropic community can do much more to foster lifelong learning.

This failure of action has led to one of the most vexing problems in the United States: whether our economy in the twenty-first century will construct a high road or low road to job creation. The high road takes us to good-paying, full-time jobs in which workers enjoy good benefits and can look forward to a secure retirement. The low road leads to part-time, temporary, or contract jobs that pay low wages and offer few benefits or employment security.

The U.S. Department of Labor (DOL) has already cited the dangers of low-road job creation. According to the DOL more than 25 percent of current jobs now fall into the part-time, temporary category, leading government officials to warn of a social time bomb waiting to go off as these workers require greater health care or near retirement without sufficient financial resources.

Adult education and upgrading of skills can help prepare workers for the good-paying jobs of the future; they are critical strategies for encouraging the growth of high-performance workplaces.

This new book on the work of the Commission for a Nation of Lifelong Learners offers a blueprint for government, business, academic, labor, and philanthropic leaders to open the doors of lifelong learning to all Americans. "Expanding educational opportunity has been central to the development of the American community," William Maehl writes in this book. He is right on target.

Maehl reviews the work of the commission and describes in detail thirty-four fine programs operated by institutions of higher learning, programs that can serve as models for the entire nation. Their characteristics vary, from Bell Atlantic's Next Step, which pays workers while they attend college, to the Truman College–DePaul University partnership to help disadvantaged adults in Chicago make the transition from two-year to four-year degree programs. But they all provide a wealth of experience to others in the field and demonstrate the wide variety of approaches that higher institutions of learning have adopted to serve adult learners.

Lifelong Learning at Its Best presents a coherent, well-organized review of the challenges that lifelong learning presents to the nation and the many ways that higher education and other providers have responded. Anyone with a special interest in the field of adult learning or who is concerned about preparing workers for new jobs and skills will find it a valuable starting point.

It is also an excellent companion to the report issued by the commission, *A Nation Learning: Vision for the 21st Century*. Indeed, this book represents yet another opportunity for the commission to get its message into the arena of public debate on this extremely important topic.

Turning our nation's culture into one of lifelong learning is no small undertaking. One of the fears I had serving as chair of the commission was that our report would be widely distributed, debated, and just as quickly, forgotten on somebody's shelf as it collected dust.

Slowly and steadily, however, the commission's work is reshaping attitudes toward lifelong learning and is influencing government policy. Vice President Albert Gore's very successful conference, "21st Century Skills for 21st Century Jobs," held in early 1999, was a direct offshoot of the commission's work. This conference resulted in many new adult education initiatives at the national and local levels. In addition it added to the public visibility of adult learning and to the debate now focusing on this topic.

I believe this issue resonates with many working Americans and eventually will be recognized by our government leaders with the same concern that they now demonstrate for K–12 educational policies.

Lifelong learning is necessary today for an economically productive life. But, as Vice President Gore said, "Lifelong learning is essential to good living as well as to a good standard of living."

The future will surely be dominated by new technologies and ever-changing advances. Changes will occur at a much faster pace than at any other time in human history. How do we understand and control these events so that we use the new technology to enhance our human values?

Lifelong learning is about much more than dollars and cents. It is our passport to a technological future that expands our human potential: the value of the work that we do and the worth of the lives that we live.

Lifelong Learning at Its Best makes an important contribution to this field and helps point the way for us.

Morton Bahr
President,
Communication Workers of America
Chair,
Commission for a Nation of Lifelong Learners

To my family

Audrey, Christine, and Peter

PREFACE

THE RHETORIC OF the learning society envelops us. Daily the media tell us that we have moved from the age of industry to the age of information. The knowledge revolution has superseded the industrial revolution, and information and knowledge have replaced coal and iron, the driving resources of the industrial age, as the elements of change. Fluid *learning organizations* are replacing the hierarchical structures that dominated businesses previously. What we learn no longer lasts a lifetime but must be replaced in a few years. Economists hammer home the message that an individual's life chances and potential standard of living are directly related to level of educational attainment. Consequently, despite some demurrer to this view (Brown, 1995; McMenamin, 1998; Rubenstein, 1998), educational credentials, especially degrees, remain a vital currency in the information age marketplace.

The recognition of the need for learning credentials has led to a remarkable influx of new learners into postsecondary education. The number of adult learners in colleges and universities has grown massively over the last twenty-five years, and it promises to grow further. During the mid-1990s, adult enrollments approached (and by some estimates, became) a majority of higher education enrollments.

There is some difference among commentators over what constitutes an *adult learner*. The most common definition, especially in statistical discussions, is learners twenty-five years and older. Others reasonably point to the fact that so-called adult characteristics such as independence and economic autonomy, can be found in people on both sides of twenty-five. However, in order to employ the existing quantitative information, most of which was gathered using the twenty-five-plus age level to define adult learners, this discussion will also use that definition. At the same time, I acknowledge that many considerations that apply to adults twenty-five years and older may also be pertinent to some younger individuals. Faculty, counselors, and institutional staff are strongly advised to exercise sensitivity and judgment in their work with persons under twenty-five whose life circumstances may place them in situations different from those of other traditional-age students and more like those of adult learners.

How well has postsecondary education served the new population of adult learners? It is fair to say that in providing degree opportunities for adults, *we know how to do, more than we do.* That is, we as a society, and more narrowly we as a profession of adult educators, have devised a great variety of responses to adult learner demands, but we have not applied them as broadly as they are needed. We have demonstrated enormous creativity, inventiveness, administrative skill, and dedication in providing learning opportunities for adults seeking postsecondary education credentials. The achievement has extended from nondegree certificates to doctoral degrees, has included content from liberal education to specialized professions, and has involved learners who are individually responsible, self-sustaining persons aged from the early twenties to the seventies and beyond.

Despite all the activity and creativity, however, we do not apply what we know as widely as we could. And often many educators are not even aware of the full range of possibilities. Many institutions, although they accept adult students, have made little or no adaptation to their special needs. Despite the scholarly publication of theory and practice in adult education, the plethora of associations dedicated to the spread of innovation in adult programming, and the recurring conferences devoted to the topic, many people engaged in education and even some specializing in adult education, do not know of successes already demonstrated. In preparing this book I attended many conferences, reviewed hundreds of questionnaire responses, and interviewed scores of people. Even among experienced practitioners, I found uneven acquaintance with the vocabulary of adult education innovation, with knowledge of practices that can shorten new program development effort, and with other helpful organizational learning resources.

Ironically, the resources of ideas, practices, and examples of success have never been greater than at the present time. Starting in the 1960s, but especially since the early 1970s, adult higher education has undergone an extraordinary period of experimentation and innovation. New developments have included special degree programs for adults, external degrees, prior learning assessment, competency-based learning, individualized educational design, flexibility in time and location, and planned experiential learning. More recently, the landscape of adult programs has been altered by the adoption of various forms of technology. We are also in a time of collaboration among higher education institutions and engagement with sponsors of adult learners to devise new learning opportunities. These experiences provide a copious store-house of examples from which to build new programs.

Lifelong Learning at Its Best is an outgrowth of the project For a Nation of Lifelong Learners and its guiding body, the Commission for a Nation of Lifelong Learners (CNLL). The commission was convened by a consortium of institutions and organizations that have been leaders in the adult learning movement since the 1970s: Regents College and State University of New York–Empire State College (ESC), the Council for Adult and Experiential Learning (CAEL), and the American Council on Education (ACE) (through its Center for Adult Learning and Educational Credentials). The consortium began its work in June 1994 when the W. K. Kellogg Foundation awarded it a generous grant to assess the state of adult higher education as we approach the twenty-first century. The commission was formed in fall 1995 under the chairmanship of Morton Bahr, president of the Communication Workers of America and a leading advocate of learning opportunities for adults. Its members included representatives from business, labor, public service, higher education, and philanthropy (see Appendix A for a list.) It met six times between February 1995 and November 1997 and also conducted four public hearings (in Davis, California; Miami; Chicago; and Dallas) and a focus group of college and university presidents (in Washington, D.C.).

The commission and its project undertook two tasks. The first was to take stock of the provision of adult learning in the late 1990s and to recommend actions that business, labor, higher education, public agencies, and philanthropies could take to advance it. The commission's report, *A Nation Learning: Vision for the 21st Century,* was introduced in November 1997 at a Washington, D.C., conference addressed by Vice President Al Gore. Gore subsequently convened, as a direct outgrowth of the report, the national summit "21st Century Skills for 21st Century Jobs" in January 1999. The second task was to collect information on adult learning innovation since the early 1970s and to make that information available to others seeking to initiate or adapt programs for adult learners. This book results from this latter effort.

AUDIENCE

Lifelong Learning at Its Best is directed to anyone working with adult learners at the postsecondary level. It is not a collection of recipes or easily replicable learning packages. Rather it is a resource from which to take ideas and identify sources of information that can be applied in a variety of circumstances. Although it draws examples from credit and degree programs, it should be useful to practitioners across adult education, whether working with credit or credit-free activities.

Persons who currently offer adult credit programs or who are considering initiating programs will find helpful models. Those already engaged in the enterprise may compare their concepts and practices to others' and find ideas they can import to their own programs. Those beginning new programs will find a generous menu of designs and practices from which they can select, imaginatively combining the approaches and elements that will work in their circumstances. From the institutions and programs cited here, readers should be able to build networks with other professionals to share ideas, solve problems, and possibly collaborate (for program contacts, see Appendix B).

Those who offer credit-free activities or conduct human resource development programs will also find helpful examples that match processes to learning objectives, lead to desired learning outcomes, accommodate the variable circumstances of learners, give learners initiative in their learning, and provide models of cooperation and collaboration with other partners in the provision of learning experiences.

Institutional administrators responsible for decisions about initiating or revising programs for adults will find useful information to aid their evaluation. The experiences of other institutions of various types may reveal options of which they may not have been aware.

Commissions, boards, and staffs of accreditation and regulatory bodies will also find this material informative as they consider guidelines for programs that vary from accustomed patterns. CNLL has urged accreditation and regulatory bodies to adopt innovative and flexible approaches to serve adult learners and to remove regulatory barriers that impede programs designed for adults (CNLL, 1997, pp. 21–22). The programs described here may not be effective everywhere because of current local and regional regulatory restrictions.

Faculty and graduate students in adult education and human resource development will find more extensive and detailed degree program models here than are available elsewhere. They can be a useful resource for either individual study or class discussion. Faculty in other disciplines who are working with adult learners will also find this book useful.

OVERVIEW OF THE CONTENTS

This book is organized in three parts. Part One, comprising Chapters One and Two, examines the challenges and important concepts in programming for adult learners. Chapter One explores the burgeoning lifelong learning movement and the threats and opportunities it presents for institutions of higher education, including the potential to apply more broadly what they already know how to do. Chapter Two reviews several sources of concepts and guidelines for creating programs for adult learners and describes a template for examining them.

Parts Two (Chapters Three to Six) and Three (Chapters Seven to Nine) discuss the needs experienced by individual learners and the contexts that facilitate or give rise to adult learner programs. The programs discussed in these chapters are grouped by themes or clusters of design or operation, that is, by shared emphases or circumstances, and also examined in terms of factors important to individual programs. Each program is discussed in terms of a recurring set of factors, although not every factor is present in every case. Readers will recognize that some of the programs might fit in one or more group categories besides the ones in which they appear. Such are the risks of classification! Yet, each program appears where it does because it illustrates well the characteristic under discussion. Four of the themes arise from learner experiences or needs: the need for individualization, for learner centeredness, for competency-based programs, and for programs for advanced professionals. Three other themes relate to the context or circumstances in which the programs are created or operate: collaboration among providers, responsiveness to sponsors of adult learners, and requirements for challenge and renewal (an exploration of the survivability of long-running programs).

Chapter Ten offers some concluding reflections on our collective experience in adult degree programming and speculation on future implications.

TREATMENT

The content consists mainly of a series of vignettes of presently operating adult degree or certificate programs that illustrate a range of models. An early steering committee of the For a Nation of Lifelong Learners project concluded that the project's exploration of exemplary practices should be guided by four program criteria: (1) programs should be conducted in the United States, because the project sought primarily to affect policymakers and practitioners in this country; (2) programs should be regionally accredited; (3) programs should be at the higher education level; and (4) programs should be credit-bearing sequences—leading to certificates, degrees, or other academic awards—rather than isolated experiences. Although acknowledging the value of many other forms and levels of adult learning, the steering group believed its research could be most effective if limited to this scope.

Within these guidelines, the project research staff undertook to gather information on as many programs as they could identify. Many programs surfaced from review of existing directories of adult programs, membership lists of adult learner–oriented organizations, awards made in recognition of excellent programs, and information from grant funding organizations. With support from the Kellogg Foundation, the staff extended this search through a survey of higher education institutions, asking them to identify and provide information on programs they offered. (For survey instruments, see Appendix C.) The survey responses were especially important for locating programs with which the staff were unacquainted and eliciting detailed information on program design and practices. As staff reviewed the body of information from all sources, certain clusters of program emphasis or approach began to emerge that eventually defined the content of the chapters of this book.

The final step in data gathering involved extended interviews with representatives of the selected programs, through either site visits or telephone interviews. In all, fifty-two interviews were conducted during visits to sites of programs and more than forty occurred subsequently by telephone. The intent of the interviews was to pursue some issues in greater depth than was feasible in a survey instrument and to collect qualitative information from persons working directly in the programs. Unfortunately, because of space limitations, not all the programs contacted could be described here, but the contribution of each was valuable to the commission's understanding.

This book presents thirty-four programs in detail, and some additional programs are alluded to more briefly. The emphasis in the descriptions is on concreteness and specificity. The intent is to examine complete operating systems that illustrate solutions to the needs of adult learners, solutions that in turn can be helpful to adult educators.

The program characteristics vary widely. The oldest one discussed here began in the early 1960s, the youngest in early 1997. Geographically, they represent most, although not every, region of the country. They differ in level from associate degree to doctoral programs. The institutions that offer them range from community and technical colleges to major research universities, and some are institutions specially created for adult learners. A number of programs are highly individualized, with most decision and control in the hands of the learners, yet some others are rigorously structured and paced to meet learner demands for predictability. The learners range from persons seeking technical or professional advancement to persons concerned with personal enrichment, and age levels extend over the full range of adult learners.

These descriptions were composed during the summer and autumn of 1998. Because vital programs develop continuously, some changes may have occurred since that time. Each section was reviewed by representatives of the programs, and many made corrections of fact. They also made other suggestions, most of which I incorporated. However, final responsibility for what is here lies with me.

The spirit behind these descriptions is to provide individual program cases in sufficient depth that persons working in other settings can judge whether a given program's character is relevant to them and worth exploring further. This approach derived in large measure from the steering group mentioned earlier. Some of its particular concerns are described in Chapter Two, but in brief its members shared a twin desire to express the philosophy and purpose of programs *and* to provide enough practical information about administration, finance, and delivery that would-be administrators could judge whether the program would be feasible for them. Hence, these sketches touch on history, mission, and purpose, and curriculum, but also deal with start-up and continuing funding, relation to the host institution, delivery system, learner services, follow-up with graduates, and future prospects for the program. Over a third of the programs make extensive use of distance learning and technological delivery procedures. Because the goals of the programs applying technology vary considerably, they are not grouped together, but examples of distance and technological delivery can be found in all the program description chapters. Because individual programs require an emphasis on their distinctive characteristics, not every element appears in all sections or is always treated in depth, but overall the same bones form the skeleton of each piece. It is my hope that this approach will assist you in selecting the parts that best suit you, and I encourage you to assemble them in combinations that fit your unique setting.

September 1999   William H. Maehl
Santa Fe, New Mexico

ACKNOWLEDGMENTS

THIS BOOK AROSE FROM a three-and-a-half-year project, For a Nation of Lifelong Learners. Recognition must go to the four institutions that initially conceived the project and then formulated its design, Regents College and State University of New York (SUNY)-Empire State College, the Council for Adult and Experiential Learning (CAEL), and the American Council on Education (ACE) (through its Center for Adult Learning and Educational Credentials). Gratitude must also be expressed to the W. K. Kellogg Foundation of Battle Creek, Michigan, for its funding of the project's activities, and to its program officers, Betty Orton and Roger Sublett, for their continuing encouragement over the duration of our effort. I must also give thanks to Morton Bahr, chair, and the other members of the Commission for a Nation of Lifelong Learners (see Appendix A), who guided the project with their advice and counsel.

Early on the project formed a steering committee of representatives from the initiating institutions. I was one of the members, along with C. Wayne Williams and Robert E. Kinsinger of Regents College, James W. Hall and Paul Shiffman of SUNY-Empire State College, Henry A. Spille and later Susan Robinson from ACE, and Pamela Tate of CAEL. My committee colleagues' many contributions to the study of innovative programs are reflected in the text. Others from the institutions who gave invaluable assistance were, from Regents College, Paula Peinovich, Mitchell Nesler, Carole Coyne, Laurie Greenwood, Marie Gerhardt, Nancy Fisher, and April Marinello; from Empire State College, Jane Altes, Timothy Lehmann, and Judy Richards; from ACE, Eugene Sullivan; and from CAEL, Thomas Flint.

I must also thank the adult educators from scores of programs who talked with me, gave me information on their programs, and reviewed my drafts for accuracy. I am particularly indebted to James W. Hall, Jerry L. Hargis, and John A. Henschke for their review of the manuscript and many helpful suggestions.

Special recognition for research support and electronic technology wizardry must go to my research associate, Tom L. Root.

Thanks also are due to friends at Jossey-Bass: Lynn Luckow and editors Gale Erlandson and David Brightman. They recognized the potential for a book early on and offered editorial support and counsel throughout.

Finally, I must acknowledge with deepest gratitude the support and encouragement of my wife, Audrey. This work would not have been possible without her patient understanding.

THE AUTHOR

WILLIAM H. MAEHL has spent his career in higher education as a faculty member and an administrator of adult degree programs. Presently, he is professor emeritus at the University of Oklahoma and president emeritus of the Fielding Institute, Santa Barbara, California. He received his BA (1950) and MA (1951) degrees from the University of Minnesota and his PhD degree (1957) in English history from the University of Chicago. He joined the history faculty of the University of Oklahoma in 1959 and also became a faculty member in the university's bachelor of liberal studies adult degree program. He later served as dean of the College of Liberal Studies and as vice provost for continuing education and public service. He retired from those positions in 1987 to become the second president of the Fielding Institute, serving until 1993.

He was a founding member of the Association of Graduate Liberal Studies Programs and executive secretary of the association in 1979–81. He has been a member of Council for Adult and Experiential Learning (CAEL) Committee on Graduate Experiential Learning (1979–81) and served on the CAEL/American Council on Education Commission on Higher Education and the Adult Learner (1981–85). From 1981 to 1983, he served as president of the Southern Conference on British Studies. He also served on the boards of The Alliance: An Association of Alternate and External Degree Programs and of CAEL from 1989 to 1993. He joined the council of the National Center for Adult Learning at its founding and continues to serve in that role. Most recently, he participated as principal investigator in the project For a Nation of Lifelong Learners, research from which forms the basis of this book.

Maehl has published on English history, liberal education, and adult education, and from 1980 to 1983, he served as editor and publisher of *Continuum: The Quarterly Journal* of the National University Continuing Education Association.

Currently Maehl lives in Santa Fe, New Mexico, and serves as a consultant to adult and higher education institutions.

PART ONE

MEETING THE NATION'S NEED FOR LIFELONG LEARNING

1

THE CHALLENGE TO POSTSECONDARY EDUCATION FROM AN EXPANDING POOL OF LEARNERS

OVER THE LAST GENERATION, service to adult learners has become a major part of postsecondary education's task. From 1970, the adult portion of college and university enrollments grew from under one-third of the total to over 44 percent in 1994 (National Center for Education Statistics, 1998). Some observers estimate the numbers to be even higher—perhaps a majority of all enrollments—because national statistics are based on a one-time snapshot of enrollment taken in the fall, whereas adult enrollment often varies throughout the year. Hence the total number may be understated in official statistics, and adults may actually be a majority of enrollments (Aslanian & Brickell, 1980, pp. 43–45; Aslanian & Brickell, 1988, pp. 10–11). Broader definitions of *nontraditional* learners, using characteristics in addition to age, definitely place nontraditional learners in the majority (National Center for Education Statistics, 1997a). Recent increases in youth enrollments have decreased the proportion of enrollees twenty-five years and older; nevertheless adults' proportion of the total will remain in the 40 percent range for the foreseeable future. Equally important, their total numbers will continue to increase (National Center for Education Statistics, 1997b, 1998).

The increase has been largely a phenomenon of the mid-1980s and 1990s. During the decade of the 1980s, when higher education enrollment was expected to decline because of a shrinking traditional college age population pool, total enrollment actually increased by more than 10 percent. Nearly all this gain came from the over twenty-five group

3

(Hughes, Frances, & Lombardo, 1991, pp. 13–14). The trend toward high adult enrollments maintained itself into the 1990s. Social and economic factors and personal preferences of learners suggest this growth will continue indefinitely, although perhaps with differing rates over time.

As a nation we appear to be moving toward a goal of completion of two years of college for the general population and more broadly distributed completion of four years of college than at present. The associate degree may very well replace the high school diploma as our basic national educational benchmark. Such an evolution makes education beyond high school an integral part of a lifelong learning system.

LIFELONG LEARNING AS A SYSTEM

Hitherto, lifelong learning has been seen more as a principle or organizing concept than as a functioning system of values, policies, organizations, and processes intended to provide individuals with access, opportunities, and services to support their learning from infancy to old age.

An early UNESCO statement puts the new goal eloquently: "Every person must be in a position to keep learning throughout his life. Education must be carried on at all ages . . . according to each individual's needs and convenience. We propose lifelong learning as the master concept for educational policies in the years to come. The lifelong concept covers all aspects of education . . . with the whole being more than the sum of its parts. Lifelong education is not an educational system, but the principle on which the overall organization of the system is founded" (Faure et al., 1972, pp. 180, 182). Similar views have been articulated by other sources. Peterson (Peterson & Associates, 1979) formulated them as a master concept (see also Dave, 1973, quoted in Cross, 1981). Peterson argued that in its broadest sense lifelong learning has been regarded as the development, changes, and adaptation in human consciousness that occur partly through deliberate action but even more as a result of the business of living, where learning may be intentional or unintentional. Delors (Delors & Associates, 1997) extended this concept to include acquiring greater understanding of other people and the world at large, based on four pillars of learning: learning to live together, learning to know, learning to do, and as Faure suggested, learning to be.

Yet those who work with lifelong learners have long sought a practice environment in which organized learning intersects with individual, informal, and unplanned learning experiences in a deliberate and complementary way. They have sought conditions in which, on the one hand, institutional or school-based learning becomes more flexible and adapts to learners, whatever their stage, and in which, on the other hand, the experiences, learning, and achievement outside the formal setting are recognized, and if desirable recorded, as having equivalent value. They have looked for a comprehensive and supportive system that encourages and supports all forms of learning. There is now a need for a more organized system of lifelong learning that fulfills these goals.

Two recent policy statements point in this direction. The European Lifelong Learning Initiative's first Global Conference on Lifelong Learning, meeting in Rome in 1994, enunciated this active definition of lifelong learning: "A continuously supportive process which stimulates and empowers individuals to acquire all the knowledge, values, skills, and understanding they will require throughout their lifetimes and to apply them with confidence, creativity and enjoyment in all roles, circumstances and environments" (Longworth & Davies, 1996, p. 22). Similarly, a 1998 UNESCO world conference on higher education in the twenty-first century charged higher education to embrace all forms of learning and to become an active provider of lifelong learning opportunities. Lifelong learning and adult learning concerns permeate the entire conference report (UNESCO, 1998).

There is a sense in these statements of an emerging concept that a set of services and support is needed that will ensure learners whatever opportunities they need throughout their lifetimes. It is in the light of such a proactive, operating system that this book considers lifelong learning. Further, because of the prevailing high levels of educational attainment among the U.S. population and the changing demography of adult learners, the discussion especially focuses on U.S. postsecondary education as the potential leader in providing lifelong learning in this country.

In the following pages I argue that postsecondary education faces both a great challenge and an enormous opportunity to serve not only young adults but the entire adult population. Universities, colleges, and other institutions can meet this challenge in collaboration with new partners in business, labor, government, and philanthropy. Yet to do so they must choose to make extensive changes in their accustomed policies and practices and embrace serving adult learners as a central part of their missions. Otherwise they risk being replaced by other servers ready to adapt to the new conditions and eager to take on postsecondary education's role.

Adopting a pervasive and systemic view of lifelong adult learning will require significant adjustment in conventional thinking. From its beginning the adult education movement has been shaped by a belief that human and democratic potential can be realized through increased education (Lindeman, 1938, quoted in Brookfield, 1988; Stewart, 1987; Stubblefield, 1988). Nevertheless, many persons, especially those outside the profession of adult education, still see adult learners as playing catch-up after a failure to achieve expected stages of education at the traditional age. Adult education has been considered a remedial effort to repair an earlier omission. Morris Keeton (1997), who chaired the 1981 to 1984 Commission on Higher Education and the Adult Learner, recently observed, "A moralistic attitude prevailed in the country to the effect that if an adult did not get his or her education at the appropriate time, which was between 18–22 for most, it was their own fault and completely their responsibility to make up for the defect if they wanted to. . . . From my perspective (despite some changes in outlook), we have great residues of practical consequences of the earlier attitudes and practices" (p. 3).

These comments are borne out by the persistence of phrases such as "getting an education" and "finishing their educations," which are applied to graduates, particularly from four-year colleges, whatever their age. The notion persists that education is a finite product or condition, normally obtained by early adulthood. Fortunately, new realities are beginning to change this view. Education and training are moving to the forefront of planning for the future.

These new realities are linked to the fast-moving pace of economic transformation, not only in our national economy but in the interconnected global economy. New conditions include the advent of electronic technology; the growth of services based on information and knowledge; the restructuring of the nature of work from simple, repetitive and less-skilled tasks to complicated team activities involving analysis, problem solving, judgment, and communication; and the need for workers continually to extend their learning to remain current in their fields. In the words of *The Economist,* "The new jobs in tomorrow's industries, manufacturing and services alike, . . . will require workers that are literate, numerate, adaptable, and trainable—in a word, educated" ("Education and the Wealth of Nations," 1997, p. 15).

As a result, education that was once regarded as repair of individual failings now is seen as a social need. Expanding individual capability through education now is seen to promote general economic and social well-being. For example, President Clinton's 1997 State of the Union message, which focused on educational policy, included tax and financial aid provisions that were explicitly stated to apply to learners regardless of age. In his ninth point, the president stated that "in the twenty-first century we must expand the frontiers of learning across a lifetime. All our people, of whatever age, must have a chance to learn new skills."

The president's views echoed the concerns of three major commissions over the last twenty-five years. The first was the Commission on Non-Traditional Study, whose report, *Diversity by Design* (1973), and recommendations still command attention among innovators in adult education. The second was the Commission on Higher Education and the Adult Learner, whose report, *Adult Learners: Key to the Nation's Future* (1984), pointed toward change and collaboration in federal, state, and institutional policy, some of which has been implemented. The third, the Commission for a Nation of Lifelong Learners, which met from 1995 to 1997, brought together an unusual array of stakeholders from public service, business, labor, higher education, and philanthropy. Its report, *A Nation Learning: Vision for the 21st Century* (1997), called for collaboration and change among all those parties to meet the dramatic new demands and opportunities for lifelong learning. It urged that we as a nation recognize lifelong learning as a national priority. Its recommendations fall in five areas: acknowledge the link between lifelong learning and global economic success, establish equity of access, incorporate new technologies in lifelong learning, rethink and reorganize educational delivery, and make resource commitments commensurate with lifelong learning's importance.

As this report urged, it is important that this nation create a comprehensive system of lifelong learning that not only prepares youths from their earliest days for a lifetime of growth and renewal but then continues to facilitate adults' learning beyond the traditional school years for as long as they are capable of participating. Our society can simultaneously build on the high base of education it has already attained and strive to involve persons who have not reached those levels. But first we must recognize changes in the population of learners, in their needs in the information age, and in the means available for them to learn. Many postsecondary institutions have already developed a broad array of adult learning models, geared to adult needs for flexibility in time, place, content, and recognition of previous experience. By applying and extending these already available resources, colleges, universities, and others can play an enormous role in making lifelong learning a practical reality.

U.S. EDUCATIONAL ATTAINMENT
IN THE LAST HALF CENTURY

Expanding educational opportunity has been central to the development of the American community. From Jefferson's comments about informing the discretion of the people to our present controversies over the quality and effectiveness of schools, a continuing U.S. theme has been the linkage between availability of opportunities for learning and the health of society. In particular the construction of a system of public schools and institutions over the last century and a half has positioned the United States as the world leader in years of education completed by its citizens and in individuals' broad access to learning. Adult education, a product chiefly of twentieth-century developments, has already made a major contribution to this general rise in the country's educational level. Further, a major theme in adult education theory has been that through lifelong learning adults can achieve understanding of the complex world they live in and can influence the world through their democratic participation (Stubblefield, 1988; Stubblefield & Keane, 1994).

The last half century demonstrates this achievement most clearly. The United States has made remarkable progress in increasing the level of education among its people since World War II and thereby has changed the quality of life for the broad mass of the population. In 1940, 13.7 percent of the population twenty-five and older had less than five years of elementary school, 24.5 percent had at least four years of high school and possibly some years of college, and only 4.6 percent had four or more years of college. By 1996, the corresponding figures were 1.8 percent with less than five years of elementary school, 81.8 percent with four years of high school or more, and 23.6 percent with four or more years of college. The change was even more striking among young adults twenty-five to twenty-nine years old. By 1996, only 0.8 percent in that group had less than five years, 87.3 percent had completed high school or more, and 27.1 percent had four or more years of college (National Center for Education Statistics, 1998). As a nation we are well along the way to universal high school completion and broadly distributed, rather than elite, baccalaureate completion.

These aggregate statistics mask some serious gaps and inequities, however. Despite U.S. progress in years of school completed, functional illiteracy remains a significant problem for many adults. International comparisons of educational achievement suggest lower levels of mastery among U.S. schoolchildren. Within the U.S. population, African Americans and other racial and ethnic groups complete fewer years of school than whites do. Serious high school dropout rates among Hispanic students have aroused concern for their prospects as adults. Although recent data indicate that the high school completion gap between young whites and African Americans may have been closed, observers with detailed knowledge of various underserved groups point to remaining inequities and specify the remedies needed to close the gaps. A revitalized commitment to lifelong learning at all ages must include an effort to eliminate these discrepancies once and for all.

At the same time, our generally high level of educational attainment is leading our nation to set a new universal threshold goal beyond high school completion. Demands for knowledge are also pushing us to ensure the prospect of perpetual learning for all who wish to engage in it. Our experience in attaining our current level clearly demonstrates this can be done. The challenge to postsecondary education is to respond once again as it did in the post–World War II period and the innovative era of the 1970s.

THREE EPISODES OF CHANGE

The same period that achieved such great increase in the overall educational level of the population also saw a much expanded participation of adult learners in postsecondary education. Opportunities for adults have increased enormously since World War II, or as Stubblefield and Keane (1994) put it, "In the half century since World War II, the United States entered the age of adult education" (p. 251). Led by the Servicemen's Readjustment Act of 1944 (the GI Bill), which financed education for military veterans, the attitude about access to higher education changed from a conception of college attendance as an elite privilege, available and useful only to a few, to the idea that higher education should be universally available to any who could benefit from it. As Bennett (1996) writes, "The GI Bill was a Marshall Plan for America, but one that encouraged innovation and change rather than rebuilding on old foundations" (p. 8). From Peter Drucker's point of view, the GI Bill is the strongest candidate for the kickoff of the global transformation from an industrial to a knowledge society, based on an increasingly well educated general population (Drucker, 1993, p. 3).

The development from the end of that war to the information age did not proceed at an even pace, however, but in three waves, each marked by new social demands for access and flexibility. The last of those waves is still in course, and it, coupled with new technology, promises to bring even greater change.

Post–World War II: Discovery of Adults

The postwar flood of GI Bill veterans strained higher education's capacity and ingenuity. Most institutions were caught unaware in 1946 by the scale of the pent-up demand for education after the long hardships of the Depression and the war years. Colleges and universities scrambled to accommodate unprecedented numbers and improvised to meet the demand. I remember being a young freshman at the University of Minnesota in fall 1946. Registration increased by almost 50 percent over the spring 1946 quarter, when it had already swelled beyond any prewar period. The teaching day stretched from dawn until past midnight, and the university scoured the area for additional qualified faculty, especially to teach a vast number of additional introductory sections. Without today's computerized control over registration, hundreds more students sometimes registered for courses than there were seats in the rooms. It was an exciting time of extraordinary demands, but the effort worked. And it was replicated throughout the country.

Many feared a decline of standards when the gates of formerly limited access institutions opened to so many. The reverse was true, however, and faculty were startled by the motivation and capability of the adults eager to seize the opportunity that had been offered them. By the early 1950s, the great numbers dwindled as the postwar groups completed their programs and moved on. Respect for the potential of adult students, however, had been established.

1960s and 1970s: Breaking the Mold

The pace of innovation in program design and delivery resumed in the 1960s and especially in the 1970s. Pressure both from younger students, who complained about what they regarded as static and constricting forms of education, and from great numbers of adults, who recognized their futures required more education, drove change. Innovators sought greater flexibility for all and especially worked to remove financial, motivational, and situational barriers that prevented adults from participating. New terms appeared, such as *alternative* and *external* degrees and *nontraditional education,* to differentiate the novel forms from the traditional mainstream.

It was this climate of change that led to the formation of the Commission on Non-Traditional Study. Its report, *Diversity by Design,* both defined and stimulated new approaches in higher education. Companion studies to the report described a three-step evolution of external degrees out of conventional programs: first through extension offerings, then through degree programs totally reconceived in terms of adult needs, and eventually through development of programs leading to *assessment* degrees, which focused on learners' competence or ability to perform rather than on the set of formal educational processes they had experienced (Houle, 1973; Valley, 1972; see also Medsker, Edelstein, Kreplin, Ruyle, & Shea, 1975). The bachelor of liberal studies programs of the 1960s exemplify the second step. The third step broke apart, or disaggregated, functions that higher education institutions had once linked inseparably: admission, provision of resources of learning, requirements of residence, socialization with other students, and certification or credentialing. Some called this disaggregation process *unbundling.* One specialist in monopoly law (Wang, 1975) pursued its antitrust parallels, and the concept of unbundling excited considerable interest for a while in the mid-1970s.

The external degree spread greatly during the 1970s, and variations on it developed. New institutions offering newly formed degrees appeared, such as SUNY-Empire State College, the New York Regents External Degree Program (later Regents College), Thomas Edison State College, Minnesota Metropolitan University, and the Union for Experimenting Colleges and Universities. They were joined by advanced degree institutions, such as the Fielding, Saybrook, and Union Institutes and Walden University. Other external degree programs appeared in existing institutions. By the end of the 1970s, a study on the acceptance of external degree graduates' credentials elicited responses from 244 separate external degree programs then in existence (Sharp & Sosdian, 1979).

One commentator (Martin, 1978–1979) observed, without any regret, that higher education was bifurcating into a two-track system with elitist traditional and more accessible and broadly educational nontraditional sectors. He believed the egalitarian and change values of the nontraditional sector had entrenched themselves at that time, although mistrust between the sectors still remained.

One place this division could be found was among the providers of education for adults. Those most closely allied with traditional institutional structures through extension or continuing education programs remained largely skeptical of the more radical innovations favored by those teaching in programs based on assessment, competence outcomes, and high degrees of learner self-direction. The latter also tended to have different prior experiences and perspectives.

By the late 1970s, interest in these innovations began to fade in the mainstream higher education community, although not among the innovators themselves. Martin (1978–1979) was already observing that the impetus to change arising from student unrest had abated. Some believed that the issues of adult learning had been addressed by the changes that had already occurred. The previous rash of reports on adult learning dwindled to a trickle by the early 1980s, and the later ones usually came from associations with a special mission to adults. One of the last in this period was the report of the Commission on Higher Education and the Adult Learner (1984). Fewer sessions devoted to adult learners or nontraditional innovations appeared on professional meeting programs, and funding agencies began to turn their attention elsewhere.

Yet some educators and policymakers believed more change was desirable. The awareness that lingering myths still impeded higher education's response to changed conditions prompted a critique by one of the nation's leaders in academic accreditation (Millard, 1991). And, although not speaking directly to adult learning, Ernest Boyer lamented the decline of a "network of nontraditional institutions" that experimented and introduced new methods (The Carnegie Foundation for the Advancement of Teaching, 1994, p. viii).

Late 1980s to 1990s: National Well-Being

By the late 1980s and early 1990s, demographic reality began to reverse the waning interest in adult learners. As predictions had forecast for many years, youth enrollments declined as the last of the baby boom generation reached college age in the early 1980s and moved on. Colleges and universities avoided the expected enrollment crisis, however, thanks to an influx of adult learners, who more than replaced the missing traditional students. Instead of falling, overall enrollment increased by 10 percent, nearly all due to the entry of adults (Hughes et al., 1991). A number of factors contributed to this growth—more women were preparing to reenter employment, more individuals were in transition as a result of downsizing, more workers were becoming aware of their need to increase skills, more people were coming to believe in the value of academic credentials for employment, and more older persons were developing an interest in personal improvement. By the mid-1990s, the continuing increase in adult enrollment and the repeated calls from business and labor leaders and public authorities for more educational opportunity upon which to build economic development and social equity had brought a renewed recognition of the importance of adult learners.

In the face of this interest more institutions saw the value of adding programs for adults. In particular many smaller independent colleges, which felt threatened by the combination of declining youth enrollment and increasing costs, broadened their missions to serve the new audience. They borrowed from models already in existence, but they also added such new approaches as degree completion packages and cohort systems. The gap between the traditional and nontraditional sectors began to close, and more institutions became interested in providing for adults. Echoes of the exclusively traditional perspective remain, but once again many institutions recognize the need for initiative and experimentation in adult programs.

A MISMATCH OF PARTNERS?

How ready are educators beyond the high school level to reach out to adult learners? The answer appears to be mixed. Some would argue that the response has already been made, as evidenced by the absorption of so many new enrollees by higher education in the last decade or so. Unquestionably, a great many programs and services have been added to institutional offerings in response to the presence of older students on campus. Experimentation and innovation continue to develop and offer models that can be adopted by others.

At the same time, there are signs that much of higher education has turned its principal attention back to younger students just as the new challenge of adult learners presents itself most urgently. Intense discussion and ferment, such as that fostered by the Commission on Non-Traditional Study, accompanied the last period of major innovation in the 1970s, but that interest declined in the early 1980s. Seldom anymore do conference sessions or higher education policy discussions deal with issues of adult learners. After the earlier attention to adult and nontraditional learner needs, much of policy discussion has slipped back to the youth paradigm and proceeds as though traditional age students were the only audience.

To assess awareness of and concern for the rising numbers of adults entering higher education institutions, Commission for a Nation of Lifelong Learners staff reviewed as many policy statements and other documents from national higher education organizations as they could obtain for the post-1984 period (that is, since the report of the Commission on Higher Education and the Adult Learner). To compare higher education's concern for adult learning with that of other sectors, they also sampled statements from sources outside higher education. In all, staff reviewed more than seventy publications.

These documents fell into three major groups: (1) statements of major associations or study groups with a general interest in higher education, (2) statements from higher education associations with a special mission to adult learners or expressing special concern, and (3) statements from bodies or study groups outside higher education.

Silence of the Mainstream

The documents from major higher education sources included several important national reports and statements from major national higher education associations and national public agencies. Many acknowledged the growing presence of adult learners and the importance of lifelong learning. Yet, almost without exception, they concentrated their recommendations elsewhere and did not propose action on behalf of the swelling new population. Despite the intense attention given to adult learners until the mid-1980s, including their distinctive needs in curriculum, program delivery, student services, and financial aid, adult learners' concerns rarely appeared in these inquiries and recommendations of the late 1980s or 1990s (see, for example, Education Commission of the States Task Force on State Policy and Independent Higher Education, 1990; Association of Governing Boards of Universities and Colleges, 1992, 1994; Breneman, 1995). In some cases the discussions went to the point of recommending that admission be rationed by age, with younger learners coming first. This perspective has carried over into public policy in California through an enrollment triage that prefers younger learners and in New York through reduction of financial aid that had primarily benefited adults.

A Mission to Adult Learners

The principal exceptions to these views in the higher education community were found in the materials of associations that either solely or substantially addressed adults in their missions. They included the chief voice of higher education, the American Council on Education, and various of its divisions (see Business-Higher Education Council, 1988; Labor-Higher Education Council, 1992). Others included the National

University Continuing Education Association (NUCEA, now UCEA) (1993a), the American Association of Community Colleges (AACC) (1993), and the American Association of State Colleges and Universities (AASCU) (1986). All addressed adult learners in their policy concerns and spoke out on adults' behalf. A report from the National Association of College and University Business Officers (NACUBO) made an unusually strong statement about the rapidly shifting demography of higher education enrollments, arguing that these trends were "causing a paradigm shift in higher education" that was moving it "from its historic identity as a provider of discrete learning experience for young people to a new identity as a provider of lifelong education to adults engaged in the workforce" (Hughes et al., 1991, p. 50).

From Outside the Academy

Observers outside higher education have also noted the rising interest in learning among adults. For at least a decade reports and recommendations emanating from nonprofit and corporate entities have exhorted educational institutions, and particularly postsecondary education institutions, to be more proactive in providing for workforce development and adult learning. In 1987, the Hudson Institute's report, *Workforce 2000,* listed "improving workers' education and skills" as one of its six urgent issues, remarking that "between now [1987] and the year 2000, for the first time in history, a majority of all new jobs will require postsecondary education. Many professions will require nearly a decade of study following high school, and even the least skilled jobs will require a command of reading, computing, and thinking that was once necessary only for the professions" (Johnston & Packer, 1987, p. 116).

Workforce 2020 (Judy & D'Amico, 1997), an update of *Workforce 2000,* made an equally strong case for the importance of improved workforce education, although its greatest concern was education at the K–12 level.

Reports in the late 1980s and the 1990s have echoed these views. The Commission on the Skills of the American Workforce (1990) determined that we have a choice between high skills and low wages, depending on whether or not we adopt a policy of higher educational standards and lifelong education for workforce preparation. Other warnings and exhortations followed. A Twentieth Century Fund task force report recently reaffirmed that "lifelong learning that continuously enhances the skills and knowledge of *all* workers is essential if the benefits of a growing economic pie are to be shared with a larger portion of the population" (Van Horn, 1996, pp. 3–4). Carnevale (1998) reports that "today, a 'family wage' requires two earners, each with at least a high school diploma and two years of postsecondary education. Almost seven in 10 job openings now require postsecondary degrees or certificates" (p. 14).

A special subset of such statements address small businesses. The largest growth in our economy, the majority of employment, and the overwhelming majority of initial employment occur in small to midsize businesses. Yet smaller businesses have the least awareness of the benefits of workforce development, the least information about possible resources for employee growth, and the fewest discretionary funds to devote to education and training. Workers in companies with fewer than fifty employees are far less likely to receive company-provided training than workers in larger companies (Carnevale, 1998). A group of groundbreaking studies of this sector in 1992 illustrated the need but also revealed a widely held view among employers that educational institutions were not responsive to them (Bassi, 1992; Chisman, 1992). An appeal for more worker education and training in small businesses came from the Modernization Forum's Skills Commission (1992), and statements from representatives of the National Association of Manufacturers reinforce this view, arguing that each year of additional education beyond high school increases both productivity and earnings (Carnevale, 1998; "The Multifaceted Returns to Education," 1998; "The U.S. Labor Market," 1998).

CONDITIONS OF PERMANENT CHANGE

Four new conditions are propelling the rapid growth in adult learner needs: the changing demographics of the adult learner population, the increasingly competitive and globally oriented economy, the increasing availability of learning resources due to new technology, and the now permanent need to engage in learning.

Changing Demography of Adult Learners

It is important to understand the present makeup of the burgeoning population of adult learners, who want to carry their learning forward but who encounter a host of barriers. The new adult learner population is heterogeneous, with more varied needs than adult students had in the past. Because of their massive numbers, they possess a full range of learning needs, circumstances, and preferences. For a considerable number educational offerings in traditional settings and at traditional times and locations can serve them well. Many others, however, are unable or unwilling to participate unless greater flexibility and recognition of their adult characteristics are available.

The transformation of women from a minority in the traditional student population (32 percent in 1950) to a majority (55 percent in 1990) is one of the most spectacular changes of the last generation (Hughes et al., 1991, pp. 1–18). This is a trend among women adult learners as well. Women over the age of thirty-five are one and a half times more likely to be enrolled than men. They are also more likely to have sole responsibility for dependents, either children or adult relatives. Many of these women return to higher education after an interruption in their education, and a larger proportion of women than of men attend part time.

Part-timers are an increasing element in the higher education population overall as well. Between 1970 and 1990, part-time enrollment doubled whereas full-time enrollment grew by only 34 percent. Age makes a major difference in part-time enrollment. In the early 1990s, 75 percent of part-time students as contrasted with 22 percent of full-timers were over the age of twenty-four. Adult part-timers are more likely to work and less likely to receive financial aid; the majority enroll in public two-year colleges—3.2 million of the total 4.9 million part-time undergraduates in all colleges (O'Brien, 1992, p. 8).

Rates of participation in adult learning are uneven among various demographic groups; however, there is a strong likelihood that the next decade will see significant growth among adult students in currently underrepresented racial and ethnic groups and among non-English-speaking immigrants. With the declining proportion of white males in the general population, women and ethnically diverse persons will make up an increasing proportion of the emerging workforce. We can anticipate that like women over the last two decades, adults in other groups that delayed education at an earlier age will now seek additional learning to become full players in the information-based economy. Signs of this trend are appearing in some of the recent analyses of undergraduate enrollments by race and age, which show an increased proportion of participation for some ethnic groups by individuals over the age of twenty-five in comparison to youths (National Center for Education Statistics, 1997a). In some regions of the country with high immigrant populations, institutions have already designed programs to assist immigrants in integrating into U.S. society. Program content ranges from English as a second language to revalidation of the credentials of high-level professionals who earned their initial quali-fication outside the United States. In other cases more remains to be done (Fujimoto, 1992; Kerschner, 1992; Gray, Rolph, & Melamid, 1996; Vernez & Abrahamse, 1996).

The model envisioned in the 1960s of returning to education through-out life is becoming a reality. Rather than accumulating a lifetime stock of learning during adolescence and young adulthood, today's adults find they need to return to organized learning at many points in their lives. However, unlike the earlier conception of *recurrent education,* which alternated full-time work with full-time study, the method most persons now try is to do both concurrently. In addition, they have be-come aware that they acquire learning informally through work experi-ences, community involvement, leisure pursuits, and other activities. They would like to apply that learning toward formal credentials.

Another factor is that the entire U.S. population is becoming older, with a smaller proportion of youths and a higher proportion of young adult, middle-aged, and elderly people. Despite the echo of the post–World War II baby boom that is now increasing school and college enrollments after a period of decline in traditional age students, the long-term trends are toward an older population overall. Further, the baby boomers have passed into adulthood, and those at their front edge are now reaching middle age. This generation was better educated than any previous cohort in our society, and so will be their successors. More boomers completed high school and earned first college degrees than members of any previous group did. Prior education is a strong in-dicator of the likelihood that persons will seek further education. This group appears to have a predilection toward education (Cross, 1981).

The large numbers of the population shifting into middle or older age need a wide range of educational choices that serve those stages of adult development. This means learning that addresses not just career needs but also the personal concerns of integration and valuing associ-ated with middle age. As Kolb (1991) points out, from his work with advanced professional learners, such learning also has professional application. Young professionals begin their careers with preparation for competence in highly specialized areas. They discover, however, as they reach maturity in their professional work, that they need greater breadth, integration of their specialization with other contexts, and an ability to relate values to their practice: "90 percent or more of tomor-row's advanced professional leaders are working. . . . Their preparation for future and greater leadership responsibilities will depend on how they learn from their experiences and develop as adults in their work organizations" (p. 112). Such needs are addressed by the graduate liberal studies programs and midlife advanced professional or doctoral programs that innovations of recent years have added to the learning menu for adults. It is likely that increasing numbers of people in mid- to later life will call upon these programs.

The greater vitality and longevity of older adults also leads to increased demand for learning. Many seniors seek learning that will assist them with such things as health maintenance, personal fulfillment, and leisure activities. However, many also are engaged in *serial retirement,* that is, alternating periods of retirement and work. Often the new jobs they take up require them to gain additional competencies. Looked at from another perspective, older adults offer a rich pool of experience and talent that practitioners can draw on to enhance adult learning resources. Whether through volunteer programs, many of which already exist, or employment, they can contribute to meeting the learning needs of persons younger and less experienced than themselves (Prisuta, 1997; Scheibel, 1997; Perkins, 1997; Hubler, 1999).

Effect of the Competitive Global Economy

The new global economic competition, and the accompanying restructuring of the U.S. economy, has changed the nature of work, employment, and educational requirements with bewildering rapidity. Persons accustomed to stability and permanence in employment and slow incremental adaptations in their skills face unanticipated loss of their jobs or fast-changing demands for what they are required to perform.

The results can be confusing. For many, work opportunities appear to contract with downsizing and relocation of industries to cheaper labor markets. Job security no longer is dependable. Conversely, new job creation is stronger than it has been for years, and the majority of new jobs are highly skilled and better paying. The complexity of these trends is illustrated in a *Workforce 2020* analysis that describes the large number of low-skilled, low-wage jobs that will continue but also points out that greater growth and opportunity lie in jobs that require higher skills gained through education (Judy & D'Amico, 1997, pp. 69–83; see also "The Multifaceted Returns to Education," 1998). As Morton Bahr (1999) has observed: "U.S. workers have felt firsthand the painful consequences of economic restructuring and the erosion of long-term, secure employment. Many are concerned by the growing gap between those who have advantages of high skills and education and those who do not. The nation must recognize lifelong learning as a national priority."

The numerous career changes that adults now experience, whether or not they remain with the same employer, contribute to the sense of impermanence. All workers, not just professionals, face escalating demands for higher credentials and more capability, and job changes are more frequent for many people. The need for continual upgrading has spread from managerial and supervisory employees to the entire workforce. Often a new bargain replaces the old social contract between employers and workers that ensured security of employment in return for good and loyal work effort. Some employers now agree to maintain the future employability of workers through education and training in return for good performance. This employability, or *career resilience,* may include movement to new responsibilities within the employee's present company or assistance in a no-fault exit leading to work elsewhere (Sheckley, Lamdin, & Keeton, 1993; Waterman, Waterman, & Collard, 1994). For example, over a hundred of the largest companies in the United States have recently created the Talent Alliance, a program that assists their employees to plan their career development and to select education and training to support it and that facilitates movement toward new jobs within the participating companies (Lancaster, 1997). The emerging demand for short-term contract workers rather than long-term employees places a premium on persons who can develop and maintain multiple skills through education, even though independent contractors usually are precariously placed to make long-term investments in their own skills.

Some of workers' uncertainty centers on whether and for which groups postsecondary education is beneficial. The Commission on the Skills of the American Workforce (1990), whose main message was the importance of increased education for the U.S. workforce, perhaps contributed to this ambiguity by dividing the total U.S. workforce into three categories defined by the education and skills needed to perform different responsibilities. The first group comprises the 34 percent of workers whose jobs require less than a high school education. The second group consists of the 36 percent of workers who are mid-skilled and who do not need four-year college degrees. The final group, 30 percent of workers, encompasses highly skilled professionals who require baccalaureate degrees or beyond (pp. 26–27).

The report's conclusion was that 70 percent of the workforce did not need four-year college degrees. This led to the misimpression that

post–high school study was unnecessary or of no benefit to the nondegree group, whereas a large proportion of the mid-skilled group do
participate in and benefit from college education at the prebaccalaure-
ate level. The recent growth in certificate programs in community
colleges illustrates this phenomenon, and many of these programs are
in occupations with strong prospects for increase of employment
(Henderson, 1995).

In 1996, W. Norton Grubb took a realistic look at the educational
needs of the largest segment of workers, those he described as the *subbaccalaureate workforce*. These are people who have completed high
school but not a baccalaureate degree. They may or may not have some
college-level education, and they work in a wide variety of occupations,
mainly at the mid-skilled level. Taken together they constitute a large
and growing segment of the total workforce—Grubb estimated about
three-fifths in 1992—and they are the principal target of the recommendations of the various study groups advocating enhancement of
worker skills to meet the demands of the new economy. The subbaccalaureate population is heterogeneous, with needs that are chiefly
local, so no universal educational approach to them is applicable. Yet
for many, education that is related to their specific job role, responsive
to employer needs, and leads to a completed certificate or degree sequence can produce an economic benefit.

Grubb believes that community colleges have an advantage in mid-
skilled workforce development over other providers at that level. These
colleges' geographical ubiquity, their declared mission to prepare persons for employment, and their ability to combine special technical
training with the broad reading, communication, and computing skills
that workers now need give them a critical edge. At the same time,
Grubb has called upon community colleges to examine their own practices to ensure effectiveness with this group of learners. O'Banion
(1997) similarly foresees a critical role for community colleges if they
can overcome their inertia by putting students first and transforming
themselves into "learning colleges."

Technology's Impact on Learning Resources

Information technology has transformed the nature of work and the
structure of employment. It has already enormously increased the ways
in which people can learn, and it promises to do much more in the future. We are on the threshold of highly disseminated access to educational technology that will be more acceptable than such technology

has been in the past. After many years of less broad adoption than was anticipated of technologies such as televised courses, satellite delivery of instruction, and computer-assisted instruction, new combinations of educational technologies, presented in forms friendly to users, promise unlimited potential for adult learners. The virtually universal penetration of U.S. households by VCRs is likely to be replicated by the adoption of high-powered personal computers, whose constantly descending prices are making them available to the broad population. There will continue to be an inequity between those who can afford access to electronic communication and those who cannot, but the gap will narrow through the provisions of public policy and other means. Already many schools and libraries offer public access to computers and the Internet. *Workforce* 2020 estimates that 60 percent of U.S. households will have computers by 2000 and that the number will grow to 90 percent by 2010 (Judy & D'Amico, 1997, p. 19).

The new technology can vanquish many of the barriers that have frequently confronted adult learners. The requirement to attend at a specific site is no longer necessary, so learners save the cost and time of travel to a campus. Persons who live in isolated locations can participate more freely. Access for disabled persons is being broadened. Asynchronous methods of delivery, that is, delivery upon demand, release individuals from rigid attendance schedules and enable them to review materials when they wish. And the greater pool of learners who can be served this way may reduce the costs of education in comparison to delivery in classroom settings, despite heavy initial costs in equipment and for training faculty and staff in its use.

Many educational institutions have seized these opportunities to reach broader audiences by more convenient means. Their offerings are multiplying to include experiences from certificate sequences to whole degree programs, through the doctoral level. The UCEA/Peterson's *Guide to Distance Learning Programs* exploded in a few years from about two hundred pages to over six hundred pages (University Continuing Education Association & Peterson's Guides, 1993, 1997). New models of delivery are being proposed, including an increasing number of *virtual universities.* Among the outstanding examples are the Western Governors' Virtual University, the California State University electronic university, the International Community College, and Jones International University. Such programs envision lucrative markets worldwide.

The availability of technology is leading to a growing range of educational providers, some of them within the traditional educational sector, but many outside it. Formal education institutions will see their traditional monopoly over learning, already somewhat diminished in recent years, erode even further as they become one group among many suppliers—the public media, voluntary organizations, libraries and museums, employers, for-profit agencies, and individual self-learners.

Contemporary observers predict great changes in the landscape for educational providers as a result. Davis and Botkin (1994a) suggest that leadership in education will pass to business as it discovers customers as learners: "Business, more than government, is instituting the changes in education that are required for the emerging knowledge-based economy. . . . Over the next few decades, the private sector will eclipse the public sector as our predominant educational institutions" (p. 170; see also Davis & Botkin, 1994b).

An even more apocalyptic view comes from a specialist on the economics of information technology who has asked "whether the present (university) system can be maintained and sustained in the face of the changed flow of information brought about by electronic communications" (Noam, 1995, pp. 247–249; see also Hargis, 1996). The traditional fixed-base institution that has prevailed for millennia, with its combination of storage of information and congregation of scholars and learners, is being undermined by the explosion of new knowledge and specialization that exceed what a single institution can accommodate. In contrast, technology enables convenient distribution of knowledge without regard to distance or time. Commercial firms may replace universities as providers of content, something Noam believes is quite feasible, with "Broadway show-sized prices" for student lecture hours at many private institutions. The new conditions make the university "ready to collapse in slow motion once alternatives to its function become possible."

Perpetual Learning

As was observed earlier, many have regarded adult learning as remedial or making up for earlier deficiencies. The most important contemporary change is that adults' search for learning is no longer seen primarily as catch-up. For increasing numbers of people, learning has become a permanent condition of their lives into advanced age. This results from social and economic necessity but also from personal motivation for growth. Most important, it has become feasible because of the great variety of learning opportunities, and this accessibility is likely only to expand. Moreover, learning can now occur in much more fluid environments than the traditional higher education delivery modes. Vaill (1996) describes traditional, or *institutional,* learning as "as much a system for indoctrination and control as it is a system for learning" (p. 40). In its place, he posits a lifelong learning process drawing upon continuously changing experiences and involving a variety of qualities of learning. This process is necessary to negotiate the "white water" conditions of modern life. He calls it "learning as a way of being": "Continual learning is nothing less than a developmental process of learning as a way of being. It is certainly never over or complete; a learner can never be sure that he or she has made hardly more than a start. The more fully a person achieves learning as a way of being, the more he or she will see that there is more to learn and will also see that the learning can be undertaken in the comfort of a fuller and fuller realization of this way of being" (p. 80).

Dolence and Norris (1995) coined the term *perpetual learning* to describe this process. The development of an information-based society and the potential of technology to eliminate barriers of space, time, and sequence radically change the dynamics of the learning experience. Norris (1996) envisions perpetual learning as "lifelong learning that is supercharged by the capabilities of ubiquitous technology and learning spaces that are fused into public and private spaces." It is an experience that is integrated with all aspects of persons' lives and through which they "fuse work and learning everyday." It is interactive and collaborative and eventually may well be facilitated by "community learning centers" to provide broad-based support for learners.

The implications for traditional, formal institutions are profound. "Perpetual learning will witness the balance of power shift from colleges, universities, schools and government to individual learners, business large and small and to communities of reflective practitioners that are even now developing and have developed in the workplace and the knowledge place" (Norris, 1996). Dolence and Norris subtitled their monograph *A Vision for Learning and the 21st Century,* and concluded by offering higher education a choice: "Transformation or Stagnation."

THE CHALLENGE TO POSTSECONDARY EDUCATION

To borrow Vaill's analogy, postsecondary education may be confronting a considerable stretch of white water itself. It faces an era of increasing demand for its services but has reduced financial resources to carry out its traditional role. Many commentators describe postsecondary education as the last major economic sector that has not gone through restructuring, and they make ominous comparisons between it and the health care industry of the 1980s. Executive and legislative intervention in higher education management is greater now than it has been for decades, largely out of exasperation with the slow pace of change. And major constituencies served by higher education complain their needs are not being met. New for-profit providers have entered the field in response to these demands, some of them with sufficient success to attract the attention and investment recommendation of major brokers (Salomon Smith Barney Research, 1997; Strosnider, 1998). The president of a major university has proclaimed that higher education has lost its "exclusivity franchise" (Brody, 1998, p. 31).

The idea that colleges and universities should engage more actively in lifelong learning and preparation of knowledgeable members of the workforce is not new. Lynton (1984) lamented the gulf between employer and higher education efforts in personnel development and saw a missed opportunity for higher education to contribute its breadth and integration of perspective to people's careers. He argued, "Education and employment must be woven together into a complex web requiring a degree of cooperation quite unlike anything in the past" (p. 152). Lynton and Elman (1987) saw a new mission for the university as an institution extended into its surroundings to meet the advanced knowledge needs of society. They envisioned a special role for regional institutions that was consistent with the pragmatic service tradition of U.S. higher education. A decade after their work, during which the pace of change has accelerated and pressures for new knowledge services have increased, Rowley, Lujan, and Dolence (1998) have put the case even more urgently, arguing that lifelong learning demands are recreating higher education: "The new academy is emerging. . . . It is moving from being provider centered to being more learner centered to meet the needs of the rapidly growing worldwide knowledge society" (p. xiv).

Higher education today has the opportunity to take a critical leadership role in lifelong learning—if it will. It is one sector in a wide range of providers of learning to adults at different levels, both formal and informal. All these providers are useful and important. Yet given the already high level of education of the overwhelming majority of the population, the next step in learning for most people will likely be at the postsecondary level, that is, in higher education's bailiwick.

The resources and capability of higher education are vast. As a whole it constitutes a pervasive system, with both public and private components, that extends throughout the country and brings educational opportunity within reasonable proximity of most people. People generally have high confidence in its quality, and achievement of college or university success is a powerful motivating factor for individuals throughout society. Higher education can award credentials that are broadly recognized and upon which recipients can build toward higher levels of attainment. It can award those credentials for learning that has already occurred as well as for the study it supervises. It can—if it will—redefine these credentials into more flexible modules that reflect the steps of learning required by employers or other agencies in the community. Often higher education institutions have strong connections with their neighboring communities or the special constituencies they serve upon which they can build to develop new programs.

Most important of all, higher education houses extensive resources of talent and programmatic experience on which to base new initiatives. Many if not most higher education institutions have adult or continuing education units with experienced and skilled personnel who are already working with adult learners. Unfortunately, in the past these divisions have sometimes been marginalized and given little support, tangible or moral (Stern, 1983; Knowles, 1994a). Nevertheless, these units have often developed highly creative and responsive programs that can serve as examples to the rest of the institution. Yet internal institutional barriers, slow decision-making processes, and outdated system regulations frequently constrain other departments from making use of them.

Alongside the work of continuing education and extension units, a multitude of other special programs for adult learners has developed in many institutions. Taken as a whole, these programs constitute a pool of successful practice that can be drawn upon by institutions planning to initiate programs or to extend the effort they already have under way.

The opportunity is present, and the expectation is great. At the same time, patience grows short, especially as those seeking a greater response to adults recognize that other sources are possible. A 1995 survey report on what the public wants from higher education illustrated this point. Eighty-one percent of adults indicated that additional education is important for success in their careers, but they believed higher education institutions needed to provide learning opportunities better adapted to their circumstances (Dillman, Christenson, Salant, & Warner, 1995). A recent article, for example, quoted a Procter and Gamble executive as saying that the disconnection between what business wants and what postsecondary schools are producing poses a "tremendous education challenge" ("K–12 Reform?" 1997, p. 4). Similar laments from business appeared in the Business-Higher Education Forum report, *Spanning the Chasm* (1997).

CONCLUSION

The solution to today's adult learning issues will come through inclusiveness and innovation. Both are fundamental aspects of the U.S. higher education tradition.

The movement toward greater inclusion of adults in education has a long history. The last half century has seen a great extension of educational opportunity throughout the entire U.S. population. The inclusion of adult learners as participants in higher education is now well established. Indeed, a recent history of adult education in the United States identified the great value Americans place on education in the adult years and the ongoing demand for new forms of adult education produced by our dynamic society as two major themes of the American experience (Stubblefield & Keane, 1994, pp. 6–8).

In his book *Access Through Innovation*, James W. Hall (1991) asserted that "innovative is the most consistent descriptor of American higher education." Hall, the former president of Empire State College, knows from experience the truth of his statement. He and his institution have been leaders in the changes and innovations of the last twenty-five years that have pointed the way for responsiveness to adult learners. He describes many of them in his book, including the creation of greater access, the increase of pluralism and multiculturalism, the welcoming of part-time learners, and the establishment of external and competence-based degree programs. He argues that we are on the threshold of a new stage of innovation that will be marked by changed faculty roles, new institutional forms, and broad application of technology and distance learning. At the same time it will be shaped by enduring values of egalitarianism, individualism, and pluralism. He concludes, "The years immediately before us . . . are likely to witness one of the most aggressively innovative periods in American higher learning" (p. 162).

Higher education's ability to renew itself should encourage those who seek to respond to the emerging era of lifelong learning. Even more important, the fund of experience and models of practice that colleges and universities have accumulated are a resource for those who wish to serve adult learners. The chapters that follow illustrate some outstanding examples, though many more are available. Whether by taking existing models as direct templates or by combining elements of models to make new forms with possibilities for new faculty roles, applications of technology, and collaborations among partners, tomorrow's innovators can use this experience to gain a head start on their task. By drawing on this ready reserve, higher education can play a central role in launching the twenty-first century as the century of lifelong learning.

2

TOWARD MODELS
OF GOOD PRACTICE

AMERICAN POSTSECONDARY EDUCATION has within it a great variety of experience and practice upon which it can draw to address the new wave of demand for adult educational services. There are many cases of effective programs that practitioners can use as examples to persuade those fixed in an institutional culture resistant to new initiatives and need. Hundreds, perhaps thousands, of separate programs planned for adult learners operate in institutions of all types across the country. They employ innovative approaches, and they have developed a highly talented and experienced pool of faculty, administrators, and staff. Some have made modest changes, such as adjustments of meeting times, calendars, or instructional sites, without significantly modifying the traditional curriculum or regulations. Others have gone further to reorganize content and structure to allow individual learners more initiative in what, how, and where they learn. Many connect learning to the workplace, by giving credit for training and experience gained in employment, by offering on-site instruction, and by designing curricula that blend learning and work activities. Some work collaboratively with sponsors of learners to design programs that jointly benefit the learners and their employers, community agencies, or other sponsors. Still others, admittedly relatively few, completely scrap the customary apparatus of terms, courses, credits, fixed sites, and use of existing faculty in order to enable the greatest amount of flexibility.

The program variety is so great that it can become a barrier to planners and practitioners of adult learning who seek new concepts, practices, and models to shape the programs they are conducting or new programs they wish to launch. The busy adult educator, pressured by the demands of ongoing operations and short-term expectations, may not have time to sort through and evaluate large numbers of program examples that might hold clues for innovation. The inexperienced planner in an organization just beginning to offer adult learning opportunities may lack confidence in his or her judgment to select from the models available.

WHAT TO LOOK FOR IN A MODEL

How do faculty and administrators choose good programs to use as models? Where can they look for existing practice that meets their needs and can help them form or reshape programs to address the growing adult learner demand? There is no universal answer to these quandaries. Few program examples can be moved from one setting to another without modification and adaptation to the new setting. No fail-safe recipe for program design will fit all cases. As Knox (Knox & Associates, 1980) observed years ago, "The practice of adult education is an art based on science," (p. 2) and both art and science involve variable factors. Any given educational sequence is affected by the goals it must achieve; the makeup of its learner population; its guiding philosophy and values; its resources, human and physical; the current circumstances of its host institution; and the personal choices of all those engaged in it. Cervero and Wilson (1994, 1996), whose views are discussed further later in this chapter, argue that choice of program design ultimately lies with the planner working ethically within an institutional context.

The programmer's choice can, however, benefit from a heightened awareness of the options available. That awareness can come in part from familiarity with and examination of operating programs whose elements have some relevance to the programmer's task. Most of this book is devoted to descriptions of successful programs that illustrate settings, missions, levels, processes, and audiences in enough variety to inform the work of planners in varied circumstances. Greater awareness can also come from studying and reflecting on the work of scholars of adult education and of conscientious practitioners who have sought to identify the viewpoints, principles, guidelines, and pragmatic operational factors that contribute to successful outcomes in programs for adult learners. Acquaintance with these studies can make programmers alert to factors that matter and enable them to choose among options from existing programs of which they might otherwise be unaware.

SIX SOURCES TO GUIDE PLANNING

This chapter will explore six sources of concepts, guiding principles, and operational practice that planners can take into consideration as they create their unique and specific applications:

1. Statements of the philosophy and theory of adult education
2. Principles of adult learning
3. Program planning models
4. Professional association guidelines for good practice
5. Directories or guides to adult programs
6. Judgments of experienced adult program administrators and leaders about elements necessary for a program's continuing effectiveness and viability

None of these sources alone is sufficient as a basis for program design, but taken together they can produce a spectrum of factors for consideration. In effect, they are the headings in a menu from which planners can choose when they initiate new ventures. A review of these sources can assist a planner in forming a template of factors or domains to take into consideration in program planning. In later chapters the descriptions of individual programs will illustrate the factors in operating systems.

The approach of this study thus is pluralistic. Rather than prescribe particular models, it proposes options grounded in existing reflection and practice in the field of adult learning.

Philosophy and Theory

As adult education emerged as a discipline following World War II, and especially since the publication of the foundational "Black Book" (Jensen, Liveright, & Hallenbeck, 1964), many scholars have explored the philosophy and theory of adult learning and have built on each other's work. Over the last two decades, several have surveyed this literature and described its broad themes (Elias & Merriam, 1980, 1995; Darkenwald & Merriam, 1982; Beder, 1990; Long, 1991; Merriam & Caffarella, 1991, 1999; Merriam & Brockett, 1997). Although they use different terms in their systems of classification—such as philosophies, emphases, purposes, perspectives, or learning theories—and although the titles for categories under those frameworks vary, there are similarities in the patterns they describe. These patterns, or perspectives, relate to the mission or purpose of programs that adult educators have created.

Most of the theoretical discussion is concerned with five patterns of adult education. The following descriptions use Elias and Merriam's names for these patterns.

Liberal adult education. This concept of adult education has its origins in classical philosophy, which has strongly influenced Western educational tradition. It emphasizes organized knowledge and development of intellectual ability, often based on study of classic works, and in the twentieth century has been a powerful influence on British and U.S. adult education.

Progressive adult education. This concept of adult education is an outgrowth of the progressive movement linking politics, social reform, and education. This movement reflected the views of William James and John Dewey, and it influenced early adult educators such as Eduard Lindeman.

Behaviorist adult education. Under this perspective, adult education is based on scientific management of learning to produce specific modification in behavior. This concept of adult education reflects the views of scientific management theorists such as John B. Watson and Frederick Taylor and behavioral psychologists such as B. F. Skinner. It emphasizes definition of objectives for learning, control of the learning process, and reinforcement. Behaviorist education is associated by many educators, but not all, with competence-based education.

Humanist adult education. This outlook on adult education is based in humanist psychology, which seeks realization of individual human potential through individual freedom, autonomy, and self-direction pursued in an environment of trust and cooperation. It is strongly influenced by mid-twentieth-century humanist psychologists—Abraham Maslow, Carl Rogers, Rollo May, and others—and espoused in adult education by Malcolm Knowles and his followers.

Radical adult education. This approach to adult education is grounded in historical movements of radical political and social change and also in more recent critical and emancipatory movements that challenge individual-centered philosophies and prevailing traditions. This philosophy emphasizes the role of power and relativism in education, and it seeks, through education, to promote broader popular understanding as a preliminary to radical social action and change.

Others employ different terms but examination of their texts shows equivalent meanings—such as cultivation of the intellect for liberal education, individual self-actualization and personal growth for humanism, and critical philosophy and social transformation for radicalism. Besides these five areas, Elias and Merriam describe a sixth, philosophical analysis, which describes the application of British analytic philosophy to adult education. In a bibliographical essay in their second edition, they discuss chiefly the work of K. H. Lawson (1982) and acknowledge the declining influence of analytic thought. Other authors deal with analytic concerns in the context of liberal education or cultivation of the intellect.

Merriam and Caffarella (1991) outlined four orientations to learning—behaviorist, cognitive, humanist, and social—to which they later added constructivist (Merriam & Caffarella, 1999). Thus their classification system parallels Elias and Merriam's in part. They provide a useful tabular comparison of the elements of each orientation (1999, p. 264). In 1991, they discussed adult learning theories in terms of adult learner characteristics, adults' life situations, and changes in learner consciousness. Later, in 1999, reflecting the development of adult learning theory over the intervening decade, they recast the discussion to explore the implications for adults of andragogy and other adult learning models; self-directed learning; transformational learning; and critical theory, postmodern, and feminist perspectives.

Despite the considerable agreement that patterns of adult learning fall into these classifications, no single philosophy prevails or predominates. Rather than reaching a consensus on a best or preferable philosophical orientation, adult educators in practice have selected the approach, or sometimes a blend of approaches, that best accorded with the situation of the learning experience as well as their own preferences. Through the leadership of Knowles and his followers (Knowles, 1980; Knowles & Associates, 1985), the humanist orientation of andragogy has gained wide adoption, but not to the exclusion of other perspectives. Further, in practice Knowles's ideas have become fused with other philosophies, particularly in human resource development applications. Cross (1981) chose to focus on the distinct character of adults as learners, rather than on broad theory. She posited a matrix of Characteristics of Adult Learners (CAL) that embraced both personal and situational characteristics of adults. She hoped this matrix would accommodate what was known about adults and would develop with changing situations and the state of knowledge.

Further, several scholars who have suggested a set of classifications acknowledge that philosophical orientations are rooted in history and that history changes. The liberal education, progressive, and humanist orientations are traceable to twentieth-century U.S. movements in politics and psychology and to earlier historical roots. The critical perspectives draw in part on Marxism but also on other recently emerging movements for social change, such as postmodernism, feminism, and Paolo Freire's work among the poor of Brazil. Some would link the work of Brookfield (1986) and Mezirow (1991) to social transformation, although their writing also resonates with liberal and humanist education. Beder (1990) and Elias and Merriam (1995) draw attention to other emerging trends.

Unquestionably, with the passage of time, other philosophies will follow. The field of adult learning, which is deeply embedded in its social, political, and economic context, is not static and will develop as the context changes. Lawson (1991) observes that "terms such as *adult education* remain perpetually fluid and systematically ambiguous. We catch their meaning only as snapshots in time" (p. 290). He adds that the highly individualized and personal adult education of the humanist emphasis may be declining in the face of a rising communitarian spirit.

As a result, most of these scholars seem reconciled to the lack of a universally accepted general theory of adult learning. Mezirow (1991, pp. 199–201) reports a high degree of agreement on theory among practitioners of andragogy, but not all concur with that philosophy. Indeed, many see an advantage in variety and in the opportunity for pragmatic choice depending on the learning situation. Darkenwald and Merriam (1982) accept that "there exists no single conceptual framework, no single set of basic assumptions and principles from which all educators view the field" (p. 35) and regard this diversity as reflective of our pluralistic society. Apps (1985) encourages a synoptic approach, drawing multiple perspectives from various sources and using a normative stance of individual personal judgment based on values to assess them. Merriam and Caffarella (1991, 1999) do not foresee the formulation of a single theory to explain adult learning but rather cast their discussion in terms of frameworks to guide further research. Despite identifying six distinct strains of philosophy of adult education, Elias and Merriam (1980, 1995) demonstrate the interconnectedness of many of these strains and suggest that adult educators might use them eclectically to formulate personal philosophies of adult education.

These philosophical perspectives lay out orientations that practitioners can use to give direction to program development.

In order to move toward application from theoretical orientation, program planners can turn to the remaining five sources for program planning. Again, no single formulation dominates, but the different approaches suggest choices for application in specific cases. As with theory, certain common themes emerge.

Principles of Adult Learning

Principles of adult learning result both from adult educators' theoretical reflection and from observation during practice. Authors of principles state them in terms ranging from the philosophical, theoretical, and humanist to the baldly pragmatic and operational.

Excellent summaries of these principles appear in Brookfield (1986) and Merriam and Caffarella (1991, 1999). The authors they review overlap in considerable degree. Both discuss Kidd (1973), Knox (1977), Knowles (1980), and Brundage and MacKeracher (1980). In addition, Brookfield discusses Gibb (1960), Miller (1964), Smith (1982), and Darkenwald and Merriam (1982). And Merriam and Caffarella cite Brookfield (1986) and Zemke and Zemke (1981) and add MacKeracher (1996). Brookfield summarizes "specification of principles" under eight headings (p. 31), whereas Merriam and Caffarella (1991) group the concerns under three distinctions between children's learning and adults' learning: context, learner, and learning process (p. 302). These lists can be extended by reference to Houle's massive bibliographical study of writing on adult education (1992) and to the design and practice principles developed by Boyatzis, Cowen, Kolb, and Associates (1994).

No summary statement of these views can comprehend all the points their authors make, but it is possible to extract a number of important principles in the form of adult characteristics and the implications of these characteristics. Not all are accepted totally by any author of principles or by any practitioner. Many of the goals overlap the points stated here. Planners of adult learner programs will tend to apply them selectively, depending upon the specific learning activity.

Four main characteristics of adult learners emerge.

1. Adults are different, both from youths and, depending on their developmental stages, from each other. As a result they need learning approaches that recognize their self-concept as independent persons and that value their individual worth. Although this view is not universally accepted (Houle, 1996), the work of Tennant and Pogson (1995) lends it strong support.

2. Adults are capable of learning throughout their lives, but their learning is affected by their stage of development.

3. Adult motivation to participate in learning is usually voluntary, although job loss and other exigencies may be compelling inducements. Adults' decisions to enter education may involve competing tensions between incentives and disincentives, such as the need to improve income versus previous negative experience with school or peer attitudes (Cross, 1981). Often participation results from a transition or change for which education offers a resolution (Aslanian & Brickell, 1980; Schlossberg, Waters, & Goodman, 1995; Boulmetis, 1997).

4. Adults are complex as individuals and heterogeneous within learning groups. Their lives encompass many competing demands in addition to learning, and they differ greatly from one another in how they learn. They benefit from flexibility and individualization in their learning experiences.

Several implications follow from these characteristics.

1. The learning experience should recognize and address the experience of adult learners. Their self-concept has been formed by previous experience and learning may be facilitated or hindered by that legacy. Individual experience can be a valuable resource to new learning and to the learning group. The adult learner will evaluate new learning against prior experience and will seek to apply it to familiar settings. He or she is likely to respond to problem-centered learning and activities that involve direct experience.

2. Many adults prefer to play an active role in the planning, direction, and evaluation of their learning. However, recommendations differ on the desirability of self-direction, with Knowles (1980) strongly recommending it, and Brookfield (1986) and Caffarella (1994) qualifying that view. Most authors of principles agree that however the learning activity is formulated, it should have clear goals and sequence.

3. Flexibility and adaptability in the learning situation are desirable to accommodate learners' variable and changing circumstances. This may apply to the time, place, pacing, and mode of learning.

4. The relation between teacher and learner should reflect their mutual respect as adults and be characterized by facilitation and cooperation rather than control. There is some difference of opinion as to how strongly the facilitator should lead or pose alternatives in the learning situation.

5. Adults benefit from a positive learning environment—what Kidd referred to as "membership rather than studentship" (1973, p. 41) and what Knowles called "climate setting" (Knowles & Associates, 1985, p. 14). Such an environment embraces the physical, social, and personal settings of learning and should include regular and constructive feedback.

Program Planning Models

When it comes to application- or practice-oriented guidelines for programs, the abundant literature on program planning once again exhibits pluralism. This discussion samples four overviews from the field that illustrate this pluralism over three decades: Houle (1972, 1996), Sork and Buskey (1986), Caffarella (1994), and Cervero and Wilson (1994, 1996).

Houle wrote initially when systematic thought about adult education was still young, but he largely reiterated his views in a thorough update of his work in 1996. Starting from the perspective of the practitioner, he believes most people in the field operate from a credo, or simple statement of belief, they have worked out for themselves. Although some practitioners have gone further to construct models or organized systems of program planning, Houle describes six major tendencies of these credos in an illustrative but not exhaustive list. Four of the six are derived from the ideas of John Dewey, Ralph W. Tyler, Kurt Lewin, and Malcolm Knowles respectively. The other two categories consist of more recent views that draw on multiple sources, such as community development and systems analysis. That none of these has become dominant he regards as "a healthy safeguard against dogmatism" that benefits professionals "who must constantly meet the test of the market" (p. 5). Houle proposes that instead of choosing a specific approach, practitioners may adopt a flexible "fundamental system," or process, that first involves determining the basic category to which a learning activity belongs based on the authority and direction of its planning. A second step requires the application of a framework of decision making about the program plan in relation to the basic category. The program results from the interaction of these factors. The concept is comprehensive in order to accommodate a broad range of approaches, but its application is specific to the educational event. Houle proposes it in a spirit of flexibility, adaptability, and "pragmatic utilitarianism" in which achievement of the desired educational end is primary and guides other planning choices (pp. 70–71).

Sork and Buskey (1986) attempted to collect and analyze the growing body of program planning literature in the mid 1980s in order to make useful distinctions among various models and to facilitate future development and study of these models. Using publications that presented complete adult program planning models, they systematically analyzed the items by descriptive and evaluative dimensions and by three analytic concepts under each dimension. They made distinctions among planning contexts, levels to which programs were directed, and client groups. They also assessed the planning models for the sophistication they required of the user, theoretical framework, and comprehensiveness of design. They presented their evaluations in tabular form, indicating a classification, or ranking, for each planning model, which readers can use to guide a choice of models.

This analysis also led Sork and Buskey to observe the state of adult education program planning. Reflecting the immediacy and concreteness of planners' tasks, Sork and Buskey found little cross-referencing and cumulative development in the planning literature. Hence there was a low degree of theoretical explanation and comprehensive treatment of planning in the works they reviewed. In addition, the models employed group instruction almost exclusively, at a time when opportunities for individualized learning were increasing. Finally, the roles and characteristics of the planners themselves were rarely discussed. Sork and Buskey's discussion reiterated the tenuous linkage of theory and practice observed by Houle and the limited effort to generalize models from one context to another.

Two other studies extended the ideas of Sork and Buskey. Langenbach (1988) reduced the number of models to seven broad categories, which he discussed in conceptual terms and illustrated with case studies. Sork and Caffarella (1989) started from a belief that systematic planning is more valuable than its absence. They discussed a generic set of six steps to program planning, reflecting the earlier work of Tyler (1949), Knowles (1950), London (1960), and Sork and Buskey (1986). With some regret they observed that the theory-practice gap "has widened since . . . 1980" (p. 243), and they called for collaborative theory building and reflective practice to bring the worlds of the scholars and practitioners closer together.

Caffarella (1994) stepped aside from the previous program planning models and discussed the question of planning from the point of view of the purposes of and the changes sought by adult education programs. She argued forcibly for the use of some model in the planning process and proposed an eleven-component interactive model. Its value lies in its comprehensiveness and practical ideas for implementation. She took account, for instance, of the personal beliefs of planners that Sork and Buskey found were often omitted in planning design.

Cervero and Wilson (1994, 1996) attempted to reconcile the role of the planner, or agent, and the social context, or structure, within which the planner works. They classified previous planning theories into three categories: *classical,* the planner exercises scientific rationality based on principles; *naturalistic,* the planner engages in practical reasoning that may be informed by theory but is mainly guided by his or her judgment; and *critical,* the planner acknowledges social, political and ideological contexts whose influence needs to be confronted by the planner's moral and ethical stance. Although Cervero and Wilson recognized value in each of these perspectives, they found none of them adequate in itself.

Their solution was to describe planning as a process in which planners are agents with judgment and volition who must act but who also are constrained by social and political factors in their environments with which they must engage and negotiate from an ethical stance. Ethical practice requires planners to take account of the power and interests in their environment by democratic means, which allows input from all but also enables the planner to exercise his or her own moral judgment. The result of these interactions cannot be fully determined and may not be perfect, but the outcome situates the planner as a responsible agent striving for human betterment in a context of power and interest.

In summary, these discussions of planning models describe a number of approaches that can be taken and of circumstances that will affect planning choices. Despite a wistfulness on the part of some authors for a universal system, they accept the validity of various methods so long as planning is deliberate, respectful of the educational ends sought, and cognizant of the circumstances of the learning event. Like philosophies or theories of adult learning, then, concepts of program planning are helpful in considering options or alternatives but not necessarily prescriptive. Thus Cervero and Wilson call upon planners to act responsibly and to choose courageously, even though they cannot be certain of outcomes.

Professional Association Guidelines for Good Practice

A number of the professional associations dedicated to adult learning have articulated principles of good or ethical practice to serve as guides to their members (Council on the Continuing Education Unit [CCEU],

1984; American Council on Education [ACE] . . . & The Alliance, 1990; Coalition of Adult Education Organizations [CAEO], 1991; National University Continuing Education Association [UCEA], 1993b; Association for Continuing Higher Education [ACHE], 1997). These associations intend individual institutions and programs to use the guidelines as benchmarks rather than as requirements to be implemented in all cases. One of the largest and most complex associations, with several specialized divisions, the American Association for Adult and Continuing Education, has not adopted comprehensive guidelines, but it has expressed similar concepts in planning its association conferences and in formulating a vision statement for planning (Henschke, 1992; Grissom, 1996). The guideline documents of these associations vary in scale and scope from a thirty-six page pamphlet in one case to single-page lists in others. Some are elaborated with rationales and sub-principles; others present groups of brief sentence-long statements. Three are statements of good practice, one is a code of ethics for professionals, and another is a "Bill of Rights" for learners. Taken together they reflect the views of practitioners of adult education over the last decade and a half.

Despite their differing formats, they express closely aligned concerns. The points, although not always expressed in the same language and sometimes implied instead of explicitly stated, fall into these six major groups.

1. Learner needs should be carefully assessed and addressed fairly and equitably.

2. Learning programs should be planned in terms of the learning outcomes sought, which in turn arise from the needs assessment.

3. Learning experiences should be of high quality and be adult learner centered. This means, among other things, that they should encourage a positive psychological environment for learning, allow learner participation in the design of experiences, relate learning to the learner's prior experience and application, use varying types of learning, recognize differing learning styles, provide continuous feedback to learners, and arrange appropriate physical settings.

4. Assessment of learning should be outcome based and designed to evaluate the intended learning outcomes. It also should recognize participants' previous learning, whether formal or informal.

5. Faculty and staff should be adequately prepared to work with adult learners and should participate in ongoing evaluation and development of their own capability.

6. Programs should have clearly stated missions and sufficient resources to carry out their missions effectively. These resources include rigorous financial administration, necessary learning and student support services, policies governing learner confidentiality and other matters, and ethical standards for learner recruitment and professional practice.

In addition, ACE/Alliance and UCEA specifically call for thorough program evaluation, both to assess program effectiveness and to direct future improvement. UCEA also calls upon programs to "assume an advocacy role when needed to encourage changes in institutional, state and federal policies that affect the student's access to programs and ability to continue to completion" (p. 8).

ACE and UCEA, with assistance from CAEL, have provided a useful elaboration of these six factors in a self-study manual (ACE, 1991). It was initially issued in 1984 to assist institutions to evaluate and improve their adult programs. ACE used it in recurring workshops on program assessment and periodically revised the text, most recently in 1991, in light of feedback from institutions that have carried out self-assessments. Building on the assumptions that adult learners have different needs than traditional age students and that students of all ages are entitled to equivalent treatment, the guide presents twenty-nine inventories for institutions to consider. These inventories are organized in seven major categories: (1) mission and objectives; (2) data on present and potential adult learners; (3) outreach to potential learners and admission; (4) academic policy, practice, and curriculum; (5) supports for learning; (6) faculty and staff development and rewards; and (7) administrative structure and finance. Taken together they constitute a thorough basis for reviewing programs, and the guide also identifies key issues to consider with regard to program design. Use of the guide in workshops has been discontinued, but it is still a useful inventory of factors to look for in quality programs.

Directories or Guides to Adult Programs

The increase in adult-oriented programs and in the numbers of adult learners who seek them out has stimulated a small industry that produces guides to adult programs. On the whole they provide a good service to adult learners, many of whom lack information on specific offerings or are uninitiated in the arcana of the higher education system. All intend to lead learners to programs that serve their needs, but individual guides vary considerably in how they are compiled, the extent of information they supply, and the basis on which they include programs. Most, although not all, offer a general orientation to college-level learning, suggestions on how to clarify one's goals with regard to education, and some description of and referral to sources of information about accreditation. Usually, they focus on attributes of programs that reduce or eliminate barriers of time and place for adult learners, and they call attention to recent innovations such as reduction or elimination of campus attendance requirements, alternative calendars, and means of recording or earning credit that do not require traditional enrollment. In a few cases they provide information on how to achieve high school equivalency to enable entry to higher education; some offer advice on career or other opportunities following completion of the college credential. Most important, they provide lists of adult-oriented institutions along with contacts and information in varying depth about the adult learning programs. They may also include information on program enrollment cost.

Although they have limitations, these directories can be useful to developers of programs. Above all, they can lead planners to programs that offer helpful examples. Because the guides are consumer oriented, the information they provide may indicate attributes of the market that adult educators are trying to reach. Program planners can also discern the information, services, and procedures they must be prepared to offer in order to be successful.

However, these directories contain little information about program origins, missions, funding, curricula, administrative operations, evaluation results, and impact on their own or other institutions. To answer these questions, planners need to probe more deeply.

Guides are currently available from two main sources. The first source is institutions or organizations with a mission to adult learners. Guides from this source try to facilitate educational entry or continuation, or they seek to disseminate information about educational models. The sponsors often base the directories on surveys of programs they have repeated over a number of years, and they reissue successive editions. ACE's guide to alternative and external degree programs (Sullivan, 1993) is based on a survey and self-reports from institutions. More recently, ACE published a guide to external degree programs offered in large part by electronic means (Spille, Stewart, & Sullivan, 1997), reflecting the growing importance of that process. This electronic program guide offers useful cautions and advice on avoiding diploma mills, a topic discussed at length elsewhere by Stewart and Spille (1988). UCEA in cooperation with Peterson's Guides (1993, 1997, 1998) has issued directories of independent study courses and distance learning programs. The Regents College Alumni Association (n.d.) and SUNY-Empire State College (ESC) (1992) initially developed guides to external or innovative graduate programs for their own alumni but made the publications available to the general public in response to demand from other learners and program planners. The alumni association guide is a simple list of programs and contacts, but the ESC list, which is no longer being issued, was based on a succession of surveys. It described specific programs as well as external degrees and provided detailed information on program design and practice. Regents College has developed a listing of other institutions' course offerings that can be applied to Regents degree requirements. It is called DistanceLearn and is available for purchase on disk (www.regents.edu). The Association of Graduate Liberal Studies Programs (1994), which encourages the development of its type of program, periodically issues a list of member institutions' program descriptions, both for general information and for use as a manual in program development workshops.

The second source of guides is individuals who have collected and organized information useful to adults approaching education. They make deletions and additions in successive editions, and they invite readers to send them information on programs they have overlooked. Like the foregoing organizations, they usually provide helpful information orienting readers to the higher education system and its opportunities. The program descriptions they supply vary extensively, from rather brief entries offering information on contacts, subject matter, and cost and limited supplementary comment to extended systematic entries covering a wide range of topics. A few examples will illustrate. Duffy (1994) and Thorson (1994) focus on programs with little or no residency requirement and with methods other than class attendance of gaining credit. Butler (1994) discusses degree completion through technology-based programs, and he devotes over half his text to various planning and learning strategies related to these programs. Bear, who has published guides for over twenty years, regularly issues a guide to nontraditional programs (see, for example, Bear, 1994; Bear & Bear, 1995) and recently has added a guide limited to external and electronic degrees (Bear & Bear, 1998). He adopts an admittedly personal and idiosyncratic stance in his judgments, which his comments on individual programs reflect. Unlike most compilers of these guides, he includes unaccredited as well as accredited programs and also offers a "goodbye" index of the programs dropped from his listing. Bear, and also some other authors, also prepares indexes of nontraditional programs for specific professions.

Judgments of Experienced Adult Program Administrators

The steering committee of the For a Nation of Lifelong Learners project was an excellent source of professional judgment for identifying the qualities of good adult learning programs. The committee members, who have observed and initiated innovation in adult programs since the early 1970s, constituted an unusually experienced and well-informed cadre of practitioners.

In addition to their acquaintance with the literature and practice of adult learning, they also brought a sense of the operational viability programs must have to be successful. Their experience as leaders of institutions and organizations that have played leading roles in major change gave them a unique perspective. They looked for the characteristics of adult learner responsiveness that have been discussed earlier in this chapter, but they also were concerned about practical operation, survivability, longevity, and the impact of programs on their sponsoring institutions and surrounding environments.

To make the study of existing programs more useful to those wanting to undertake programs themselves, committee members wanted program factors such as the following to be examined:

- Administrative placement of the program in the institution
- Program origins, including sources of start-up and continuing funding
- Program mission and purpose statements
- Audience intended and recruitment and admissions processes; also numbers of persons served and number completing the program in a defined period
- Program responsiveness to the needs of learners' external sponsors, such as employers, unions, governments, and other organizations
- Processes of program evaluation, including evaluation of faculty, staff, and administration
- Indications of the recognition and impact of the program, both within and outside its institution

- Program documentation that describes, evaluates, and analyzes programs

CONCLUSION

This chapter has examined many different perspectives on adult programming and observed many factors that can be taken into consideration in planning programs. The exploration suggests no single formula or template that is applicable to all learning experiences, although there is considerable agreement about the many elements that are desirable and that benefit adults. Still, making a choice among all the elements is difficult.

It is made more complex by the heterogeneity of the U.S. higher education system. The absence of central control and the variability among regulatory jurisdictions, the multiplicity of institutions and missions, and the value we place on independence and self-direction all lead away from uniformity. In individual institutions the evolution of forms, structures, and processes is shaped by internal considerations that are not transparent to the outside observer. Abstract concepts usually do not determine choices. Traditional goals and practices; internal politics; unpredictability of resources; and local idiosyncrasies of organization, terminology, and regulation do.

The discussion here does not resolve these difficulties, but it does suggest some domains for consideration. The remainder of this book applies those domains to select a group of programs for discussion that have demonstrated success, that have fulfilled many if not all of the expectations of the domains, and that can serve as examples to others.

These domains, embracing and distilling the concepts from the scholarly or professional practice literature and the judgment of practicing professionals, are

- Clarity of mission and purpose
- A strong commitment, including funding, to undertake the program
- Appropriate match between learners and the program, as exhibited through recruitment, admission, entry, and continuing practices
- Provision of a favorable climate of learning, including advising and other services

- Provision of a learner-oriented curriculum and modes of learning
- Adaptability to learner circumstances, either individually or in context
- Recognition and involvement of learner experience
- Commitment and development of faculty and staff
- Clearly identified administration and governance
- Ongoing program evaluation and documentation
- Positive program impact and future prospects

The programs discussed in the chapters that follow were selected from among those identified from a variety of sources—personal acquaintance, networking among colleagues, membership lists of organizations of adult learning programs, and others. The largest number of them were respondents to the Commission for a Nation of Lifelong Learners' project survey questionnaire designed to identify and collect information on adult programs (see Appendix C for survey instruments).

The programs selected differ in level, geographical location, mission, and learner population. They represent multiple points of view and reflect different goals and values. Some are highly individualized and learner centered. Others prescribe particular curriculum goals but progress through processes attractive to their participants. Some are associate degree programs; others offer master's or doctoral degrees for advanced professionals. Some make extensive use of distance learning and electronic technology; others place greater value on intense, face-to-face contact.

Their chief value is that they represent models, or cases, of programs that work in terms of the goals and objectives they set themselves and the needs of the learners they serve. Individually and collectively they offer a resource bank of practices other institutions can draw upon as they adapt or create their own programs.

These cases are by no means exhaustive. Many other excellent programs could stand alongside them as examples. Nor should the practices described here be considered prescriptive. The choice of how to proceed rests with each operating organization in relation to its values and goals. The purpose of these models is to be illustrative and heuristic and in the process to provide resources that can be applied in a spirit of creativity.

INNOVATIVE RESPONSES TO LEARNER NEEDS

3

INDIVIDUALIZATION AND
SELF-DIRECTED LEARNING

A CHARACTERISTIC OF ADULTS is that they have a strong self-concept of themselves as individuals and they want to manage their own affairs. Scholars and practitioners make this characteristic a recurring theme in their discussions of adult learning, examining adults' need to play an active role in their educational experiences. Thus Knowles argued that adults develop a self-concept of being self-directing personalities and an intense need to be perceived as such by others (1980, pp. 45–46). The review of principles and professional association guidelines in Chapter Two illustrated scholars' and practitioners' considerable agreement on the need to respect the individual identity of learners, to acknowledge their experience, to facilitate their goals, and to involve them actively in the planning, direction, and evaluation of their learning. It is not surprising, therefore, that many innovative programs for adults have sought to recognize both learners' individual differences and their adulthood by loosening or abandoning general requirements in favor of individual choice. This chapter explores several examples of programs that provide a high level of individual learner choice and control but do so within an institutional framework.

Self-directed learning has become a pervasive concept and a positive value in adult education during the last generation. This view of learning has antecedents in the experiments in undergraduate education for traditional students conducted at colleges such as Antioch and Goddard earlier in this century. Adult educators began to apply it following the publication of several influential works in the 1960s and 1970s.

In a study of a number of adults continually engaged in learning activities, Houle (1961) identified a *learning oriented* group (p. 38) for whom learning was not instrumental to another end but was embedded in their lives. Somewhat later Tough (1971, 1979) described a group of adults who regularly initiated and carried out their own learning projects independently of formal educational structures. He and others then replicated the original study in varied settings and cultures and appeared to demonstrate a predilection of adults for self-directed learning. Shortly after, Knowles (1975) published a manual for learners and teachers in which he argued that self-direction was appropriate to adult development and necessary for survival in a world of rapid change. Knowles elaborated this view in later discussions of the concept of andragogy (Knowles, 1980, 1989; Knowles & Associates, 1985).

These ideas proved attractive to adult educators for a number of reasons. They accord with the humanist goal of developing human potential and encouraging self-development that has been influential in the United States since World War II. Although much of the traditional liberal arts curriculum is prescriptive, liberal education has valued turning students into informed and self-initiating persons who can "live responsibly and joyfully, fulfilling their promise as individual humans and their obligations as democratic citizens" (Association of American Colleges, 1990, p. 15). The self-direction goal resonates with these values. Candy (1991) also argues that adult educators find self-directed learning compatible with values of democracy and individualism, with the belief that mature adults are actors equal to teachers in the learning process, and with relativist views about the nature of knowledge. Further, self-directed learning has proved to have value in human resource development, professional development, and learning through cultural institutions such as libraries and museums (Brookfield, 1985; Hiemstra & Brockett, 1994).

The intense interest in and application of self-directed processes have in turn led to major research efforts on the subject (Knowles, 1975; 1980; Brookfield, 1985, 1986, 1993; Candy 1991; Brockett & Hiemstra, 1991; Hiemstra & Sisco, 1990; Sisco & Hiemstra, 1991; Jarvis, 1992; Flannery, 1993; Collins, 1991; Garrison, 1997–1998). Candy (1991) and Brockett and Hiemstra (1991) offer overviews of this work and also discussions of the implications of self-directed learning. Long (Long et al., 1991), Caffarella (1993), and Merriam and Brockett (1997) present briefer summaries. For about a decade Long has convened symposiums on self-directed learning that have issued proceedings and other publications on developments in the field (Long et al.,

1988, 1990, 1991, 1992, 1993, 1996). Merriam and Caffarella (1999) provide a comprehensive review and critical analysis of the literature on self-directed learning to date.

These explorations reveal self-directed learning to be a much more complex matter than was initially envisioned or has been understood by many practitioners. Is self-directed learning a process or a goal? That is, does it entail giving learners a high degree of initiative and control over what and how they learn, or does it mean developing individuals who are capable of completely unassisted learning? Is genuine self-directed learning compatible with institutionalized learning? Are varying degrees of self-direction or individualization possible? Is individualization or learner control appropriate for all learners? What is the role of the teacher or facilitator in self-directed learning? Does the individual focus of self-direction overlook sociological and cultural factors that affect education? Is self-direction possible if knowledge is socially or culturally constructed, and is self-direction therefore limiting to the individual? Or is self-direction a deceptive charade whose goal is to accommodate learners to prevailing social or political beliefs while conveying an illusion of individual control? Or alternatively, does self-directed learning have a radical emancipatory potential; can it help individuals break through a constricting political environment?

Merriam and Caffarella (1999) seek to bring greater clarity to this multifaceted discussion by grouping the research in three categories: the goals of self-directed learning, self-directed learning as a process or form of study, and self-directedness as a personal attribute of the learner. The programs discussed in this chapter illustrate the second of those groups, self-directed learning as a process.

Structured learning experiences leading to credentials, however flexible, may seem to contradict many concepts in self-directed learning. Certainly, they stand apart from the self-learner as autodidact that Candy (1991) describes. Also, self-direction is not for everyone. Houle (1961) described only one group of the several he studied as learning oriented, and some authors discuss means to overcome resistance of learners to self-direction (Hiemstra & Brockett, 1994). Yet many structured programs, such as those that follow, seek to provide frameworks that are respectful of individual goals, nurture the initiative and exploration of each learner, and encourage the formation of unique syntheses of understanding. Their design guides participants toward some goals, such as general education, professional outcomes, or values of the institutional mission but nevertheless allows considerable learner self-management and control. In this respect these programs illustrate Merriam and Caffarella's second, or process, category. They also envision participants' development of continuous initiative in learning as an ultimate program goal.

This set of programs presents a range of models from several different types of institutions. The institutions are State University of New York (SUNY)-Empire State College, the University of Memphis, Atlantic Union College, and Prescott College. One is a special-purpose public institution devoted primarily to adult learners. Another is a large public university. The two others are small, independent colleges rooted in liberal arts traditions but with distinctive missions. Three offer baccalaureate programs to adult learners. One offers a graduate program at the master's level. Their experience with their adult programs extends from six years to twenty-seven years. Program enrollments vary from nearly ten thousand in one case to fewer than one hundred in another.

All the programs screen applicants for motivation and indications of ability to manage their own learning, although none applies assessment instruments such as the Guglielmino Self-Directed Learning Readiness Scale. They all recognize variations in learning style and in capacity to take responsibility for one's learning program. Consequently, their admission processes are responsive to individual characteristics but usually discourage applicants whose goals are not clear or whose skills and discipline seem unpromising for success. They differ in the degree to which learners control the process of learning, but all provide much greater freedom than traditional programs. Some set fairly firm guidelines for content, whereas others apply only general and porous lines of definition. All use learning contracts or some other form of mutual agreement between learners and faculty as a basis for degree planning. The learning resources allowed vary from existing courses of the institution to whatever experience, structured or informal, learners can demonstrate relates to their goals. Several programs are very receptive to transfer and prior learning assessment credit and also to the use of courses given by cooperating institutions in the learning plan. One program allows none of these. Faculty are specially prepared to work with adults or have had experience with them, although the faculty development programs differ in their depth. All these adult learning programs have specially dedicated administrative structures through which they operate.

PUTTING INDIVIDUAL LEARNERS' NEEDS AND INTERESTS FIRST

SUNY-Empire State College—Saratoga Springs, New York

Baccalaureate Degree Program

The most experienced of these programs, SUNY-Empire State College (ESC), has concentrated its mission on the individual learner from its inception. A prospectus from the time of the college's origination states that the college "will place the central focus on the individual student learning at his own pace," through a process that "will place the responsibility for learning on the student in return for his freedom to pursue his education according to his individual needs and interests" (Bonnabeau, 1996, p. 19).

The college originated amid competing pressures in the late 1960s and early 1970s, as confidence in traditional higher education structures declined and surging demand for education threatened to swamp the existing and anticipated facilities of New York's public higher education system, the State University of New York. Faced with these simultaneous conditions, the newly appointed chancellor of SUNY, Ernest L. Boyer, convened a meeting of his chief associates in November 1970 that led to a planning task force. The task force in turn generated several proposals. On the strength of those ideas, Boyer secured commitments for major grants from the Carnegie Corporation and Ford Foundation. In January 1971, he persuaded the SUNY Board of Trustees to adopt a unanimous resolution to establish a "non-residential, degree-granting college" that would draw upon the resources of the entire university and provide access for "young people and adults for whom an off-campus individualized instructional pattern will be most effective" (Bonnabeau, 1996, p. 18).

By the following September the college enrolled its first students. It improvised rapidly to deliver on promises articulated in a February 1971 prospectus to build a learner-centered institution. Organization, procedures, and practices that have evolved since that time represent experience drawn from trial and error, interplay of competing philosophies, and adaptation to changing conditions. The system now in place has grown to a comprehensive organization serving nearly ten thousand learners. It functions at more than forty locations across New York state, at several sites outside the United States, and through a distance learning program that extends as far as its communication technology allows. It is an excellent example of an institution that, by emphasizing process and collaboration rather than structure and facilities, provides cost-effective educational opportunity to a large audience of learners across a wide geographical area. Yet the focus on the individual remains paramount. The following discussion profiles ESC's current baccalaureate program.

Six Program Features

Six distinctive features characterize the Empire State baccalaureate program: (1) the individualized degree plans and semester learning contracts, (2) the mentor role of faculty, (3) the breadth of learning resources, (4) the comprehensive program of prior learning assessment, (5) the flexible and dispersed administrative structure, and (6) the thorough program documentation, which has played an important role in program evolution. Although some of these elements now appear in many other adult programs, it is useful to remember that most of them were adopted at Empire State well before they became part of the common discourse in adult learning. Indeed, ESC's initiatives provided early guidance for the later models that evolved.

Empire State College is open to persons of all ages who have high school completion or its equivalent or who can demonstrate ability to benefit from the program. From the beginning, somewhat to its initial surprise, it has overwhelmingly attracted adult learners as applicants, chiefly persons in the thirty to fifty age range, most of whom have had previous college experience. The college now acknowledges adults as its principal population, and college publications point out its advantages for mature persons with strong motivation and well-defined goals. No standardized tests are required for admission, but applicants are asked to present a statement of personal goals and to attend an orientation session. Applications from persons whose goals cannot be served by the college, for instance, those seeking to prepare for a licensed profession, may be declined. Enrollment is possible on a year-round, rolling basis, as student and college resources permit.

DEGREE PLANNING AND LEARNING CONTRACTS. In a major departure from undergraduate program tradition, learners design plans of study in terms of their individual goals and preferences. ESC borrowed concepts previously used at Goddard and Sarah Lawrence Colleges, but developed them further in the ESC environment. A critical debate took place early in the life of the college over whether individual planning should be completely open or guided by previously formed curriculum elements. The college compromised by formulating eleven broad areas, or frameworks, of study, including interdisciplinary studies, which are registered with the New York State Education Department. Within each of these areas individuals may develop unique programs of study directed to their personal goals that include work in both general liberal arts and a concentration. Learners spend considerable time and effort at the beginning formulating their degree plans. Plans are subsequently reviewed at the learners' local centers and the college's central office. Upon approval they become the basis for the learners' later learning activities.

Students progress in their plans by a variety of study methods, including tutorials with specialists, guided independent study, group study, classroom instruction in one of the ESC units, cross-registration in courses at other SUNY or private institutions, experiential projects, and distance learning. These activities are mediated by *learning contracts* formed between learners and their chief faculty members, or *mentors,* for each semester. Within the context of their degree plans and in collaboration with their mentors, learners propose goals, means, and resources for their study, what their activities, outputs, and duration of effort will be, the amount of credit they seek, and the basis for evaluation of their achievement. They may enroll with full- or part-time status. Upon the approval of the mentor, the students proceed to fulfill the terms of their contracts and to submit their work for evaluation. Contract evaluations are regarded as part of the learning process; this feedback facilitates learning and understanding by the learner. Evaluations may include letter grades from classroom course experiences but normally are narrative, reflecting the judgment of the mentor on the contribution of the result to the learning plan.

FACULTY. The college decision to shift to a learner-driven process transformed the faculty member from professor to a multifaceted figure (Hall & Bonnabeau, 1993). Faculty members, now called mentors, became persons with disciplinary expertise who additionally fulfill facilitative and advising functions, assisting students with all aspects of their programs. One mentor (Belasen, 1995) describes eight faculty roles: creator, ambassador, standard-setter, energizer, assessor, process specialist, coach, and collaborator. Mentors need to form partnerships with learners and at the same time expand learners' awareness of content, relationships, and possibilities. The mentor is a bridge between the learner's aspirations, the learning resources and values the college represents, and the standards expected of the degree credential. The college's success has depended on recruiting mentors with the academic breadth and depth as well as the range of personal qualities necessary to perform all these roles—and a continuing issue has been the workload that recurring personal attention to individual learners requires of mentors.

Because mentors are dispersed over more than forty sites, programs for faculty networking and continuing development are important to the system. The college has facilitated easy communication among faculty and staff, which has evolved with technology. It holds recurring systemwide faculty meetings as well as meetings at regional sites. The Mentoring Institute, conducted by mentors, guides mentor development activities and issues a mentoring newsletter. Throughout the program's history, college institutional analysis has included the mentoring role and has resulted in several publications on the mentoring function (see bibliography in Bonnabeau, 1996).

LEARNING RESOURCES. Empire State students draw on a broader array of learning resources than is usual at a single institution. Along with the mentoring and tutorials that they arrange as part of their learning contracts, learners may participate in study groups organized voluntarily to pursue common learning goals, complete parts of their program through an array of courses offered through the college's distance learning program, and benefit from the college's technology services and published handbooks.

Additionally, part of the college's original concept was that the resources of the entire SUNY system would be available to learners. Cost-effectiveness would be achieved through sharing of library facilities, cross-enrollment in courses at other institutions, and use of SUNY faculty beyond the college for tutorial assistance. As the college has developed, both college and other resources have expanded. Learners, so long as it is consistent with their degree plans, may enroll in courses offered by SUNY and by private institutions; participate in courses offered by an electronically linked consortium through the SUNY Learning Network; plan field experiences through community-based institutions, government and social agencies, and employers; and gain international experience through a statewide group of cooperative programs. Opportunities are as broad as the resources of the state.

RECOGNITION OF PRIOR LEARNING. ESC was one of the earliest institutions to make recognition of previous learning, either formal or informal, an integral feature of its academic program. Well before the broad acceptance of assessment of prior learning elsewhere, ESC made identification of previous learning part of the degree plan development, allowing transfer credit and providing review of learning from other sources. Typically, entering students fulfill somewhat more than half of their credit hour requirements with previous learning—about two-thirds from other institutions and one-third on the basis of standardized testing, review of sponsored noninstitutional learning experiences, and review of portfolios of informal or specialized learning. In addition, the college encourages the application of experiential learning in the degree plan and provides extensive support to learners who do so. To facilitate the process of evaluation, the college has created an assessment staff and is considering centralized services for this process.

ADMINISTRATION. ESC's founding president has described the principal and unique innovation of the college as structural (Hall, 1991). ESC's charge was to serve people throughout the state, especially those whose geographical or other circumstances made access to existing higher education services difficult. To fulfill this charge, ESC needed a decentralized and dispersed organization that also exhibited coordination and consistency. This paradoxical structure was achieved through the establishment of eight regional centers, each staffed by a director, an associate dean, and a critical mass of nondepartmental faculty representing a range of academic interests. The dispersed centers have considerable autonomy and have added outreach units staffed by one or two faculty and support personnel to reach rural or other specialized populations. The centers maintain communication with and respond to a central administration in Saratoga Springs. The college has benefited from a strong and participative governance system, clear articulation of policy, regular gatherings of faculty and professionals, continuing collegewide professional development activities, and in recent years a strong computer-based communication system. A strong team spirit and nonhierarchical culture characterize operations. The combination of dispersal and effective communication knits the structural elements together as a system.

PROGRAM DOCUMENTATION. Because the college was an early innovator, challenging accepted views, it has always emphasized evaluation of and research on the effectiveness of its programs. It conducts student evaluations, faculty evaluations, program reviews, and external assessment reviews, and it prepares for accreditation reviews as regular procedures. It also has scored well on a SUNY systemwide student satisfaction survey for over fifteen years. Documentation on the college is also very strong. ESC has maintained a strong historical archive, which includes the Empire State Oral History Project. Publications arising from institutional and other studies can be accessed through the bibliography in Bonnabeau (1996) or by consulting college staff.

Summary

Today ESC has become an integral part of the SUNY system, serving a significant portion of the state's public higher education adult enrollment and some out-of-state students as well as some through distance learning. The flexibility of its undergraduate degree format enables it to fulfill learners' individualized goals within a framework of emphases that are meaningful to people outside the institution. The same flexibility also allows ESC to customize its programs when employer or trade union sponsors of learners (see Chapter Eight) have special needs. The mentor-learner relationship, demanding as it is on faculty, facilitates this adaptability and provides supportive contact as learners otherwise work independently. In recent years ESC has extended its methods into several areas of graduate study. Expanded technological facilities and organization for distance learning will increase the college's outreach services to the state and beyond.

AN INDIVIDUALIZED COLLEGE IN A TRADITIONAL UNIVERSITY

University of Memphis—Memphis, Tennessee

University College

Bachelor of Professional Studies

University College (UC) at the University of Memphis (unlike ESC, which is a separate institution in a state system) is an innovative, individualized college embedded in an otherwise traditional public institution. UC was established in 1975. Like many new educational ventures of that time, it responded to students' and educators' ferment and desire for change in that period.

The university, then Memphis State University, undertook a self-assessment of its position in this environment and considered possible innovations. The vice president for academic affairs appointed a group of task forces, one of which was charged to consider a new nontraditional, or experimental, college with an interdisciplinary core curriculum. The task force of about twenty members, largely faculty from various disciplines, took their assignment seriously. They surveyed and visited other experimental programs that had appeared in recent years, including the New College of the University of Alabama, Empire State College, Central Michigan University, the College of Liberal Studies at the University of Oklahoma, and Evergreen College. They drew ideas from many of these organizations and incorporated them into a concept for a new college that would offer flexible, individualized degrees. They also decided at the outset to create an interdisciplinary core curriculum, which has subsequently influenced general education requirements across the university.

The college that resulted from their recommendations has been created as a degree-granting college, equivalent to the five other colleges in the university, and like them, reporting to the chief academic officer. Students pay regular university tuition, and the college receives state funding in parallel with other colleges. University College differs from the others, however, in that it does not have its own faculty. Instead it draws on the other colleges and community members for faculty. It initially sponsored an individualized, interdisciplinary baccalaureate degree program that has now grown to include a Bachelor of Professional Studies (BPS) degree, a Bachelor of Liberal Studies (BLS) degree, and a newly launched Master of Arts in Liberal Studies (MALS) degree, as well as some special programs. The college also serves as a host for the exploration of interdisciplinary ventures that may later be subsumed in other university units and of alternative instructional methods. The discussion here concentrates on the BPS.

The Bachelor of Professional Studies Degree

The BPS can accommodate individual learner choices all the way from uniquely planned programs of study to partially planned specialty tracks shaped by UC advising guidelines. The guidelines ensure that graduates are prepared for sophisticated professional roles yet still permit students considerable individual choice in course selection. The curriculum also presumes students will take initiative in planning their degrees. Within this context the program seeks to develop students' theoretical understanding across disciplines and to relate that theory to the considerable practical experience they often bring to their studies. It also strives to cultivate skills of synthesis and integration.

DEGREE PLANNING. The basic degree plan is a shell composed of five elements: (1) general education; (2) coordinated studies, which may be individualized or follow curricular guidelines; (3) electives; (4) upper-division thematic studies; and (5) an integrating senior project. Coordinated studies, an interdisciplinary major, may include core courses, related supporting courses, and internships or other experiential learning.

Students who wish to pursue a wholly individualized degree form an interdisciplinary advising committee upon entry composed of two or three faculty from different departments. They discuss with this committee their academic goals, tentative special project topics, course selection, potential assessed credit for experiential learning, and independent study and internship possibilities. Based on this planning, students make detailed statements and choices related to each of these topics. Within three months after admission and with approval of their advising committee, they submit a baccalaureate contract form to the college for contract committee review. The contract committee may request revisions, but when these revisions are complete, the contract becomes the student's degree plan.

If students choose one of the fifteen career-oriented specialties that the college has developed, their program is shaped by the established advising guidelines. After studying the guidelines, students meet with an adviser to select courses that best suit their needs within the guidelines, and as soon as possible, to begin planning later experiences such as internships, experiential learning, independent study, and the final special project.

One area, paralegal services, has slightly different procedures from the others, and the Fire Administration and Fire Prevention Technology areas are planned in conjunction with the Degrees at a Distance/Open Learning Fire Service Program in which UC participates. UC provides the fire service tracks through independent study procedures to firefighters in a seven-state region.

RECOGNITION OF PRIOR LEARNING. Students in either the individualized or advising guideline tracks may apply relevant previously earned transfer credit and assessed experiential learning to their degree plans. University regulations allow up to ninety-nine credits of transfer credit. A portfolio preparation workshop led by a faculty member and a student with experience in assessment shows students how to apply for and document prior learning in a portfolio that is then assessed by university faculty. A maximum of thirty-three credits can be awarded through assessment.

CURRICULUM: HUMAN SERVICES AREA EXAMPLE. An example from one of the Bachelor of Professional Studies sequences governed by the advising guidelines, the BPS in human services, will illustrate the curriculum. All degrees require 132 semester credits. Of these, forty-two to forty-five credits are general education requirements from a number of specified areas, although often some choice is possible and some courses are specially created University College courses. The human services professional core requires twenty-two credits selected from guideline-approved choices in the basic core courses: statistical methods, professional writing, and rehabilitation and social intervention. Twenty-one more credits in support courses are selected from course groupings on individual development, the individual and the community, and the individual and the system. In addition, six credits of internship or advanced experiential learning are required. Finally, students take six credits in University College Thematic Studies and six to nine credits related to their special project. Other tracks may require different distributions of activity. The BPS in alcohol and drug abuse services requires more experiential learning and that in commercial aviation a minimum amount of professional instruction in aspects of aviation.

LEARNING RESOURCES. The BPS program is based on enrollment in traditional course formats supplemented with individualized activities such as independent study, internships, and field experiences. However, special areas such as the Open Learning Fire Service Program are exceptions to this pattern. University College offers some of its own courses, but most are drawn from existing offerings in other university departments. Clearly designed forms have been developed to record and monitor the baccalaureate contract and individually designed activity such as internships, field experiences, independent studies, and final special projects.

The Learners

University College was never planned exclusively for adults. Like University Without Walls institutions and Empire State College, which began during the same period, UC envisioned students of all ages who sought a more individually responsive degree. In practice, the college has preponderantly attracted adult students, who make up 90 percent of its current enrollment. Average age runs in the mid-thirties, and over 76 percent of enrollees fall between the ages of twenty-five and forty-nine. About one-third of enrollment is from people of color, mainly

African Americans. Most students are strongly career oriented in their goals. Recent figures indicated about 765 active students enrolled in various UC programs, overwhelmingly in professional studies sequences. Of these, over half were in three BPS options: individualized baccalaureate contracts, 31 percent; paralegal services certificate and degree programs, 29 percent; and Open Learning Fire Service Program, 17 percent. Other areas had considerably smaller enrollments.

Applicants must meet general university admission requirements, which are flexible for persons with a semester's equivalent of previous college enrollment or who are twenty-four or older. University College has an additional admissions procedure in which applicants state their goals and anticipate some of their choices about their programs. The college looks especially for a demonstration that the applicants' goals can be met only in University College and that applicants are prepared to cooperate in developing their degree programs. UC is also considering instituting a minimum grade point requirement to screen marginal applications, although the requirement would be waived for exceptional candidates. Some of the BPS professional tracks have additional requirements, such as relevant work experience. Most applicants have some previous college experience, and many bring credit equivalent to beginning junior level.

Learner Services

The most important service provided by UC is academic advising. From their entry experience through their final integrating courses, students work with advisers to shape their programs and make specific choices related to their goals. Often the advisers become personal mentors, and students rely on them closely.

General university services are available to UC students, and the college has been a successful advocate of maintaining evening office hours for adult students. Such advocacy is also supported by the Adult Student Association, which dates from early in the history of the college. Among the services UC offers is child care. And UC publishes a special newsletter three times a year for distance learners in the Degrees at a Distance/Open Learning Fire Service Program and believes this contributes to retention. UC also issues periodic newsletters with program information for other students.

To maintain some connection between students who otherwise are dispersed, UC offers recurring informal meetings. By letter, UC invites students from a specific area to meet in the late afternoon with faculty, advisers, and staff at the UC offices. UC provides some snacks and offers a setting for students to get acquainted and establish connections with each other and with faculty and staff that are not usually feasible for part-time students.

Faculty and Administration

UC has a pool of about seven hundred faculty upon whom it can draw for advising and other services, and it believes it can meet almost any individual student interest. Many faculty are regularly appointed faculty of the university, who usually work at UC on an overload basis, but occasionally in-load assignments are negotiated with departments. The balance are adjuncts, many of whom are professionals in the community. In the paralegal services area, for instance, a number of local attorneys and judges participate as faculty.

Faculty play a central role in UC academic planning. New proposals for advising guidelines in career areas are developed by small groups of faculty, college staff, and community professionals. After UC reviews other college offerings to avoid duplication and consults with college deans, faculty and related community professionals complete the guideline design. Proposals are then referred to a college curriculum committee and a fifteen-member UC faculty council for review, after which they are sent to the provost for final approval. Guidelines are considered emphases under the basic UC BPS rubric and do not require degree approval at a higher level.

Students have opportunities to evaluate faculty on their teaching and advising, and results are shared with faculty. Annually, the college recognizes superior faculty service with the University College Advising Award and the Part-Time Faculty Award. Each year it also gives the Distinguished Faculty Award to honor outstanding overall service to the college.

Outcomes and Evaluation

UC staff express commitment to access combined with quality. Over its history UC has provided a valuable route for persons in the Memphis metropolitan area who are capable of achievement in higher education but who have lacked opportunity. Many are people with considerable prior education or learning from experience who cannot afford the time for a traditional degree program. A recent study of the time students took from application to graduation, covering the period from August 1992 to May 1997, showed over 20 percent completing their degrees in the first year, 25 percent in the second year, and nearly 20 percent in the third year. Given that most students attend part time, these completion rates suggest extensive prior college credit and assessed credit from prior learning. Some participants were former students at the university who had experienced difficulty focusing on more prescribed programs but established a clearer direction for themselves in the individually responsive and advising-intensive UC degree program.

UC conducts regular alumni surveys, and the respondents indicate strong satisfaction with the program. Comments on the value of the integrating senior project are especially positive. Fifty percent of respondents to the 1997 survey reported going on to further education, mainly at the graduate level. Many also indicated that the degree had been helpful to them in job promotion and advancement.

In addition to the BPS, UC offers a Bachelor of Liberal Studies, which includes special tracks in Judaic studies, African American studies, and women's studies. In fall 1998, the college began a master of arts in liberal studies degree for which early enrollment seemed promising. It will be the first graduate offering of the college and increases its recognition within its parent graduate research institution.

Future

Presently the UC degree programs are doing well and continue to find a constituency in their environment. UC enjoys a good acceptance level in the institution and community. Its role is expanding somewhat through offerings at a university center in Jackson, Tennessee, the hub city in a developing area about eighty-five miles northeast of Memphis. The college does a limited amount of distance learning delivery, although primary responsibility for learning technology is located elsewhere in the university.

A possible area for development is study in nonprofit management. UC currently offers a BPS in nonprofit development and administration through an advising guideline track, and it is discussing collaboration with other regional institutions and a national project to prepare persons for entry-level positions in nonprofit management.

TRANSFERRING INITIATIVE TO ADULT LEARNERS IN AN ALTERNATIVE FORMAT

Atlantic Union College—South Lancaster, Massachusetts

Adult Degree Program

Baccalaureate Degree Program

Atlantic Union College is a much smaller institution than either ESC or UC. It had followed a traditional pattern of educational offerings, but as it considered work with adult learners, it concluded that it should provide a learner-driven program in a novel format.

The Adult Degree Program (ADP) at Atlantic Union College offers an external, highly individualized baccalaureate program leading to BA and BS degrees in several fields. As is common in other institutions, the program borrowed some ideas that originated elsewhere, but it adapted and developed them in ways that were innovative and also feasible given the college's mission, traditions, and capabilities. It retained the familiar four-year baccalaureate pattern based on general education and a major specialization, but it took a fresh approach to the design of the curriculum and the processes by which it would be fulfilled. By transferring initiative for the planning of content to the learners, and by freeing them from all but brief attendance at the campus, ADP turned old assumptions upside down. The means by which it did this have significant educational benefits and hold lessons for others.

Atlantic Union College is an independent institution in central Massachusetts, located about fifty miles northwest of Boston and near Worcester. The college was founded in 1882 by the Seventh-Day Adventist Church to educate workers for the worldwide church organization, and although it continues that denominational goal, it also prepares persons for professions and occupations in the larger society. Its educational perspective reflects religious and liberal education values, which in the case of the Adult Degree Program include a mission of service to persons with limited college opportunities. It also meant that the new program took shape in an existing context rather than starting with no antecedents, as did Empire State.

The initiative to establish ADP arose in the early 1970s from discussions among the president, the academic dean, and some interested faculty. They recognized the desire of many adults to complete interrupted college study and the barriers that extended campus attendance posed for these persons. They also were aware of short-residence distance learning programs at a number of institutions, particularly Goddard College, which they visited. Goddard had initiated an adult degree program in 1963 that had parallels with other adult special degrees of that time, such as the Bachelor of Liberal Studies degree at Syracuse University and the University of Oklahoma. All these models, in turn, owed debts to European residential adult study experience, which began to influence U.S. practice in the 1950s (Benson & Adams, 1987). Finally, the people at Atlantic Union knew they had residence and class meeting facilities that lay dormant during vacation periods. After a short planning period, ADP was launched in February 1972, basically on the Goddard model.

Start-up funding for the program came from internal college resources and were initially marginal. The program was accommodated in college facilities when they were not in use by the traditional programs. No special program administrative office was established until 1974. Faculty initially assumed teaching responsibilities in the program as part of their regular load. The program now sustains itself from student tuition and contributes to college overhead. Tuition is priced lower for ADP learners than for full-time residential students—presently about 60 percent of on-campus charges—due to ADP's lower demand on college resources.

The boldest innovations of the program lay in its reconception of the academic calendar and the transfer of responsibility to the learners to plan and carry out their studies independently. To make this design work, new systems had to be put in place.

CALENDAR AND SEGMENTS OF STUDY. ADP redefined the academic year as two semiannual periods rather than the traditional nine-month cycle. Within each six-month session, instead of enrolling in a group of discrete courses, students pursue *units* of coherent and integrated study. Students, with faculty collaboration, plan units that will earn between 15 and 18 semester hours of credit. The degree requires eight units with a total of 128 credit hours. Students may enroll in full or half units. In some cases units may be planned to extend over twelve months, and if necessary, students may apply for extensions of the time period.

Details of each unit plan, including subsection specifics, are recorded upon registration and become part of the student's academic record when completed. In education degree units, which must satisfy state certification requirements, specific course equivalents and credit hours are recorded. If transfer credit or prior learning assessment is applied to unit study, this is indicated.

The unit concept enables students to plan a large block of study with interrelated and integrated areas and to pursue it in a self-paced fashion. This avoids the intellectual fragmentation often associated with enrollment in a series of unrelated courses. Students are expected to devote twenty hours per week to study, to maintain journals of their activity, and to maintain communication with a faculty supervisor during each six-month period.

Curriculum

ADP provides students with both a framework to guide individual planning and the flexibility to make unique choices within the framework. The curriculum has its roots in the liberal arts tradition and encourages humanistic values of exploration and expansion of awareness. Approximately half of the degree, or a unit each in humanities, social science, science, mathematics, and in reflection of the college's tradition, religion, are required in individually designed study. Majors and areas of emphasis are offered in a broad selection of liberal education and professional fields, and interdepartmental majors can be arranged with approval. Majors require two or three units of study, which are normally planned as a coherent whole. The two final units, including half a unit in the major, must be taken in ADP rather than being met by transfer or assessed credit.

Residence and Independent Study

Unit enrollment extends over a six-month period, but it includes two distinctly different periods of activity: a short, intensive residential seminar on campus followed by an extended period of guided independent study. It is this combination that makes the program feasible for many adults who are unable fulfill semester-long attendance requirements at a campus site.

The seminars, which convene twice a year, in January and July, play a pivotal role in the program design. Entering students and education students requiring certain certification requirements attend for eleven days. Others spend nine days on campus. The seminars include several intensive minicourses and related library study that reacquaint newcomers with college-level study expectations, provide group contact for these learners who must spend much of their time studying alone, and open up new areas of content to all participants. In some cases the experience may demonstrate to individuals that external degree study is not appropriate for them.

A large portion of the seminar is devoted to planning the forthcoming unit's study plan. Early in the seminar students brainstorm ideas for their units with faculty, staff, and other students with similar interests. Subsequently, they submit tentative topic proposals for review. On approval of the proposal, each student meets individually with a study supervisor to create the details of a plan of study for the next six months. The plan includes a method of procedure, a preliminary bibliography and other resources, a plan for communicating with the supervisor, a timetable for completion of segments of the plan, and a statement of the expected specific products of the study and its credit hour value. The activities that satisfy the unit requirements can vary widely, depending upon the agreement between student and supervisor. They may include reading and research; application of theory to such practical situations as job experience, creative work, and travel; and other activity that is relevant at the college level. In the second week of the seminar students submit drafts of their proposals for ADP review and carry out revision if necessary, after which the proposal is registered as a contract for the plan of study.

Newly entering students initially exhibit considerable anxiety about the independent study planning process. The program uses the regular group meetings to facilitate their entry and also conducts daily newcomer meetings to respond to questions, clarify understanding, and anticipate next steps. It also provides a notebook of materials that guide the proposal planning process.

The seminars also include evaluation sessions where returning students present and receive feedback on their work. Students summarize their previous unit's work and present it for discussion with fellow students. As part of their learning experience, the students also present their supervisors with a self-evaluation of their work in relation to the original proposal, and they also make an evaluation of their supervisors. The supervisors, in turn, evaluate the academic quality of the work, assigning a letter grade and writing a short narrative comment that become part of the student's record. Students are also evaluated on seminar attendance, participation, and work done in minicourses. Graduating students attend their final seminar for only one week but participate in a special integrative capstone minicourse for graduates and in the graduation ceremony.

Recognition of Previous Learning

The program accepts previous learning for credit toward the degree if it can be documented. Students may transfer up to 75 percent of their required credit from courses taken previously at accredited higher education institutions. They may also gain credit from challenge examinations such as CLEP (College-Level Examination Program), or by preparing portfolios that document learning from professional, applied, or other nonacademic learning experiences. Application of previous learning to the individual student's learning plan is negotiated with ADP upon entry to the program.

Admission and Recruitment

Application is open to anyone twenty-five years or older who holds a high school diploma or the equivalent. Provisional admission may be granted to individuals who are not high school graduates but who demonstrate ability to benefit. Applicants must provide indications of writing ability, motivation, and a commitment to spend at least twenty hours per week in independent study. ADP admission criteria are flexible and responsive to individual strengths. Nevertheless, because the independent study modes require strong self-direction and communication abilities, applicants whose writing skill or motivation appears weak may be discouraged or counseled to seek alternative preparation.

ADP recruitment is directed toward adults who desire a college degree but who are unable or unwilling to comply with traditional attendance schedules. ADP largely recruits in its immediate locale and its region through local media and regional church publications. Word-of-mouth plays a major role in recruitment. Some recruitment occurs serendipitously through Adventist connections, even though the recruits themselves may not be church members. For example, a cadre of education students from Washington's Olympic peninsula learned of the program from an Adventist graduate working in their area. In another case, students from Bermuda learned of the program through church members or church publications. Inquiries from further afield are attracted by ADP information on the college's Web site. In a recent twelve-month period, the program enrolled about 140 students, of whom 26 completed the program. Total college enrollment is approximately 700.

Faculty and Administration

The program is closely linked to the college's governance structure. ADP has a full-time director who is a member of the regular college faculty and also carries the title of associate dean. The director reports to the college's academic dean and also chairs a program faculty committee that oversees program operation and recommends on academic and administrative matters. Critical policy matters are referred to a collegewide academic affairs committee and, if necessary, may be reviewed by the college faculty as a whole.

ADP faculty are drawn from regular faculty of the college. Although this was not the case in the beginning, they are now paid a stipend upon students' completion of units that they supervise. The program conducts informal faculty development through ongoing peer relationships. The college has a tradition of teaching, and there is strong commitment to the program among faculty. One member expressed great appreciation of the program's flexibility and especially praised the seminar component.

Future

Program staff see possible additional growth ahead for the program, although it may entail adding adjunct faculty because recent seminars have strained the capacity of existing faculty. The college is exploring use of distance learning technology, although what application it might make of it is not yet clear. It could establish a new program organized on a different basis, or it could make distance learning a function of the Adult Degree Program.

AN INDIVIDUALIZED GRADUATE PROGRAM IN A MULTICULTURAL AND ENVIRONMENTALLY CONSCIOUS SETTING

Prescott College—Prescott, Arizona

Adult Degree Program

Master of Arts Program

The Prescott College Master of Arts Program (MAP) is a small, individualized graduate program focused on a well-defined audience. It emphasizes its distinctive environment and cultural setting, and it illustrates how a small institution can reflect its character and values through an innovative program.

MAP describes itself as designed for highly motivated adults who are "ready to work creatively and independently" and who wish to "consider and explore the environmental and multicultural dimensions of the subjects they are studying." It brings together an alternative calendar; a combination of limited residence and guided independent study; a learner-initiated curriculum based on theory, practice, and research; and planned use of community resources in a way that enables adults to pursue the degree while holding full-time employment and remaining in their home locations. Study is interdisciplinary but can lead to specialization, including certification in teaching.

Prescott College originated in a local community initiative to establish an undergraduate liberal arts college. A planning and fundraising effort continued over several years. This deliberation culminated in a Ford Foundation–funded symposium that concluded the new college should be nontraditional and experimental and its programs should be interdisciplinary, experiential, and multicultural. The college adopted a mission "to educate students of diverse ages and backgrounds to understand, thrive in, and enhance our world community and environment." From the outset it built on the ethnic diversity and environmental awareness of the Southwest, and it has developed a culture of directly experiencing the regional landscape.

The college began in September 1966 by enrolling traditional age students in a residential program; however, it floundered financially, and its original board closed it in 1971. A dedicated group of faculty and students refused to disband and continued their work under the name of Prescott Center for Alternative Education. They met in faculty homes and sought accreditation from the North Central Association of Colleges and Schools. Through determination they succeeded, and the college was resurrected. One consequence of this experience has been a strong faculty and student voice in the governance of the college; faculty and students each elect a board member, and the entire board slate is submitted for confirmation to faculty, students, and alumni.

In 1978, Prescott College expanded its mission and original values and added the baccalaureate Adult Degree Program to its other studies. The Master of Arts Program was added in 1992, adapting the model developed for the adult undergraduate program.

The Learners

The program design begins with learner initiative. The college provides a framework, or shell, within which the learner "seeking something different" can pursue individual goals. Prospective enrollees therefore must approach the application process with a preliminary proposal for a degree study plan already formulated. Applications do not require any standardized test scores but do ask for recommendations, personal goals statements, and the preliminary study plan. Autobiographical statements, nonacademic achievements, and evidence of motivation are taken into consideration. Admissions reviewers place heavy emphasis on evidence of good writing skills, a strong focus on goals for study, and an ability to work independently. About half of initial applications may be declined, usually because of insufficiently developed study plans. Those rejected often are encouraged to reapply after they review and redraft their proposals. The college also rejects study proposals for which it does not have appropriate faculty resources.

Recruitment for the program is largely by word of mouth, although the program does some focused advertising through Arizona media and presents face-to-face information sessions to groups when there is sufficient interest. Because both the adult bachelor's and master's degree programs require brief campus attendance twice a semester, most enrollment comes from Arizona and the immediately surrounding region, in contrast to the undergraduate resident program, which draws nationally.

Curriculum and Calendar

Learners may pursue study proposals that fall into one or more of six broadly defined content areas that the college is accredited to offer: counseling and psychology, cultural and regional studies, education, environmental studies, humanities, and outdoor education/wilderness leadership. Participants may combine two or more areas, and in addition to gaining general mastery in their area, they usually focus on one or more specific topics, applications, or issues within that area.

Like Atlantic Union College, Prescott has reconfigured the academic year for its adult programs into two long segments—in its case two terms of twenty-one weeks each. Two weekend residential meetings, or *colloquia,* are held each term, and students are required to attend. The first occurs at the beginning of the semester and the second about two-thirds of the way through. The colloquia provide opportunities for contact and dialogue among faculty and students that reduce the isolation of independent study. Activities include adviser-student planning meetings; student presentations of work in progress; faculty-led workshops; various settings for brainstorming, networking, and discussion; and workshops on MAP's operational details. In addition to the graduate advisers, resource faculty and staff are available for consultation. A critical product of the colloquium at the beginning of each semester is a detailed study plan, or learning contract, for each student for the coming semester.

Entry and Degree Planning

Upon admission new participants attend a day-and-a-half orientation session immediately prior to their first colloquium to gain direct experience with MAP planning and study methods. They also meet with a graduate adviser to develop their preliminary study plan more fully. Advisers are recommended by MAP staff based on their appropriateness for the student's proposal, but the match with an adviser must be confirmed by the student after an initial meeting. Together student and adviser create a working plan for the whole degree and a more detailed plan for the first semester's work. The agreement between the student and graduate adviser can establish the degree plan, but if there are problems in reaching agreement, the plan is reviewed by a curriculum committee composed of all core graduate faculty.

Most degree plans are designed to extend over three semesters, but in some cases, due to certification or other requirements, they may continue to four. All work must be taken with Prescott College, and neither transfer nor prior learning assessment credit may be applied. A semester each is devoted to theory, practicum, and research, and the study plan includes examination of the environmental and multicultural dimensions of the area of study. The theory segment includes exploration of the conceptual base and issues of the field. The practicum involves a supervised internship, a field placement or other active project that connects theory and practice. The thesis requires a unique research study or exploration that results in a written or creative product related to the field. Midway through the degree process, each student submits a qualifying paper that demonstrates the research, writing, and critical skills necessary for the thesis.

Following the planning colloquium at the beginning of each semester, students carry out the activities described in their plans. They are expected to spend twenty to twenty-five hours per week on their studies, and they maintain communication with their advisers by visits, telephone, mail, and electronic means. To maintain pacing, at three-week intervals they send study packets of written materials document-ing their activities to their advisers. These materials may be critical analyses of reading, research papers, internship evaluations, or thesis chapters. Students also supply an update on their progress and on any obstacles or new considerations they have encountered. To develop articulation skills, students must submit their reports in writing. Con-versations may supplement but not replace written reports. Advisers respond in writing, offering comment, support, advice, and challenge.

Students may complete segments of their semester study plan at any time within the term. At the end of the semester the student submits a written description of the work completed, and student and adviser each write a narrative evaluation of the work done. The adviser evalu-ations may include comments from other resource persons who have consulted on the work. The student and adviser course descriptions and evaluations, along with course titles and credits awarded, are incorpo-rated into an official narrative transcript. No letter grades are recorded.

In addition to the student and faculty evaluations, MAP regularly conducts program reviews to assess success in meeting planned out-comes. It also has invited outside reviewers to examine student prod-ucts for their quality.

Faculty and Administration

MAP has a core group of full-time graduate faculty and is adding more as the program grows. It augments the core group with resident faculty and adjuncts as necessary to serve individual student needs. In particu-lar, it will seek qualified adjuncts to match students' specific individual goals. Adjuncts need not be resident at the college site and may live in the vicinity of the students they advise.

A graduate adviser serves as the primary faculty member for each stu-dent for the duration of the program. Advisers' roles are to help plan, carry out, and evaluate all stages of the program, and to offer guidance, support, and challenge as the student progresses. Advisers, in collabora-tion with students, may call on other faculty for assistance in particular areas of study. In addition, a *practicum supervisor* is designated to pro-vide on-site supervision of a student's practical experience, and a *second reader* with special expertise is selected for the thesis committee.

Orientation for new faculty is conducted at the colloquia, as are developmental meetings for all faculty.

Oversight for MAP is provided by a faculty council chaired by a faculty member with the title of *coordinator* who administers the program. Administratively, the program is located in Prescott's Adult Degree Program, which is supervised by a dean who reports to the academic vice president. The Adult Degree Program functions separately from the resident degree program and exercises its own decision making about its functions.

MAP was initiated with internal college resources, and it sustains itself and contributes to college overhead from its tuition income. MAP tuition is lower than residential baccalaureate tuition but somewhat higher than adult baccalaureate tuition, reflecting varying levels of cost.

Future

MAP currently enrolls between ninety and one hundred students, with a new intake of about twenty-five each semester. Due to its semester-by-semester pacing and relatively low attrition, MAP graduates approximately half its enrollment each year. The program continues to attract interest, and growth of 5 or 6 percent a year is anticipated. Total college enrollment is about nine hundred, with slightly less than half that number in the Adult Degree Program, of which MAP is a part.

Because of the flexibility of the curriculum and its adaptability to different needs, MAP's basic structure will probably not change. For instance, the current pattern can be adapted to needs of employer sponsors of learners, and a number of students are attending on employer tuition reimbursement plans. Some demand is appearing for master's level qualifications in licensed professions such as school counseling, and the program may consider whether it can serve those needs through its model. The college has a relationship with the Navajo Nation to sponsor tribal members for both bachelor's and master's degrees in education through a Center for Indian Bilingual Education, and this effort may grow.

CONCLUSION

Although the four programs just described differ in many respects, they also share many characteristics and elements that contribute to individual learner choice and self-direction. At the heart of each of them is intensive advising that fulfills a supportive and nurturing, but not directive, function and involves learners in what Knowles (Knowles & Associates, 1985, pp. 17–18) called *mutual planning*. Whether conducted by professional staff, faculty, or mentors, the interaction on the one hand introduces participants to the program, assists as they design study plans, and provides ongoing encouragement. On the other hand it changes faculty from teachers to facilitators and counselors, a change that leads many programs to provide recurring faculty development through coaching, workshops, and seminars in working with adult learners.

Because most of the programs depend heavily on self-managed independent study by learners, they seek evidence of the capability for that independence in their admission processes. They also try to counteract the isolation of independent study through recurring contacts, whether through advising or periodic intensive seminars. The program flexibility enables learners to use a variety of study methods, which can be adapted to their learning styles and personal schedules. Similarly, learners can draw on learning resources beyond the program's campus. Almost all the programs recognize participants' previous learning and experience through generous credit transfer policies and procedures for assessing informal prior learning. Because individual learners' plans are so variable, most programs have developed careful procedures to document learning plan agreements and amendments.

Finally, the programs strive for integration of the learning experience through such continuing activities across the program as journal keeping; culminating, or *capstone,* requirements; and seminars. These activities bring closure to the stage of learning the participants are completing and contribute to the goal of cultivating a disposition to lifelong learning among program graduates.

4

LEARNER-CENTERED DESIGN

ASK ANY GROUP of adult education practitioners what principle is most important to their professional work, and most will probably reply, "Start with the learner," or some variant of that phrase. Centering on the learner has been the distinguishing characteristic of practice in adult learning practice since early in this century. In 1926, Eduard Lindeman wrote, "In adult education the curriculum is built around the student's needs and interests. Every adult person finds himself in specific situations with respect to his work, his recreation, his family life, his community life. . . . Adult education begins at this point" (Lindeman, 1989, p. 6). Change has also begun at this point as adult educators, such as the initiators of the adult special degree programs of the 1960s, have sought ways to reshape existing forms to fit adult learners' circumstances, backgrounds, and needs.

The same focus on learners runs through the adult learning principles and their implications summarized in Chapter Two. Rather than discuss institutional structures or definition of content, theorists and practitioners have called for mutual respect between learner and teacher, flexibility, and learner involvement in the learning situation. These ideas were probably most fully developed by Malcolm Knowles, whose thinking on this topic extended over many years, culminating in his *Modern Practice of Adult Education* (1980; see also Knowles, 1989; Knowles & Associates, 1985).

Starting from the democratic and humanist perspective that given sufficient information, people will make the right choices for themselves and that democracy releases human potential, Knowles (1980, pp. 67–68) believed that learning activities should be based on participants' interests. Further, learners should have maximum participation

in decisions about the experience. These premises led Knowles to advocate approaches that have been broadly adopted and practiced. An
adult learning program should facilitate access by providing easy
approach, a welcoming environment, supportive services, and adaptability to individual circumstances. The program should establish a
friendly climate of learning for adults, both in a physical facility that is
suitable and in a psychological environment that is warm, mutually
respectful, trusting, supportive, and collaborative. The program should
involve learners in diagnosing their learning needs, setting learning
goals, designing a plan of learning, managing the learning experience,
and evaluating learning outcomes. An important device for accomplish-
ing all these steps in learner involvement is the learning contract that a
learner and a teacher, or facilitator, develop mutually. Knowles also
believed the process should be characterized by respectful acknowledgment of the learner's previous experience; adaptability to changes in the
learner's circumstances during the course of learning; ongoing supportive engagement between the learner and the facilitator; and positive
reinforcement, or feedback, to the learner. Knowles developed these
concepts into the system of *andragogy*, "the art and science of helping
adults learn," which has influenced a generation of adult educators
(Knowles & Associates, 1985, p. 6; Pratt, 1993). Not all authors on
adult education practice have accepted Knowles's full formulation, but
many propose practice that parallels his sensitive and nurturing spirit
(Hiemstra & Sisco, 1990; Sisco & Hiemstra, 1991). Brundage and
MacKeracher (1980) especially reflect Knowles's empathy with adult
learners. These views have permeated many adult learning programs,
including some of those this book describes.

Taking a somewhat different approach, Cross (1981) reviewed literature on motivational factors that affected adults' participation, and
by implication persistence, in learning activities. She also analyzed various theories of adult learning, including Knowles's andragogy, in
order to develop a framework for research and action. She noted the
attention Knowles's relatively new concept had attracted but also the
criticism it had drawn, and she took a neutral position until more research could test it. From her review, she proposed two models for
adult educators and researchers to consider in their work. The Chain
of Response (COR) model dealt with negative and positive motivations for participation and their valences which might be affected by
interventions. The other model, Characteristics of Adult Learners
(CAL), described a set of personal and situational characteristics that
distinguish adults from children as learners and therefore could sug-

gest different approaches to be used by educators of adults. The follow-up study that she suggested to examine these formulations has not occurred (Hiemstra, 1993; Merriam & Caffarella, 1999). However, many of the factors that she noted with regard to both adult learner motivation and characteristics are addressed by the recommendations of Knowles and other adult-centered authors.

All the programs discussed in this chapter place adult learners at the center of their concern, especially through well-developed advising systems. At the same time, each works in a different institutional or community environment and that leads to varying approaches and to greater or less guidance for program participants. Although they started their work with adults at different times and under differing circumstances, most of these programs take a holistic approach to learners and learning, an approach they encourage through continuing reflective and integrative experiences. Regis University offers flexible scheduling and individual degree planning. Capital University and St. Edward's University, in interestingly similar programs, provide a high degree of responsiveness within the context of strongly specified curricula. Central Maine Technical College enables learners to shape customized individual sequences in an occupational program as they build on their previous technical education. In contrast to these programs, three cohort-based programs, at Columbia Union College, Thomas More College, and Northwestern College, illustrate how highly prescribed curricula and pacing can serve learner interests. Finally, Cambridge College demonstrates how a positive *climate of learning* can achieve success with populations that sometimes are overlooked.

FLEXIBILITY AND RESPONSIVENESS TO ADULT LEARNER NEEDS

Regis University—Denver, Colorado

School for Professional Studies

Baccalaureate Degree Programs

The School for Professional Studies (SPS) of Regis University is a major provider of adult higher education opportunities in the Denver metropolitan area and, through off-campus centers, on the eastern and western Colorado slopes of the Rocky Mountains and in Wyoming. Introduction of distance learning procedures has begun to extend its reach even farther, and it will be a major participant in the emerging Western Governors' Virtual University. More than 3,800 persons enroll each term in the undergraduate program, on which this discussion will focus, and about 25 percent of them graduate each year.

Regis has offered adult-oriented programs for about twenty years, over which time it has developed a distinctive learner-centered approach, a wide choice of curricula, a cadre of faculty and staff experienced in assisting adult learners, and program flexibility sensitive to both learner and community needs. In recent years the adult programs have been brought together in the School for Professional Studies.

SPS evolved from Regis University's involvement with adult learners from the late 1970s. That involvement began with an accelerated degree completion program for military personnel in Colorado Springs in 1978. Based on success there, Regis shortly after opened a program in Denver on a similar model and added a Master of Business Administration degree. In 1988, a sister institution, Loretto Heights College, closed, and Regis absorbed many of its adult programs, including a University Without Walls option that has since been absorbed into a *guided independent study* model. In 1992, a new dean, who still is with the program, studied a number of adult programs and recommended that for better direction, coordination, and student support services, Regis should consolidate its adult programs in the School for Professional Studies into three distinct divisions: graduate programs, undergraduate programs, and academic delivery systems. The latter is the major support unit for adult student services. Since then, SPS has had a large degree of academic autonomy over its programs and has been able to oversee all aspects of their presentation.

Learner-Centered Elements

The programs of SPS bring together complementary elements that contribute to success with program participants. These elements are an accelerated calendar, a flexible curriculum, adaptable instructional modes, a strong program of prior learning assessment, faculty and staff committed to facilitation, and convenient learner services.

CALENDAR. From its beginning, the foundation concept of Regis's programs has been an accelerated calendar that enables busy adults to use learning time efficiently and flexibly. The university initially offered eight-week units of study, then experimented with four-week blocks, and finally settled on five-week course periods. Students attend four-hour classes one night a week or, in some cases, two-hour classes twice a week for the five-week period. Most participants concentrate their attention on one course at a time, and their class attendance is supplemented with out-of-class work that includes projects and applications. In recent years the prevailing five-week module has been supplemented with eight-week courses in subjects thought to need more class contact time. Some courses are also available with weekend classes. Each course yields three semester hours credit. Students may complete nine three-credit courses in a twelve-month period, although completion of six is more typical. With permission they may take as many as twelve courses in a year, but that is unusual.

The earliest design of the program organized students into cohorts whose members worked through the program as a group, but this was soon abandoned for an open system in which students choose their enrollment sequences individually. The adult program operates within the context of conventional fifteen-week semesters, so participants can complete three five-week or two eight-week modules each term. They may also combine the five- and eight-week modules in different combinations, and with permission, they may enroll in semester-long courses in the university's traditional program. The open system appears to work well for the SPS population. It accommodates the emergencies and other exigencies that caused people to leave their groups in the cohort system and brings learners in contact with a broader mix of their peers than they could meet in cohorts. SPS still uses cohorts on a limited basis, to serve groups at specific employer sites or remote rural locations where groups might otherwise be difficult to assemble.

In recognition of Colorado's sometimes severe winter climate, the calendar also builds in planned *make-up days,* in case weather or other unanticipated events force cancellation of scheduled classes.

CURRICULA. SPS offers learners considerable choice in both degree specialty and content. Students may chose between predetermined classroom majors or individualized, self-designed models in up to sixty approved majors, each requiring 128 semester hours. In either case, degree requirements include 45 hours in general education, a major component that varies in credit hours with the subject concentration, an optional minor, and general electives. Some majors have more specified classes than others, but all afford learners a considerable role in planning, design, and evaluation of their study. Broad choice is possible in meeting general education requirements, and many majors include approximately thirty hours of electives. Similarly, a variety of learning modes is available.

In keeping with the university's Jesuit tradition, all curricula include a strong values component. This is expressed in part through general education requirements in philosophy, religious studies, and ethics. Faculty also are encouraged to address values across the curriculum through applications and issues they raise. A current concern of the program is how most effectively to present values to an increasingly diverse and mobile body of learners, many of whom participate through distance and mediated learning. Recently a senior capstone course has been added whose aim is to integrate study in general education, the major, and values in a summative experience.

LEARNING RESOURCES. SPS offers a variety of learning formats, and students may move freely among them. The majority—approximately 80 percent—of enrollment is in instructor-led classes in five- or eight-week modules. Specific class procedures vary with instructors and content, although faculty development encourages all faculty to use a variety of teaching approaches with adults.

In addition, the program provides several methods of distance learning. Building on its University Without Walls experience, it gives students the opportunity for individually designed guided independent study courses that can apply to degree requirements. An increasing number of courses are offered through Regis Distance Learning packages including video, print-based modules, and Internet communication. Video material may be purchased or viewed over the Knowledge TV Network of Jones Education, a Denver-based company. SPS is also offering courses over the Internet. One undergraduate degree, the Bachelor of Business Administration, and two graduate degrees, the Master of Business Administration and Master of Non-Profit Management, can be completed through distance learning procedures.

RECOGITION OF PRIOR LEARNING. Because most SPS enrollees enter with previous college study and are required to have at least three years' full-time work experience, they usually bring a considerable amount of academically equivalent learning. An important aspect of their degree planning is the application of this learning to degree requirements. Thirty credits of their degree total must be taken with Regis, but they may transfer up to ninety-eight hours from other institutions, although that maximum is seldom achieved. Alternatively, they may apply up to forty-five hours from various forms of prior learning assessment.

The program for recognizing learning from noninstitutional sources is comprehensive, and it has been recognized by the Council for Adult and Experiential Learning for its excellence. It includes the services of a testing center that administers CLEP (College-Level Examination Program), DANTES (Defense Activity for Non-Traditional Educational Support), National League for Nursing, and Regis University challenge examinations. Credit recommendations from the American Council on Education for military or PONSI (Program on Noncollegiate Sponsored Instruction) courses are also applicable toward degrees.

Students may also acquire credit for experiential learning by means of portfolio assessment. They enroll in a one-credit portfolio course, Experiential Learning, in which they learn how to prepare essays supporting their applications for credit. If the experiential learning is deemed academically appropriate, the credit is normally applied to their degree plans in three-credit blocks.

FACULTY AND STAFF. SPS has developed graduate and undergraduate faculty, qualified at the master's level and above, who have experience of theory and practice in their fields and who are oriented to adult learning. There is a core group of approximately 55 full-time faculty and a pool of 300 to 350 part-time affiliate faculty.

The core faculty function in two roles. A main group serve as academic advisers to the students in the degree programs. They also serve as faculty of record for guided independent study courses. Most are prepared to serve as general advisers for all areas of study, although members of a specialist group work with students in the teacher certification program. SPS has found that establishing a one-to-one relationship between each student and an adviser helps retention, but if necessary, students are always able to reach alternate advisers. Students and advisers communicate largely by telephone but also in person at the campus. Traveling advisers serve the off-campus sites. A second group of core faculty serve as faculty chairs in degree concentrations and oversee content.

Affiliate faculty are academically qualified persons and preferably also practicing professionals in their fields. The process of inducting affiliate faculty into the program is a key element of quality control for SPS. Prior to appointment prospects spend a full day in assessment of their suitability. If selected, they spend another day in formal orientation to the university, SPS, and the program in which they will teach. Then, before assuming responsibility for a course, they participate in an internship with an experienced teacher throughout an entire course.

Both core and affiliate faculty are governed by an extensive faculty handbook that outlines procedures, responsibilities, and rights. Both core and affiliate faculty participate in SPS governance. SPS conducts an ongoing program of faculty development, using workshops and consultants on various needs. The program maintains an annual fund of $25,000 for individual faculty development grants. Faculty performance is regularly evaluated and recognized. Retention of faculty, including affiliate faculty, is high, and faculty express a strong commitment to the program.

LEARNER SERVICES. The most important learner service in the Regis model is continual access to faculty advisers, as described in the section on faculty. Each new student comes to campus or one of the remote sites for a meeting with his or her adviser to get an overview of the program and orientation to program services. Following entry, advisers are available to work with students on their degree plans. Subsequently, periodic *student services days* at the main and remote campuses offer a selection of workshops on learning styles and learning skills; time management; job skills such as résumé writing, interviewing, and networking; and procedures for the guided independent study. Limited career counseling is also available.

Other services also are learner friendly and offered at convenient hours. Students may register by telephone, fax, or mail as well as in person. Financial aid is provided through a general university office. Deferred tuition payment plans and direct billing to employers are possible for students on employer tuition reimbursement plans. Regis provides libraries in Denver and Colorado Springs. An extended campus library service assists faculty and students at remote sites and distance learning students. The main campus bookstore provides its services to remote sites. SPS students receive a program newsletter and have access to general student services at the main Denver campus.

Partnerships

SPS has exported its successful program through licensing relationships with thirteen other institutions. Through a university-wide consulting service, the Office of New Ventures, it has entered into mutual agreements with partner institutions who adapt its model to their institutional settings. SPS encourages each partner college to exercise initiative and independence as it customizes the new processes to its setting. At the same time, the partner institution benefits from SPS's previous experience in program operation. SPS continues an advisory relation with the partner during the start-up contract period of two to six years. For these services, SPS charges an initial fee and a portion of program income.

Outcomes and Evaluation

SPS conducts regular evaluations by students and faculty, periodic program review and external assessment, and surveys of alumni and employer sponsors of learners.

Recently, in cooperation with some of its partners, SPS has initiated an extensive program outcome evaluation. With the assistance of Raymond Wlodkowski, it has launched a three-phase, cross-institutional research study. The first phase compares learner satisfaction at the end of courses and expert evaluation of learner performance. A second phase compares results of accelerated and traditional calendar courses. The first two phases have been completed and reported on (Wlodkowski & Westover, 1998). A third phase will examine distance learning outcomes.

Summary

Through its flexibility and responsiveness, SPS has established itself as a major adult learning provider in Denver and surrounding areas, especially among employers. Its degree programs' adaptability, breadth, and applicability; recognition of previous learning; well-developed full-time and affiliate faculty; and personal attention given to students in advising and learner services all contribute to credibility. The accelerated calendar, in which learners concentrate on one course at a time but take courses at a pace they set themselves, fits well with learners' individual circumstances.

In addition to its undergraduate degrees, SPS offers six master's degree programs in professional and liberal studies. It also has close, cooperative relations with Denver-area employers. Through its Corporate Education Services, it can provide employers with a group of services that include both credit and credit-free courses offered on site or through various other delivery modes. It can also work with employers to design specific courses or certificate sequences.

EXTENDING THE INSTITUTION'S MISSION TO ADULTS: TWO CASES

Capital University—Columbus, Ohio

Adult Degree Program

St. Edward's University—Austin, Texas

New College

Bachelor's Degree Completion Programs

As some colleges and universities have undertaken degree programs oriented to adults, they have experienced a growth in their basic missions and positive benefits to the whole institution. Not only have they learned how to serve new audiences, the new practices and academic understandings have positively affected all their programs and deepened their links to their surrounding communities. Such was the case for Capital University in Columbus, Ohio, and St. Edward's University in Austin, Texas.

These two totally separate midsize universities are over one thousand miles apart. Historically they have been shaped by different denominational and educational traditions. Yet in the last quarter century they have developed similar adult bachelor's degree programs that benefit and reinforce the parent institution.

This section discusses these programs together because they illustrate how adult learner–centered programs can develop as extensions of and complements to existing traditional institutions. Capital's Adult Degree Program (ADP) and St. Edward's New College are separate adult-oriented operating units in their respective universities, yet each draws on and reinforces the older sectors of its university as it also contributes new elements to it. In both institutions the adult and the traditional programs gain strength from each other.

Similarities

Capital and St. Edward's have some significant similarities in circumstances and background. Both are located in state capitals that also are hosts to large public universities and many other higher education institutions. Both cities have experienced recent booming economic growth.

In addition to state administrative and higher education employment, Columbus is home to operations in administration, finance, and insurance, and Austin has become a center for high-technology industry. All these employers require highly educated workers and frequently offer educational benefits.

Neither institution had much experience with adult learners before initiating its present program—St. Edward's in 1974 and Capital in 1979. Since beginning work with adults, however, they have drawn similar groups of students. These learners are mainly fully employed adults living in the vicinity who seek to improve their future job opportunities through more education. In age they cluster in the thirties and forties, although some are younger or older. Most have between one and two years' previous college credit and learning from experience that may be creditable. Women predominate, numbering 60 to 65 percent of the total enrollment in both programs. Both programs enroll over one thousand current students, amounting to a quarter of university enrollment in one instance and nearly a third in the other.

Because of the students' background, their study sequences might be called *modified degree completion programs*. Although, with some exceptions, neither program requires a minimum amount of previous credit, as some accelerated cohort programs do, degree planning usually involves supplementing previous learning with the remaining degree requirements students have to fulfill. For the most part the programs assist students to complete major sequences that already exist in the university's traditional offerings by allowing them flexibility in how they meet those requirements. Both programs offer special courses that support the adult learning program and are adapted to adult learners. For those who need unique content, both programs have individualized degree options, which many students use, and St. Edward's has some degrees that only New College offers.

Each program has a separate administrative unit with considerable autonomy and its own full-time faculty who are eligible for tenure even though their responsibilities differ from those of other faculty in the same institution. In both programs the interface that helps them be learner centered is a highly developed faculty and professional staff advising system.

Distinctiveness Within Similarity

Despite these many similarities the programs have unique characters and differ in detail. The following discussions highlight their separate learner-centered approaches to advisement and degree planning, prior learning assessment, administrative organization, and impact on the rest of the university.

ST. EDWARD'S NEW COLLEGE. St. Edward's University grew out of an academy for boys founded on land south of Austin by the founder of Notre Dame University and head of the Congregation of the Holy Cross. It became a college in 1885 and a university in 1925. Through collaboration with the Sisters of the Immaculate Heart, it became coeducational in 1970. It retains its Catholic character and draws faculty from religious orders as well as from among laypersons. New College was initiated by an enterprising sister, and is now headed by a lay dean. The college's mission is to serve adults in the context of the university and help them achieve their potential as lifelong learners.

New College offers thirty-six undergraduate majors leading to bachelor of arts, liberal studies, science, or business administration degrees. Entering students with associate of applied science degrees in areas not available at St. Edward's may take an inverted degree, basing the specialization on their associate degrees and taking two years of liberal education at St. Edward's. An accelerated, cohort-based Bachelor of Business Administration degree is also available through New College's PACE program. In addition to a major concentration, all students complete required New College courses in critical inquiry, ethical theory and analysis and moral issues, and critical issues (two courses) and a sufficient number of electives to total 120 credits. The required course Introduction to Critical Theory serves as an orientation to the college as well. The moral issues course is a capstone, integrative course taken near the end of the program. New College students also take general education courses that are unique to the college although they parallel the traditional degree program's pattern.

Faculty and professional staff of New College play a pivotal role in assisting students to realize their goals. Upon entry each student is assigned an advising team of a New College faculty member and a professional staff member. Because students bring considerable prior credit and experience to the program, two early processes, guided by faculty, affect learner approaches to the curriculum. These are the development of a detailed written degree plan in close consultation with the advising team and a review of prior learning for creditable content. While students take their initial required courses, New College faculty, who come from a broad range of fields, and staff members work with students individually to identify their goals, to plan their programs, and to select means to fulfill them. Program personnel believe that the early experience of the program's possibilities and responsiveness contributes to student success, as does the continuing supportive adviser relationship.

An important adviser role is to assist students in selecting the instructional mode through which they will complete their courses. Though general education and major content is heavily prescribed, the distinctive modes in which the college presents its own and major courses afford great flexibility in matching individual preferences, schedules, and learning styles. Most courses can be taken in one of three methods, as small-group seminars, as self-paced individualized studies with a faculty facilitator, and increasingly, as on-line courses. The college publishes planned offerings annually, and students select the modes most suitable to them. Students may register for individualized studies once a month and must complete them within four months. Some major courses cannot be offered in these modes and must be taken in the classroom format.

Concurrently with degree planning, students may request assessment of prior learning by submitting a portfolio. Administrative Services, attached to the dean's office, screens entering students' possibilities for earning credit by assessment and refers them to appropriate services. A centralized service, the Center for Adult Learning Services, coordinates all aspects of portfolio assessment, including the New College Research Seminar, which is required for portfolio preparation; advisement on portfolio content and documentation; and coordination of faculty assessors. The center also informs students of other forms of assessment, such as standardized examinations and credit for military experience, which are handled by other advisers. When assessment is complete, the relevant credit is applied to student degree plans.

New College faculty and professional staff cover most of the academic tasks of advising, offering courses, and conducting assessment, although departmental faculty on overload and adjunct faculty sometimes assist. New College faculty are eligible for tenure and university faculty development and recognition. The college mentors new faculty and staff as they work in the program, and assessors and adjunct faculty receive special training. It also conducts an ongoing evaluation of its program, including faculty performance, and ambitious monitoring of learner outcomes.

The college functions in a complementary and collaborative manner with the rest of the university. New College faculty meet with departmental faculty and remain professionally active in their own specialties. Some New College curriculum concepts have been adopted in the traditional program, such as emphasizing diversity in U.S. society and studying non-Western cultures. Major departments usually have agreed to adapt content and applications to make courses more appropriate for adult learners. University student services are open to all students. New College participates in faculty governance equally with the other university schools. Recently a *dual focus* reorganization acknowledged the importance of adult programs by establishing a vice president of professional and graduate studies and the College of Professional and Graduate Studies, which includes New College.

CAPITAL'S ADULT DEGREE PROGRAM. Capital University was chartered in 1850 to benefit German immigrants in Columbus, Ohio. An Evangelical Lutheran institution, it began with a mission to offer service and higher education to those who were not wealthy. Recent administrators have seen work with adults as a continuation of that mission. Capital's Adult Degree Program began in 1979, when Capital purchased from the Union of Experimenting Colleges three University Without Walls centers in Dayton, Columbus, and Cleveland. They comprised an operating program, supported by its own tuition, of more than one hundred students. ADP has developed its own program model from that base. The program aligns itself with the missions of the university and the College of Arts and Sciences and seeks to provide alternative learning experiences through integrative advising and teaching, program flexibility, self-directed and interdisciplinary learning approaches, and a commitment to experiential and lifelong learning. A major goal is to assist learners to consolidate previous learning into a foundation for degree completion.

Capital has twenty-five majors leading to bachelor of arts, general studies, or social work degrees, and in collaboration with its School of Nursing, a Bachelor of Science in Nursing degree. In addition, a multidisciplinary option enables students to create individualized plans to meet special needs. ADP also offers a number of credit-based certificate programs in cooperation with community-based agencies, such as a substance abuse counseling certificate. Degree students complete the university's general education requirements and the requirements for the major that they select. A large number of ADP students, 38 percent, choose the multidisciplinary option, often to complete bachelor's degrees based on associate degree specialties that are not offered at Capital.

Entering students, in collaboration with ADP advisers and assisted by a detailed student handbook, work out individual degree plans to meet the requirements of the various majors. An optional orientation course, Focus on Learning and Development (FOLD), is available to entrants who want to assess their skill needs for college work, and all students receive entry orientation. Students organize their degree plans on *degree planning grids*. Plans for standard programs are reviewed by faculty and plans for more tailored programs by a degree review committee. ADP encourages students to seek out multidisciplinary, integrative, and experiential learning opportunities as they fulfill their degree plans. A final ADP requirement, the Significant Project, fulfills an integrating role and demonstrates student ability in research, analysis, and synthesis.

Advisers assist students to apply previous learning to their degree plans. ADP has a generous transfer policy for credit taken elsewhere, and it conducts a highly regarded prior learning assessment program based on portfolio review. ADP also assigns credit on other bases, such as recognized evaluations of military or other nonsponsored learning. Students interested in portfolio assessment may take a special course, but the course is not required to apply for assessment. Portfolios are evaluated by the University Competency Assessment Panel (UCAP), a panel of faculty serving regular terms and drawn from across the university. Assessment has become embedded in the entire institution because 35 to 40 percent of the whole faculty participate on the UCAP at different times and assessment is available to all university students, whether traditional or adult. Challenge examinations and other advanced standing assessments are also available.

ADP attributes much of its success to the effort of its faculty in advising and teaching. An ADP faculty job description explicitly states key elements and expected activities in four areas and indicators of successful performance in them. ADP advising employs a holistic and personal approach over an extended period that goes well beyond managing course choice and registration. Faculty describe the process as individualized and continuous, helping students set goals, following students closely, and encouraging self-management. The task is challenging because faculty are expected to devote half their workload to this process, and they meet each student at least three times a year. Advisers must command a broad range of information to work with the diverse interests of students and the numerous fields of their study.

ADP's flexible instructional modes also depend on faculty capability. ADP instruction modes center on a combination of small-group interactive learning and individually planned independent study. ADP faculty bear the load of most of this instruction, especially in general education, popular major areas, and the Significant Project. Most faculty are full time, but part-time and adjunct appointees are also used, especially at the Dayton and Cleveland centers. The program actively promotes cohesiveness among the faculty at the three sites, increasingly through electronic communication. The Dayton center, especially, seeks to integrate its adjunct and full-time staffs. ADP undertakes a regular program of workshops for faculty development.

The relationship between the adult and traditional programs at Capital has grown closer over their nearly two decades of mutual experience. Leading administrators speak of collaboration and mutual engagement between the faculties, including joint faculty participation in departments and recurring visits of major department chairs to the Cleveland and Dayton sites. In recent years ADP faculty have become eligible for tenure, and this has reinforced parity. ADP faculty comment on the development of a culture of adult learning in the institution and the creation of a university community of undergraduate scholars who regard work with adults as enriching. Some ADP practices, such as prior learning assessment, focus on learning outcomes, and capstone courses, have been adopted by other departments.

Summary and Future

The parallels between New College and the Adult Degree Program are striking. Although they arose separately, both stress careful entry and planning processes supported by well-trained faculty and staff whose duties explicitly include important advisement responsibility. Each assigns critical importance to recognition and application of previous learning in the degree program. Although each unit offers its own courses and individualized degree programs, it also relies on the curricula and academic strength of the rest of its institution. The programs' alternative instructional modes give participants the ability to adapt their learning to their needs, and specially planned courses and assignments allow them to achieve coherence in their learning. Perhaps most striking of all is each program's integration and cross-support with the rest of its institution while it also maintains sufficient organizational autonomy to carry out its distinct role.

Both New College and ADP have experienced recent growth in numbers, despite reduction in some employer tuition benefits, and both are optimistic about the future. St. Edward's, for instance, has shifted from a policy of capping New College enrollment to a strategy for adult program growth over the next five years. Each program is confident about its achievement and its contribution to its institution's mission and enrollment. The new administrative structure at St. Edward's that includes New College reinforces this view, and ADP faculty are hopeful for similar recognition at Capital. Both programs envision more outreach in their regions, in ADP's case through addition of new degrees, work with community agencies, and greater access to the underserved, and in New College's case through cooperation with other regional institutions and in-house services to employers. ADP and New College anticipate greater use of technological delivery and distance learning, although both have apprehensions that these new learning resources might erode the current close personal relationship between students and faculty.

AN INDIVIDUALIZED OCCUPATIONAL DEGREE

Central Maine Technical College—Auburn, Maine

Associate of Applied Science

Trade and Technical Occupations (TT0) and General Technology (GET)

Central Maine Technical College's individualized associate degree programs address members of the subbaccalaureate group in the mid-skilled workforce (described by Grubb, 1996). It enables two groups—one with highly focused technical achievement and another with a more varied credit and experiential background—to plan unique programs to extend capabilities they already have. Often many two-year degree programs, especially those in technical fields, are highly structured and prescribed, allowing participants little individual choice. However, Central Maine Technical College has designed two technical tracks that are primarily student oriented and enable individual learners to customize programs toward their goals. These tracks are two associate of applied science degree programs: Trade and Technical Occupations (TTO) and General Technology (GET). These programs offer examples that could easily be applied in other settings.

The college is a two-year institution in the Maine Technical College System. It opened its doors in 1964, as the result of a state referendum to establish a technical institute in its region. In 1989, the state legislature changed the college's name from Central Maine Technical Institute to Central Maine Technical College to clarify its status as a higher education institution. It is authorized to confer associate of science and associate of applied science degrees.

The college is located in the Auburn-Lewiston metropolitan area, Maine's second largest urban concentration. This area is in the south-central region of the state, in a mix of urban and rural settlement about thirty-five miles from both Augusta and Portland.

The Learners

Both the TTO and GET programs are targeted to populations who already have or are concurrently gaining considerable technical background. TTO is designed for persons who have completed or are currently engaged in formal apprenticeship programs. In the mid-1980s, the college found it was receiving inquiries from persons with apprenticeship qualifications who wanted to earn associate degrees, often tailored to special applications they wanted to make of their technical background. Following discussions with state and federal labor authorities with responsibility for apprenticeship programs and with the state technical college system, in 1985 the college launched TTO for persons with apprenticeships validated by state and federal authorities.

The GET program followed later after persons approached the college for an option that would recognize extensive technical training and work experience even though it was not as focused as an apprenticeship qualification. As a result the participants in the two programs are distinct from each other, but all are highly motivated and already highly qualified.

Admission to the college is open to all persons who have completed high school, a requirement also for entry into apprenticeship programs. TTO students tend to be younger, usually in their early twenties. Because a portion of TTO degree credit is based on apprenticeship completion, degree completion is contingent upon finishing the apprenticeship. TTO staff have described an unfortunate incident in which a TTO student nearing degree completion suffered a disabling injury that prevented him from completing his apprenticeship, thus disqualifying him for the TTO degree route. He could, however, apply his accumulated credit to the GET program rather than the apprenticeship track.

GET students more often are in their late thirties. Typically, they have accumulated considerable work experience and formal training, although not organized toward a systematic qualification such as an apprenticeship. Often their background has required college-level skills, such as the ability to learn from books and manuals and to prepare written work, that they can apply to their degree programs.

TTO applicants who have been through apprenticeships have experienced rigorous, goal-directed programs, and those currently pursuing apprenticeships are highly intentional. GET enrollees, although normally lacking the highly structured experience of the apprenticeship, exhibit a high level of motivation. Program staff attribute a large degree of the two programs' success to the self-selection and goal orientation of the participants.

Curriculum

Once students are admitted, their most important relationship is with their advisers. Advisers begin the program planning process by interviewing students on their career directions and prior background relevant to their goals. The college has created documents to assist in the degree planning process; they inventory previous learning and lay out the study plan the student and adviser agree on. Advisers assist students to select courses that will further their goals.

The associate of applied science (AAS) degree requires sixty-nine semester credit hours, of which twenty-one are in general education subjects such as communication; social science; humanities; and mathematics, science, and business. Depending on the specialization, apprentices may receive between eighteen and twenty-four credits for the apprenticeship. The remaining twenty-four or more credits may be selected to increase technical competence or to fulfill career goals. GET students, who lack apprenticeships, apply the background they have to degree credit requirements, planning an individual specialization that addresses their objectives.

In both programs, career goals and personal objectives vary with the individual. Some may wish to increase their business and management ability so they can operate their own businesses. Others may wish to supplement their technical backgrounds to move into more specialized areas. Still others may wish to prepare for careers as trainers or teachers, and they will select additional education from that area. The program optimizes choice for them and program faculty offer experienced guidance to help them use the college's resources for their plans.

The college offers a program of prior learning assessment that especially benefits the older GET students, who tend to have more work and noninstitutional training experience. Applicants for prior learning credit spend a semester preparing a portfolio and documenting their experiential learning and informal training. Portfolios are reviewed for credit awards by specially assigned professors representing both industry and education perspectives. In addition to portfolio documentation, the college accepts standardized and institutional challenge examination results and the recommendations of recognized guides to military and noninstitutional training experiences as bases for awarding credit.

Once enrolled in one of these programs, the students have equivalent standing to other students of the college, and they pay standard college tuition. They take courses from the college's existing offerings along with other students. Many of the college's courses are already scheduled for evenings and therefore accessible to working adults. All college services are available to TTO and GET students.

Program outcomes have been very good. The programs administer structured exit interviews to finishing students, and feedback has been positive as well as useful in program development. Each year 100 percent of graduates are placed in jobs, in contrast to the lower rates for graduates of the college's other programs. The college has established an articulation agreement with the Department of Technology at the University of Southern Maine so that program graduates can enter the university with junior status. The university has expressed satisfaction with the performance of these students. Staff caution, however, that their graduates are not ready for university programs that presume strong science and mathematics backgrounds, such as engineering, and they advise additional preparation before graduates apply to those programs.

Future

The college believes that the TTO and GET programs make a significant contribution to local workforce resources, and it expects them to grow, in a reflection of the regional economy. Neither program is very large, and the administrative burden is light. One person who has other responsibilities as well handles advisement and supervision in each of the programs. The programs allow persons with the nucleus of a technical background to extend their capabilities in individually appropriate ways. They also demonstrate the potential for colleges to adapt existing resources creatively to new roles.

THREE APPROACHES TO COHORT-BASED DEGREE PROGRAMS

Columbia Union College—Takoma Park, Maryland

Adult Evening Program

Northwestern College—St. Paul, Minnesota

Focus 15 Program

Thomas More College—Crestview Hills, Kentucky

Accelerated Degree Program

Some readers may question the appropriateness of a discussion of cohort-based programs in the context of programs centered on the individual adult learner. Those seeking characteristics such as Knowles associated with a favorable climate of learning for adults may find elements he recommended missing and the cohort group requirements inimical to individual flexibility. In contrast to learner-centered programs that stress flexibility, responsiveness, individualization, and freedom from strictures of time and space, cohort programs may appear to be structured, highly prescribed, behaviorally controlling, and based on strict schedule and content discipline, with penalties for failure to comply.

Cohort Benefits

For many participants, however, the security they gain from the definition of responsibilities and commitments makes cohort programs feel user friendly and learner centered. It is a truism that adult learners lead challenging lives, full of conflicting responsibilities and unpredictable demands and emergencies. One member of the Commission for a Nation of Lifelong Learners, herself a person with a disability, drew an analogy between adult learners' lives and those of persons with disabilities. Managing continuing requirements of life, although different for both, is very difficult and demanding for both. Therefore anything that adds stability or security in one area of activity lightens the overall burden of uncertainty.

For some, undertaking a higher education degree program over a period of many months or even years is a daunting task, filled with risks that may prevent completion. For others, reaching defined goals may be something they must do within a specific time. In either case, cohort programs provide the security of a new educational commitment that is defined, predictable, and has a clear duration. The programs promise an accelerated calendar with a fixed schedule of meetings, content, and sequence that will remain stable, and they often guarantee cost so long as the learner maintains the cohort pace.

A further benefit, which some participants realize only after they have had experience in these programs, is that cohorts become valuable contributors to the success of their individual members (Saltiel, Sgroi, & Brockett, 1998). Over time the cohort itself gathers a momentum that carries members forward and sustains motivation that they might not have as individual learners in routine courses. Programs report cases of students who, when faced with discouragement or personal emergencies, have been persuaded to persist by their cohort colleagues. Often small, supportive study groups arise within cohorts, either informally or from deliberate program design. In addition to allowing their members to work on course assignments as a team, these groups maintain members' morale and desire to continue.

Without question, cohort program learners trade some independence to get this predictability and mutual support. But to many cohort members the security of the program plan is more important than these other factors. And some cohort programs may offer both appropriate discipline and individually sensitive provisions or exceptions that enable participants to devise unique applications through workplace assignments or extended projects or to interrupt the cohort sequence for emergency reasons and to join another cohort at a comparable point later.

The cohort program concept has been in existence for a number of years. Some early examples are the programs at the University of Redlands' Alfred North Whitehead Center, dating from the early 1970s, that are discussed in Chapter Nine. The number of programs employing the cohort model has grown greatly in recent years. Often cohort plans are adopted by smaller, independent institutions that have limited or no previous experience with adult degree programs. Cohort-based programs have offered such institutions a new way to apply existing resources and faculty capability. The growth in these programs has also been stimulated in part by the exportable models developed by larger organizations and institutions and adopted by smaller institutions.

Examples are the Institute for Professional Development in Phoenix, National-Louis University in Evanston, Illinois, and Spring Arbor College in Michigan.

Three Cases

Columbia Union College, Northwestern College, and Thomas More College are three institutions that illustrate cohort-based programs and some of the differences among them. Each is a relatively small institution. Each is located in a large metropolitan area in proximity to a number of other higher education institutions, but each has identified unfilled needs in its area. They have developed their adult learning programs over the last fifteen years, since 1984, 1990, and 1993 respectively, and these programs reflect an evolution of the cohort concept.

THE PROGRAMS. *Columbia Union College.* Columbia Union College is a Seventh-Day Adventist institution founded in 1904. It began as a training institute in the liberal arts, then became a missionary training institute, and in 1914 changed again to a liberal arts college giving baccalaureate degrees. It took its present name in 1961. Columbia Union is located in Takoma Park, Maryland, just north of the District of Columbia and within the Washington, D.C., Beltway. The population within driving distance includes many government workers, professionals, and military service personnel. The Adult Evening Program (AEP), which began in 1984, resulted from planning initiated by the college president and a group of administrators and faculty to serve this population. The planners reviewed and visited other programs, including that of the University of Redlands, but Columbia Union eventually developed its own unique program.

Northwestern College. Northwestern College is a nondenominational but Christian-oriented college in the Roseville-Arden Hills suburban area north of St. Paul and Minneapolis. The college was founded in 1902 as a bible and mission training school, and it was served by its first president until 1947. It second president, from 1948 to l952, was Reverend Billy Graham. In the early 1970s, the college moved to its present suburban campus. It offers traditional and adult programs both at that campus and at off-campus locations. In 1990, it began to serve the large Twin City adult audience with its Focus 15 program, a cohort model it obtained from National-Louis University through a contract relationship.

Thomas More College. Thomas More College is a Roman Catholic institution, founded in 1921, in Crestview Hills, Kentucky, about ten miles from downtown Cincinnati. From its beginning Thomas More has provided education for adults. Its Thomas More Accelerated Program (TAP) originated with a faculty member's report to colleagues on a presentation he had heard at a professional meeting about cohort programs obtained through contracts with other institutions. The concept was discussed within the college and explored with the Phoenix-based Institute for Professional Development (IPD), which had formed contractual agreements with a number of colleges. Thomas More faculty approved entry into a relationship with IPD, and a cohort-based Bachelor of Business Administration degree was launched in September 1993.

SIMILARITIES. In addition to origin, size, and location, the three programs share some other characteristics. They all attract mainly adults and two have minimum age requirements, twenty-five at Northwestern and twenty-three at Columbia Union. Previous work experience is required, both as an indicator of maturity and as a source of learning that can be applied to the program.

Each of the programs is a degree completion program that requires applicants to have an associate degree or two years of college credit when they apply. Two have specific background requirements, such as an introductory algebra course at Thomas More. Although many of each program's general education and elective requirements may have been met by previous work, learners are expected to complete any remaining requirements in addition to the concentration they take in the cohort. Two of the colleges provide accelerated opportunities to earn this credit.

All the institutions have programs of prior learning assessment, and preparation of portfolios or an effort to qualify for assessed credit is an integral part of early enrollment in the programs. Often general education or elective requirements can be met through institutional or standardized examinations, official credit recommendations, or portfolio-documented learning.

In reflection of their origins, all the institutions require some study of religion and ethics. At Thomas More, this is a three-credit theology course in the general education component and a business ethics course in the major sequence. Columbia Union requires two courses, Issues in Religion and Culture and Ethics in Modern Society, as part of its cohort major sequences. Northwestern is most demanding in that it requires a statement of Christian belief and commitment to a religiously oriented code of behavior on the admission application as well as courses in ethics in the major sequences. These requirements are attractive to Northwestern's core audience but sometimes limiting to others.

Upon enrollment, each program states a commitment to total program cost. Northwestern cites a total tuition figure that is guaranteed if the student maintains continuous enrollment; this program also offers several payment options. Thomas More guarantees members of entering cohorts that their tuition will remain the same throughout their planned program, although rates for later cohorts may increase. Columbia Union guarantees tuition will remain at the entry rate if students maintain continuous participation in the program, and it also gives a discount to enrollees who pay their entire cohort enrollment tuition at the outset.

COHORT PLAN. The central component of each program is a major concentration that leads to the degree specialization and is pursued through the cohort format. The concentration courses total from thirty-six to fifty-seven semester hours and must be taken in sequence. There are some significant differences among the programs in how the cohort is managed.

Columbia Union offers three bachelor of science programs based on eighteen-month concentrations of twelve courses, totalling thirty-six credits in business administration, health care administration, and organization management. A program in information systems requires an additional cognate course and takes twenty months. Students pursue one course at a time, attending one evening meeting a week over six weeks. Learning modes vary with instructors, but small classes enable group activity, teamwork, problem solving, and theory-application linkages. Early in their enrollment, Columbia Union students begin work on a guided independent study project that continues concurrently with their coursework throughout the whole concentration. With the assistance of project advisers, students select a project focus that they can relate coursework to and use for integration of their concentration study. A written report based on 250 hours of independent work is required at the end of the concentration.

Northwestern's Focus 15 program offers five bachelor of science concentrations ranging from sixty-one to sixty-five quarter credit hours in organization administration, managerial leadership in business, psychology, early childhood development, and ministries. The program's name comes from the fifteen months required for active study, although, when holidays and breaks are included, participation extends over five quarters and approximately seventeen or eighteen months.

Classes meet once weekly for four hours on evenings or Saturdays. Individual courses provide from one to six credits, and learners complete several courses within a given term. Student assignments stress workplace applications, and the program places unusually heavy emphasis on writing ability and assesses student writing at the end of each course.

The Thomas More Accelerated Program offers a single undergraduate degree, the Bachelor of Business Administration. The college also initiated an accelerated Master of Business Administration degree in January 1996. The undergraduate program operates independently of the rest of the college's academic cycle. TAP plans to start ten cohorts of twenty or more students a year, and it will launch more if demand warrants it. The sequence is organized in four semester blocks totaling ninety-five meetings. Courses, several of which are completed each semester, vary from two to four semester credits, and the whole totals fifty-seven credits. Cohorts meet one evening a week for four hours, and small groups of cohort members meet for an additional three to five hours weekly. The total sequence normally requires slightly under two years to complete.

Two distinctive features of the TAP program are the deliberate formation of small study groups of three to five students, and the provision of laptop computers to enrollees. In the first course, Introduction to Business, students are asked to self-form into small groups to meet and work on course assignments three to five hours each week between class meetings. Members of these groups usually bond closely and stay together for the duration of the cohort. The success of the groups has led program faculty to consider additional orientation in group process to facilitate their work. In addition, because facility with computers is vital to students' success in the program, tuition has been priced to enable TAP to lend each participant a laptop computer for use in the program, with the option to buy the computer at a deep discount at the end.

FACULTY AND GOVERNANCE. All three programs depend on both regular and adjunct faculty and in about the same proportions. Columbia Union faculty are 40 percent regular faculty and 60 percent adjunct; Northwestern has a slight majority of adjuncts; and Thomas More uses 40 to 45 percent regular faculty with the remainder adjuncts. Often adjuncts are long-term, experienced faculty with close familiarity with the program, and many others are working professionals in the field.

As is common among faculty, informal networks and advice help new members fit in, but each program also reports an explicit orientation process. At Columbia Union the program director and chairs of degree programs interview new faculty candidates and inform them on the programs. Each year an orientation for new faculty is held at which senior faculty share their experience. Columbia Union faculty also receive the results of course evaluations at the end of each course. AEP faculty hold several faculty meetings a year, from which recommendations for changes may come. Northwestern is a smaller program, and the director personally interviews new faculty and extends ongoing coaching. Faculty receive regular student evaluation results and personal recognition from the director. At Thomas More all faculty meet for orientation at the beginning of the year, and a special meeting is held for adjuncts. TAP faculty also meet once a year to discuss program issues and needs, such as special training on new methodologies or improvement of computer skills.

Each program reports to the president or vice president for academic affairs of its institution. Columbia Union's AEP has a faculty committee structure parallel to that of the college's traditional programs, and when necessary, decisions can be referred to the whole college faculty. Northwestern's programs are subject to review by departmental faculty. Thomas More's TAP offers the same degree curriculum as the traditional department, and academic control is located in the department. The TAP administrator, the vice president for graduate and continuing education, maintains close coordination with departmental heads.

RECRUITMENT. Because all the colleges are in metropolitan areas, they can use mass media to reach potential students. Columbia Union employs paid advertising on radio and cable television and in metropolitan and local newspapers and the Washington Metro subway system. In addition, it attends education fairs, makes corporate visits, and holds campus open houses. Northwestern uses media advertising and especially benefits from announcements to its chief target population over a noncommercial network of Christian radio stations owned by the college. Thomas More's marketing is handled on a cooperative basis under the college's contract with IPD. IPD maintains a marketing manager and accounting and marketing representatives on site and develops a marketing plan subject to college approval. Admissions applications are processed and student portfolios are prepared by IPD then turned over to the college for admission evaluation. IPD also collects student tuition and remits the college's contracted share at regular intervals.

All the programs stress similar critical factors for admission and will decline admission to weak candidates. The chief factors sought are maturity, previous work experience that can be related to the program, and time management skills to handle multiple demands. They may also seek managerial experience and look for strong communication skills.

OUTCOMES AND EVALUATION. All three cohort-based programs want more follow-up information on their graduates and are implementing efforts to do so. Anecdotal evidence indicates that graduates do experience job benefits, such as salary increases, promotions, or new job hires. A number also seem to proceed to further study in graduate or professional fields, as evidenced by their requests for references and statements of intention. Thomas More has the best-documented evidence of change resulting from the program. Students there have been given the Educational Testing Service's majors tests on entry and completion. Results have shown impressive gains following participation in the program.

Summary and Future

These three programs had different origins. One invented its own design, whereas the other two imported preexisting models, although from different sources.

Yet in large degree they exhibit similar features that contribute to their efficient use of time. All are cohort based, although the designs are derived from different sources and they strictly guide participants through the program sequence. They are degree completion programs offering a limited number of content tracks. They use accelerated formats with heavy assignments outside class to supplement in-class work. Courses, often of different durations, are arranged in modules, and at least one program departs from the traditional academic term pattern. Classes are small, relying on discussion and use of out-of-class experience to a considerable extent. Either informally or by design, these programs also expect students to work in subgroups. In all cases, the programs have clear lines of administrative responsibility and academic control to the parent institution.

All the programs have produced a major positive impact on their institutions and are confident about the future. At Columbia Union,

AEP students make up almost half the college's enrollment. At Thomas More, TAP and other adult students in continuing education evening and weekend courses are 45 percent of college enrollment. At Northwestern the enrollment share is less but still near 20 percent of the college total, which is substantial.

Each of the institutions anticipates program growth in some degree. All are looking toward using additional sites to expand participation, and one such site is near implementation. The colleges also want to expand program offerings from their present base by adding new content tracks, by designing modular groupings of courses (instead of whole degree sequences), and by extending both credit and credit-free offerings at the workplace.

All express satisfaction with their experience with adult programs, deriving inspiration from adult motivation, a sense of entrepreneurial success from starting something new, pride from their own creativity and agility in responding to new and unforeseen demands, or pleasure from the appreciation of students on completion.

A MISSION TO THE CITY AND ITS PEOPLE

Cambridge College—Cambridge, Massachusetts

Graduate Programs

Master of Education Program

Cambridge College originated in 1971 from plans of a group of visionary leaders to start an alternate graduate program. After brief associations with Newton College of the Sacred Heart and Antioch College, New England, they decided to create their own college.

Their ideas evolved into a master's degree–only institution dedicated to innovation to support adult professionals and based on commitment to diversity in students and faculty, excellence in educational and professional standards, and access for learners beginning from differing starting points. Cambridge College set out to provide a learner-centered, collaborative educational model that emphasized students' capacity to learn rather than their deficiencies. It sought to draw on the varied experience of individual students to enlarge the understanding of all. Initially, it focused on learners in the Boston area and especially on urban professionals and working adults seeking professional qualifications. About twenty years ago, it extended its activities to a center in Springfield,

Massachusetts, and more recently to a number of suburban sites. It added a national institute for teachers in 1991 and a bachelor of arts program in 1992. Cambridge College also began to train paraprofessionals in 1992 in order to educate teachers who would reflect the diversity of children in urban classrooms. The content of its programs includes education, counseling psychology, and management.

Key Elements of the Cambridge Model

The Cambridge model of centering on the adult learner is a system planned to maximize the potential of experienced adults, and to engage them with new learning. It establishes mutually respectful partnerships between faculty and students and among the students themselves. It provides program flexibility and adaptability to individual circumstances. It has developed processes to acknowledge and apply students' previous experience and to give continuing support. College publications describe an educational design "in which advising, learning, teaching, and assessment work together as an integrated process" (Cambridge College, 1997, pp. 7–8). A statement of philosophy and assumptions declares, "Learning must be student-centered to be effective," and it must affirm each learner's uniqueness and capabilities (Cambridge College, 1998, pp. 7–8). The key components of this system are advising, collaboration, and peer support, integration of experience with learning, a flexible calendar and instructional modes, and assessment and learning services. This discussion focuses on the graduate degree programs, especially the Master of Education.

ADVISING AND COLLABORATION. Advising begins when prospective enrollees first contact an admissions representative. This may occur in a group session called a Discovery Workshop or in individual interviews. The representative introduces the college's programs and philosophy and discusses their fit with prospects' backgrounds. Those who then wish to proceed follow one of two courses. Applicants who have baccalaureate degrees complete application documents and attend a financial aid workshop, following which they learn whether they are admitted to the graduate program.

Applicants without bachelor's degrees must participate in the forty-hour, three-credit Academic Planning Seminar. The seminar is planned and paced for reentry students. It is heavily based on group process, and it helps persons evaluate their skill levels for college work. It also helps applicants review previous college credit, identify possibilities for credit assessment, and choose an educational path to achieve their goals. At the end of the planning seminar, the seminar leader and each applicant evaluate the applicant's status and choose whether to complete a degree in the bachelor's program, to proceed in the Graduate Studies Program (GSP) of introductory graduate-level courses, or to apply for direct admission to the upper-level master's program.

Applicants with ninety or more transferable credits are reviewed for direct admission to the master's degree program but may be required to complete specific GSP courses to demonstrate competency. GSP is a thirty-credit sequence of seminars, academic skills and perspectives development, and a capstone project that leads to upper-level graduate study. GSP accepts the Academic Planning Seminar credit and continues with the remaining requirements, some of which may be met by prior learning assessment. Advising complements each GSP segment up to completion and entry into the master's program. Recent Massachusetts legislation requires persons in certified or licensed professions such as teaching or counseling to have earned bachelor's degrees, but GSP provides entry without a bachelor's degree to master's programs in education for those who do not plan to teach and to the master's in management.

Those who complete GSP or are admitted directly to the upper-level master's program receive orientation to their academic department. They then join a group of about twenty in a *professional seminar* or *management seminar* in that department. The seminar is led by a faculty member who will remain their principal adviser for the duration of the program. Seminar groups meet on a regular basis throughout the year, and the leader also arranges periodic individual meetings. The professional and management seminars provide the foundation for graduate study not only by exploring professional issues but also by relating individual backgrounds, perspectives, and concerns to that study through group process and individual discussions. The seminar environment is collaborative, nurturing, and affirming of uniqueness and differences while also engaging peers in group learning. Cambridge quotes one student as saying, "The true growth in my understanding of teaching and learning was made possible because of the nurturing experiences such as the Professional Seminar and the people in it. I contributed to this process and others affirmed me" (Cambridge College, 1998, p. 9).

Although the seminar leader and the seminar members remain the chief supports to learners throughout the program, program directors and coordinators and college deans also supplement the leader's role. The college attributes its unusually high 90+ percent completion rate to the supportive partnerships between faculty and students and among students themselves.

LEARNING RESOURCES AND CALENDAR. Beyond the professional and management seminars, content is presented in other formats and time schedules that allow students a menu for choice. Semester-long courses earning three credits are the main curriculum vehicle in the graduate program. Some courses may be taken as four- or five-day *intensives,* although there are some limitations on the number of intensives students may take. In addition, each degree sequence requires an independent learning or research project related to the student's program and professional development. The project's end product is intended to show student ability to use resources, collect and organize data, draw conclusions, and organize a report. Projects continue throughout the program and are guided and evaluated by the seminar leaders. In fall and spring the college offers ten-hour workshops for one credit each, and students may take a series of integrated workshops totaling ten hours for a *directed study*. Students may also, with approval, design an independent study course to pursue a special interest. Students in the Graduate Studies Program maintain a continuing portfolio record of their activities, both to assess their progress during the program and to provide documentation at the end.

A combination of course schedules also enables flexibility. The college conducts semester-length terms in fall, spring, and summer. During these terms, seminars meet at times decided upon by the groups; other courses meet weekly, in alternate weeks, on weekends, or as week-long intensives; and workshops too can follow variable meeting times. Students can pursue individual activities according to their own convenience. This range of course and time choices allows students to adapt their study plans to their other responsibilities.

ASSESSMENT AND LEARNER SUPPORT. Cambridge values the application of previous or current experience to the learning process as a means of advancing students in their programs, as an affirmation of the value that each individual brings to the program, and as an enrichment for others. Seminars and courses encourage participants to bring their experience to the discussions and to relate study to experience outside the classroom.

At the same time, the college provides opportunities for students to qualify for credit in the bachelor's program and Graduate Studies Program by taking challenge examinations or presenting portfolios for experiential learning assessment. The assessment process is managed through the Christian A. Johnson Center for Learning and Assessment Services (CLAS) and is described in a handbook, *Learner Guide to Prior Learning Assessment at Cambridge College* (Boornazian, 1997). Assessment is oriented to learning outcomes, and with a few exceptions all bachelor's and GSP outcomes may be demonstrated by assessment.

In addition to assessment for credit, CLAS provides many other learner support services. The center is open and staffed seven days a week, including weekday evenings. It offers students means to self-assess their college-level skills and provides computer-based learning skill development programs, writing and math labs, peer tutors, and English as a second language (ESL) assistance. Thirty-hour *academic skill improvement modules* are also offered each semester in writing, math, and ESL. CLAS also provides career counseling and résumé and cover letter preparation support, and it maintains individual learning portfolios of each student's progress in the Graduate Studies and the Bachelor of Arts Programs.

FACULTY. Cambridge College faculty fall into three groups: full-time core faculty, part-time regular senior faculty, and a limited number of adjunct faculty, who teach less frequently. The latter two groups, who make up over 70 percent of total faculty, consist of practitioners whose work the college values highly because of their direct connection to the fields students are preparing to enter. New faculty are introduced to the college culture through direct experience as adjuncts. Aspiring candidates observe current faculty for twenty-four hours as *teaching assistants*. They then team teach with experienced faculty in the Academic Planning Seminar. They are given formal training for the professional and management seminars and team experience with a seminar veteran. Later, seminar leaders meet once a month for ongoing training. Some funds are available for professional development, such as attendance at professional conferences.

Master of Education Program

The Master of Education Program illustrates the functioning of the Cambridge model. Cambridge has offered programs in education since its founding and has provided in-service training to many teachers in Massachusetts. Its graduates, drawn from a diverse population and often from education paraprofessionals, form a cadre of role models for student bodies that are increasingly heterogeneous. In addition to school professionals, the Master of Education Program also attracts human and health services managers and training specialists. Students from other Cambridge degree programs also elect to take some of its courses. In addition to a generic master's degree curriculum, the program offers a degree completion sequence for persons who enter with up to twelve previous graduate credits and Urban Teacher Preparation, a program for elementary teachers. It offers certificates in school administration, special education, and library media. These various programs meet current state guidelines.

The program requires thirty-two credits, including a core of three professional seminars, the independent learning project, and two workshops. In addition, participants select one course from each of four groups (general teaching methods, content area methods, thinking skills, educational psychology and philosophy) and one course from a final two groups (social dimensions of education and educational administration). Students complete the degree with two electives from any department in the college.

While working in the core, students are engaged with their seminar leader and peers in ongoing advisement, professional development, and peer support through the seminars and workshops and independent learning project. The courses in each course category offer a broad choice of content, using any of the several instructional modes and schedules. Throughout students can relate earlier or current experience in job or other activities to the theory and application of their study. They also can use the resources of the Learning and Assessment Center as needed for support.

The Master of Education Program has also reached out beyond the Boston and Springfield areas with the two-semester program, National Institute for Teaching Excellence. Students with twelve previous graduate credits can complete a master's degree with a summer's attendance in Cambridge followed by a fall semester in their home locations. During the fall they work independently to complete work begun in the summer and conduct a practicum, applying their ideas in classroom settings. The curriculum, which largely follows that of the basic master's degree, and the delivery method enable persons from throughout the United States to participate.

Future

Cambridge College embodies many of the characteristics that Knowles (1980) described as a positive climate of learning. These include mutual respect, involvement of learners throughout the process, recognition of learner experience, and supportive learner services. In addition, the strong peer support of the ongoing seminars and the affirmation of the worth of diverse individual contributions overcome the disincentives and motivational barriers that deter many learners from entry and completion.

Cambridge has experienced considerable growth in all its programs in the recent past, and it anticipates more demand for its education programs as teacher shortages become more acute. It expects to continue its work to upgrade the qualifications of urban paraprofessionals, especially those likely to remain involved with inner-city schools. At the same time, expansion of its programs in the suburbs and at its Springfield site are carrying it beyond a Boston and Cambridge emphasis.

In both Boston and Springfield, Cambridge College expects more participation in areas other than education, and it may broaden its offerings at the bachelor's level. The college anticipates increased use of technology in all of its programs, and it is inquiring how to integrate technology into its highly personal model. Cambridge has previously entered into partnerships with community and business organizations to provide programs to their members, and this activity will continue, especially with community and nonprofit groups. As a result of the National Institute experience the education program may also become more national and international.

CONCLUSION

The eight programs discussed here have many differences in size, situation, and history. Some of the institutions date well back into the nineteenth century whereas others are relatively recent creations. Most have a religious origin, but several do not. Most also came to serve adult learners after extended experience with traditional age students, although Central Maine Technical College and Cambridge College were founded as adult-oriented institutions. Yet in looking at their efforts to provide a supportive environment for adult learners a number of similarities stand out.

First, all are in mission-driven institutions. Most of these institutions derive their missions from a religious heritage that they have extended to a broader group, and that in turn connects the programs' work with adults to historic values of the college. In others the mission is to serve the neighboring public by applying college resources in a special way. And one has a mission of social betterment by honoring diversity, valuing experience, and encouraging potential among persons who might not otherwise have aspired to higher education. Each program plays a nurturing role that reflects its value commitments.

Second, the programs participate in all or nearly all of a set of practices that support and affirm the learners they work with. They have strong advising systems which begin in the preadmission stage and carry through the entire experience. In some cases the learner remains with a single person or group until completion, gaining encouragement from that relationship and participation in the trusting, collaborative psychological climate of which Knowles wrote. All the programs honor and apply the experience the learner brings to the program and encourage its application in courses and projects. Similarly, most, if not all build in opportunities for individuality in learning activities, even in the cohort programs, which provide opportunities for individual or group project work. Many incorporate individualized degree options or planning processes that respond to personal choices and goals. The use of variable calendars and differing learning modes makes the programs adaptable to individual and changing circumstances. Most faculty, regular and adjunct, receive recurring development of their skills for working with adult learners, and often the faculty are practitioners in the field, with experience that learners value highly. Most programs involve learners in continuing reflective or capstone experiences that enable them to integrate and find significance in their learning.

5

COMPETENCE-BASED FOCUS

COMPETENCE-BASED DEGREE EDUCATION is a relatively recent movement in higher education and especially adult higher education, dating
in the main from the early 1970s. However, in other sectors competence-based concepts arose much earlier. It has been an attractive idea
because competence-based processes appeared to ensure not only mastery of technique or information but also the ability to make active
application of that learning.

Development of interest in competence assessment has been closely
associated with the rationalization of work processes and the development of employee skills. The competence approach has especially affected technical training and human resource development and has
influenced the education of professionals who work in those fields
(Henschke, 1991). Through much of its history the movement has been
characterized as behaviorist and functionalist, and there has been ten-
sion between educators interested in competence-based processes and
educators dedicated to holistic liberal education and humanist values
(Harris, Guthrie, Hobart, & Lundberg, 1995). More recently, some
educators have applied competence-based processes in liberal education
settings and have argued that the approach is compatible with humanist and liberal education values. The programs described in this chapter
illustrate both applications, and one school brings them together in a
holistic professional program.

Educational writers have wrestled with definitions of competence-
based education because of the generality of the concept and disagree-
ments about what it should embrace. Grant and his colleagues made a
useful attempt by describing it as "a form of education that derives a
curriculum from an analysis of a prospective or actual role in modern

society, and that attempts to certify student progress on the basis of demonstrated performance in some or all aspects of that role" (Grant & Associates, 1979, p. 6). Characteristics of competence-based programs often include close analysis of explicit learning goals necessary to achieve competence, design of methods and criteria (with alternatives) for achieving these goals, continuous evaluation, feedback and individual attention to learners, and assessment of goals attainment by processes that third parties will regard as valid. Hertling (1980) describes similar attributes of competence-based programs, as do Harris et al. (1995).

Sources of the competence-based education movement can be found in late nineteenth- and early twentieth-century progressive secondary school reforms that emphasized efficiency on one hand and preparation for life adjustment rather than command of subject matter on the other. Later the scientific management theories of Frederick Taylor and his followers, by requiring close analysis of jobs and creation of training to prepare workers to perform them, encouraged behaviorist and functionalist worker education. The demand during both World Wars for rapid and effective training of persons to perform skilled tasks reinforced Taylorism, as did the emphasis during the interwar period on job analysis in preparation for training (see Neumann, 1979, for a detailed discussion of these influences). This history has contributed to the continuing dichotomy between education and training that may only now be eroding as employment requirements become more complex and of a higher order (see Glaser, cited in Neumann, 1979, p. 87).

More recently the competence-based adult education (CBAE) movement has attained great influence. Many associate it with the Adult Performance Level Project, sponsored by the Texas Education Authority and the University of Texas between 1971 and 1975 (Dorland, 1978; Shelton, 1983). The study examined the skills necessary for adult functional literacy. Federal policy favoring adult basic education that seeks to make adults more employable and independent encouraged the spread of the competence-based approach to adult basic education and technical-vocational education. Two-thirds of the states adopted programs based on the Texas study results within a few years. The CBAE approach also excited considerable discussion, including critical comment in educational literature at the time because of its perceived mechanical character (Parker & Taylor, 1980; Collins, 1983, 1984, 1991; Barnett, 1994).

The influence of competence-based education on higher education, although present before World War II at some colleges, such as Stephens and Hollins, did not become a major factor until the early 1970s. At that time the newly created Fund for Improvement of Postsecondary Education (FIPSE) encouraged its development through grants continued for a number of years. Some of these awards were made to liberal arts colleges that had adopted humanist and liberal education goals. Faculty saw in the competence approach a means to lead students to new cognitive and performance levels while preserving traditional values. They also perceived an opportunity to refresh faculty and curriculum with new ideas.

These initiatives were not specifically addressed to adult learners, but the competence approach offered adults in particular many benefits. Progress became linked to performance rather than to required time in attendance. Competence assessment could acknowledge the previous learning, whether from institutions or other sources, that many adults had acquired. The greater ability of mature adults to plan their efforts and to demonstrate performance became an advantage.

FIPSE's support achieved great success at Alverno College in Milwaukee, which in turn has influenced many other institutions. Alverno, a women's college of the School Sisters of St. Francis, did not set out to become competence based; however, it discovered that option when working its way through a crisis of enrollment and purpose in the late 1960s and early 1970s. (For accounts of Alverno's transformation, see Ewens, 1979; Read & Sharkey, 1985.)

A newly selected president, charged to undertake a radical self-examination of the college, engaged the faculty in discussion that probed the rationale for what they were teaching. A consensus formed among faculty that the key educational issue was not mastery of content "but what students should be able to do with their lives as a result of having gone to college" (Read & Sharkey, 1985, p. 199). The faculty reformulated Alverno's liberal arts degree, devising a structure of competencies and creating a means of implementing the competence framework through existing liberal education disciplines. The first students enrolled in fall 1973. Alverno also resolved to seek out the same student constituencies it had before, continuing as a women's college open both to younger women and, increasingly, to women in their twenties and beyond. Not surprisingly, the college experienced initial difficulties in implementing a new and complex system, and it lost some enrollment, but it proceeded, bringing the full four-year curriculum on line by 1976. Even at present, Alverno is still a work in progress, in that it continually monitors the college's programs and issues publications on them and also conducts periodic workshops on its model. The college's example continues to influence other degree programs and also credit-free programs.

Recent needs for workforce development have revived interest in the connection between competence development and worker preparation. Unlike early technical-vocational training, however, today's training focuses on more generalized and often less technical competencies. Instead of Taylorism's behavioral approach, more humanist and liberal education approaches such as Alverno's are demanded today. The National Skills Standards Board is seeking to identify skills needed in various technical occupations, the education necessary to attain them, and procedures to assess them. Other studies describe the skills necessary to maintain employability in today's economy. The capabilities cited are usually those associated with postsecondary education and liberal education at both the associate and the baccalaureate degree levels (Carswell, 1997; for skills, see Carnevale, 1991; Sheckley, Lamdin, & Keeton, 1993). Expectation of competence in these areas was stressed by a recent Canadian study of skills needed by university graduates entering the workforce. The study described four general skills areas: (1) managing self, (2) communicating, (3) managing people, and (4) mobilizing innovation and change (Evers, Rush, & Berdrow, 1998). The study calls upon universities to incorporate the key skills into their programs to form a bridge between formal education and work.

Toward this end, Morton Bahr of the Communication Workers of America has argued, "A liberal arts education is not just learning for its own sake; . . . it is also a great asset in the workplace, as technology is advancing so rapidly that even a state-of-the-art technical education is quickly rendered obsolete. By comparison, the skills gained through a liberal arts education—communication, critical and abstract reasoning, human values, self-esteem, and most importantly, the ability to learn—will always be essential" (personal communication with the author, July 6, 1998). There is a striking parallel between Bahr's comment and the goals of a liberal education that were recently articulated in terms of competencies by William Cronon (1998). Clearly, there is an opportunity for liberal education faculty and human resource development professionals to collaborate to serve their mutual goals.

The following programs—one community college program, two undergraduate programs, and one master's degree program—illustrate a spectrum of behaviorist and humanist-liberal education elements. Regents College, though offering no direct instruction itself, is a leader in learning guidance and competence assessment. Bringing together liberal education and professional education content, it serves a national and international student body with associate, baccalaureate, and master's degree programs. Among them is a program for nursing degrees that combines holistic education with detailed assessment of clinical proficiency. DePaul University's School for New Learning has created a learner-responsive, highly individualized bachelor's degree based on competence demonstration. Rio Salado's Educational Service Partnerships work with community organizations to develop specific job competencies, and the college adds academic content to qualify participants for associate degree status. The McGregor School at Antioch University has applied competency methods at the graduate level to prepare bachelor's degree holders for teacher certification and master's degrees.

LEADERSHIP IN ASSESSMENT AND DISTANCE OUTREACH

Regents College—Albany, New York

Assessment Program

Nursing Program—AS, AAS, BS

Regents College's degree programs have characteristics that make them eligible for discussion in several of the classifications that this book addresses. Valley (1972), Houle (1973), and Medsker and colleagues (1975) described Regents in its nascent form as an *examination,* or *assessment,* model of the external degree. In fact, it soon developed procedures that placed it in Valley's *validation* and *credits* categories, too. It also has distinctive elements of liberal and professional education, distance learning, adult learner centeredness, self-direction, and electronic technology use. Most important, over nearly three decades Regents has evolved assessment processes that place it firmly in the competence camp.

The Assessment Concept

Regents College programs are based on the premise that what individuals know is more important than how or where they learned it. The college turns upside down the usual higher education focus on providing instruction in a required set of content necessary for a credential. Instead, Regents asks entrants what they already know, and how, after a series of planned experiences, they can demonstrate they have supplemented that initial learning to reach the level of mastery and competence that their desired credential represents. This approach surmounts the barriers of time and place and the academic residence requirements that have previously blocked many adults from furthering their education at other institutions.

The core concept of Regents College originated with Ewald B. Nyquist, president of The University of the State of New York. In this role he also served as commissioner of education and chief executive officer of the New York Board of Regents. He proposed in his 1970 inaugural presidential address that the regents of the university award undergraduate degrees to persons who could demonstrate achievement equivalent to degree recipients at the New York colleges and universities whose programs the regents oversaw (Nolan, 1998). The regents were able to build on a long history of administering examinations for high school achievement and college-level proficiency. The state also had experience with proficiency examinations in professional areas such as nursing. A year later in 1971, with support from the Carnegie Corporation and Ford Foundation, The University of the State of New York Regents External Degree Program was launched. Since then, it has expanded the range of its assessments and degrees and has taken the name of Regents College, although it remains under the control, albeit as a private entity, of the state regents. In April 1998, Regents College began a new phase in its history when the board of regents granted it a charter, thus giving the college, like other private institutions in the state of New York, its own board of trustees.

To illustrate the Regents College approach, I first examine general characteristics, such as enrollment and degree planning, assessment processes and sources of credit, learning resources, and learner support. A discussion of the college's largest program, nursing, then illustrates those factors in operation.

The Regents College Model

Regents College's programs differ significantly in many respects from those of more traditional institutions. The college awards degrees based on achievement that students can demonstrate rather than on enrollment in classes. It marks progress in terms of semester hour credits, but it does not offer courses. Credits are awarded based on transfer of relevant previously earned credit, a range of assessment procedures for evaluating noncollegiate learning, and competence as measured by the college's own examinations or by demonstrations of clinical practice. Core faculty, who almost without exception hold tenured appointments at other institutions, work in committees to establish credential requirements and set academic standards but do not provide instruction. The college, although not a teaching institution itself, facilitates student access to pertinent learning resources through an advising system staffed by professional academic degree advisers. Student learning is self-paced and flexible, with students enrolling for yearlong periods of access to the Regents College system. During their enrollment period, they may progress as their individual circumstances permit, drawing on college resources as they need them. Regents provides extensive learning resources, including annotated study guides for all examinations. Increasingly, the college is applying electronic technology to expand its range of services. All these processes enable the student population to be highly dispersed, with 85 percent living outside New York State and an increasing number outside the United States. Regents describes itself as America's First Virtual University, serving sixty thousand adult learners a year and awarding five thousand degrees annually (Regents College, 1998). At Regents College, being *virtual* means recognizing learning wherever it occurs.

ENROLLMENT AND DEGREE PLANNING. Most Regents entrants have had previous college-level study, some a great deal, so their first step is to seek evaluation of that previous work. They begin by submitting an enrollment form that indicates their preferred degree program, and an enrollment fee that covers their initial evaluation and first year of participation. They include documentation of previous learning experiences, such as transcripts from regionally accredited colleges and universities, score reports from recognized testing agencies, and evidence of completion of approved military, employer, or other noncollegiate education programs. After evaluating the documents, Regents responds with a *status report* indicating how this previous learning will apply to the program selected. The applicant may then proceed to advisement and planning for completing the remaining requirements. Persons not yet ready to enroll may request a credit review, based on submission of the same documentation. After the report indicates how much of their previous work will apply to the program, they can decide whether to proceed to full enrollment.

Enrollees work with an advising team from their selected program to design their individual degree plans and to select methods for completing the remaining requirements. These methods may include traditional courses, distance learning procedures, and proficiency examinations or other additional assessment sources. In all cases the method of demonstrating learning should receive prior adviser approval to assure its acceptability. As enrollees complete steps in their plans, they submit official documentation to their advising teams, who update their status reports.

Entry and enrollment function on a rolling basis, so persons may begin and complete at any time. After the initial year of enrollment, participants pay an additional annual student services fee until they complete their degree. Various other fees apply to special services, such as degree or program changes, Regents College examinations, and graduation.

ASSESSMENT AND SOURCES OF CREDIT. The most distinctive characteristic of Regents College is its assessment of learner competence and mastery. Through direct assessment by its own procedures and carefully screened recognition of the assessments of others using national quality assurance systems, the college enables its enrollees to demonstrate their fulfillment of degree requirements. The credit may be earned prior to enrollment or subsequently as part of the individual degree plan.

Direct assessment. Regents offers several mechanisms in which the college acts as the primary judge of students' learning. These include its own written examinations in a variety of fields; criterion-referenced, clinical performance examinations; specialized assessments; and portfolio assessments by the college and collaborative partners. Regents is the only collegiate institution in the United States that also functions as a national testing agency, in parallel with the College Board's CLEP (College-Level Examination Program) and the military's DANTES (Defense Activity for Non-Traditional Educational Support) programs.

Written examinations. Currently, Regents offers a series of forty written examinations that correspond to the content of one- or two-semester courses at accredited institutions. The examinations provide opportunities for adults to demonstrate college-level learning in arts and sciences, business, education, and nursing, and they are administered worldwide. Faculty working with Regents College psychometric staff develop the examinations, which are then normed on students in campus-based programs. Most are multiple choice, although six are essay exams and one combines these two formats. Initially, examinations were at the associate or baccalaureate level, but in 1998, two graduate-level examinations were introduced to support the college's new master's program in liberal studies. In 1999, a master's degree in nursing is being introduced using graduate examinations under development at this writing. The college employs a continual monitoring process to plan introduction of new examinations and retirement of old ones. All examinations are fully reviewed and updated continually, using item response theory, the most modern technique in test development. They are recommended by the American Council on Education (ACE) Center for Adult Learning and Educational Credentials for the award of college-level credit.

Examinations are administered daily by computer in the United States and Canada through the services of Sylvan Technology Centers. Persons who register for examinations receive a tutorial packet on the technology, and may take the tests within a ninety-day period after registration. Multiple-choice examinees receive their results on-site at the time they finish the tests, and the college provides examinees with expanded score reports detailing strengths and weaknesses of their performance. Military personnel may take the examinations through the DANTES system. Other international examinees can arrange administration directly with Regents. About sixty thousand Regents College examinations are administered each year.

Criterion-referenced performance examinations. The Regents College nursing degree program includes four clinical performance examinations; students must succeed on these exams to complete requirements in the nursing major. The performance examinations are *criterion referenced;* that is, they match a student's test performance against a preestablished level of performance in a specific content domain. Nursing faculty determine the minimum standard acceptable for beginning associate- or baccalaureate-level practice. Each examination is administered according to a standard protocol in an active situation designed to test the desired competencies. To reduce stress in the test situation, the college offers orientation to the test, provides a student advocate, and schedules break periods. The college solicits student feedback at the end of the examination, and an appeal process is available for persons whose attempts are unsuccessful.

The performance examinations, some of which require multiple days, are administered throughout the year by appointment only. They are available through the four Regional Performance Assessment Centers, located in the South, West, Midwest, and Northeast, each of which operates multiple examination sites.

Portfolio assessment. Regents College assesses individual learning by portfolio evaluation based on models of the Council for Adult and Experiential Learning or of collaborating institutions. Regents internal portfolio assessments serve special needs of its nursing and technology programs. These assessments were developed by faculty in consultation with psychometric staff. Collaborative assessment partnerships with Ohio University (1993), Empire State College (1994), and Charter Oak State College (1995), each of which offers portfolio assessment at a distance, have enabled Regents to benefit from cost-effective partnerships with institutions that have well-developed comprehensive portfolio assessment systems.

Regents also offers special assessments in certain fields. The Clinical Portfolio Assessment in nursing is an alternative to the eight-credit Clinical Performance in Nursing Examination. It is available to students in the baccalaureate program who are already registered nurses. The program recognizes the clinical skills required by their licensure and enables these persons to demonstrate their current clinical competence in a written presentation supported by documentation. Students in the electrical and nuclear technology programs synthesize, apply, and explain their learning in the Integrated Technology Assessment, a capstone experience for the baccalaureate degree. These assessments contribute to the professional accreditation the technology programs have received.

As interest in individual assessment, either by portfolio or by specialized processes, has increased, Regents has strengthened its assessment advising system. On entry, students are asked to complete a *significant learning outline* in which they define learning they wish to have assessed and indicate how it will be documented. The outline is reviewed by a *flexible assessment team* drawn from advisers and the psychometric staff, after which the team recommends the most appropriate assessment options for each student and refers them to liaisons who assist in preparing the assessments.

Specialized assessments. Special individualized assessment is available for students who have in-depth knowledge in fields for which other assessment or adequate documentation of learning is not available. Assessment applicants present their knowledge and competence in person to a special panel of two faculty subject matter experts. In the last five years, special assessments have been conducted in addiction counseling, certain foreign languages, histotechnology and cytotechnology, American Sign Language interpreting, and other areas. Although used less frequently than other Regents assessment procedures, special assessments provide options for unique cases.

Recognition of others' assessments. In addition its own assessments, Regents accepts and transcripts credit from other recognized sources. In this respect it serves as an educational integrator and broker. The college will accept credit only from regionally accredited collegiate institutions. It maintains an expert transcript evaluation staff from both U.S. and international institutions who review about sixty thousand transcripts annually. It also accepts credit recommendations from ACE for military training, national credit-by-examination programs, and corporate and industrial training programs. Regents also actively seeks additional extrainstitutional sources of credit, and in recent years has evaluated programs such as the Physician Assistant National Certifying Examination and the Rural Leadership Development Network.

GUIDED LEARNING AND LEARNING RESOURCES. Regents College has developed a guided learning system to help students become resourceful, independent lifelong learners. It provides services in three areas: learning how to learn, learning how to use the Regents College system, and learning subject matter content. The goal is to enable students to use alternative means to gain mastery of the knowledge and skill necessary to succeed in the college's assessments.

Regents provides integrated packages of learning materials and resources to guide students' preparation for each of the written examinations and criterion-referenced performance examinations. Expanded learning packages have been developed for some of the college's upper-level examinations.

Staff of the Office of Learning Services serve as consultants to other college units that are developing learning resources and delivery systems to support learners studying at a distance. These services include face-to-face workshops, electronic teleconferencing, audio teleconferencing, print-based correspondence, tutorials, and combinations of those methods. Regents encourages students to form study groups among themselves, and the college facilitates this activity through the Electronic Peer Network (EPN) on its Web site, where students can communicate and form study groups. The college also provides study guides for adults, such as *How to Study Independently* and *Research and Writing at the Graduate Level*. To help students locate learning opportunities, it has developed DistanceLearn, a searchable database of over eight thousand college-level courses and examinations available at a distance from regionally accredited colleges, and each of which is keyed to Regents College degree requirements. Learning services continue to develop toward goals set for 2001.

Regents students' principal contact with the college comes through the advising team of their degree program. These professional advisers are available to assist students to obtain assessment of previous learning and to plan additional education that will complete their programs.

The Nursing Program

Regents has thirty different degree programs at the undergraduate and graduate levels in business, liberal arts, nursing, and technology. Each curriculum includes general education and specialization components and opportunity for electives. Over half the college's enrollment is in health-related fields, primarily nursing.

Regents' nursing program was one of its earliest degree offerings, and it was developed with extensive support from the W. K. Kellogg Foundation. The college offers nursing curricula leading to associate of science, associate of applied science, and bachelor of science degrees. All sequences draw on the liberal arts, humanist, and behavioral philosophical orientations discussed in Chapter Two. They seek to integrate a liberal education, a holistic approach to persons, and competence in practice. The associate and baccalaureate degrees differ in the extent of content and competence required and the levels of responsibility degree recipients are prepared for. The associate of science has a somewhat stronger arts and sciences content than the associate of applied science. The degree programs are accredited by the National League of Nursing.

ENROLLMENT. Regents has been very successful in attracting participants for its nursing program. Currently, it enrolls over ten thousand persons, about 70 percent at the associate level and 30 percent at the baccalaureate level. A substantial proportion are people of color. Program graduates provide strong word-of-mouth promotion, but the college also uses convention exhibits, advertising in nursing journals, and direct mail to distribute information to prospective students.

Entrants follow general college procedures for enrollment and initial evaluation. A study several years ago indicated a low success rate in the program for persons with limited prior clinical experience or acquaintance with health specialties. Evidence of that experience is now required, and completion rates have improved. Now 75 percent of associate degree entrants are licensed practical nurses who already have accumulated considerable content background, skill, and experience.

CURRICULUM AND METHODS OF COMPLETION. The following discussion focuses on the Bachelor of Science in Nursing (BSN) program. The BSN curriculum requires 120 semester hours of credit: 69 credits in general education and 51 credits in nursing. The general education component is distributed over humanities, social sciences, and natural sciences and mathematics, with a requirement of a nine-hour depth in one discipline, plus nine hours of electives and three hours in written English. It is also possible to minor in one of several areas as part of the general education component. Students meet these requirements through credit recognized at enrollment for previous learning and through newly taken college courses or proficiency examinations, many offered by Regents College's own examination program.

The professional component is expressed in a series of ten knowledge and performance areas that are tested by written examinations and performance assessments. Emphasis is placed on integration of nursing knowledge and related sciences in a variety of care situations. The examination areas are health restoration, health support, professional strategies, research in nursing, clinical performance, health assessment performance, teaching performance, and professional role performance; each has an assigned credit hour value. Enrollees may request a waiver of one or more of the examinations if they have relatively recent accredited baccalaureate coursework that is equivalent to the examination content. Faculty review requests for waivers quarterly.

No waivers are allowed for the nursing performance examinations, but registered nurses enrolled in the program may elect to present the clinical portfolio described above. Regents provides study guides for each of the performance assessment areas and schedules appointments for the examinations. The Professional Role Performance Examination is a major assessment, requiring three days, that is taken near the completion of the program.

LEARNING RESOURCES. The nursing program supplements general Regents College advisement and learning resources in several ways. Guided learning support is one of the most critical services of the program, and it is staffed by a cadre of nurse educators in Albany with faculty experience. They maintain contact with students to provide guidance and support on both academic and clinical content. These nurse educators do not set the curriculum, but they administer it through their communication with students. In addition to supplying their own support, they can refer students to educational experiences in the students' own locales to supplement clinical preparation. The nurse educators also travel to present workshops and to train clinical examiners in the field.

Regents provides study guides for the nursing assessments as well as access to the nurse educators in the field for advice on exam preparation.

The college also offers workshops in study skills and test-taking strategies, as well as videotapes, workbooks, and workshops in clinical performance examination preparation, and teleconferences on nursing diagnoses and clinical portfolio preparation. While in the program, students have access to an electronic network of current Regents College students and graduates.

CORE FACULTY. A core group of seventeen faculty, shortly to increase to twenty, maintains academic control and oversight of the program. These faculty hold appointments at other higher education nursing programs, meeting three times a year to consult on Regents' program curriculum and operation. They normally work through a series of subcommittees with differing program responsibilities: for example, reviewing applications for written examination waivers.

Core faculty are a key element in program maintenance in a rapidly changing field. They work with the college's nurse educators and clinical examiners to keep assessments current and to update processes as well as to monitor consistency in the regional assessment system. In addition to periodic regional and professional accreditation review, Regents does five-year follow-up studies with graduates, and also surveys employers of graduates for performance ratings (for follow-up studies on the nursing program, see Nesler, Hanner, Lettus, & Melburg, 1995; Newman, Stahl, Pierce, & Borelli, 1995; Kelley & Joel, 1996).

FUTURE AND SUMMARY. The nursing program hopes that it can increase participation in the baccalaureate degree. At present the proportion of associate degree graduates who proceed to the bachelor's degree is higher than national averages, but the program would like to improve that rate. It also offers a certificate in home health care nursing and is in the process of adding a certificate program in health care informatics to respond to changing needs in the profession. The former is planned for associate degree nurses, and the latter for postbaccalaureate nurses. A Master of Science in Nursing Degree is in development, and the informatics certificate component will apply to that curriculum. As access to electronic technology becomes an increasing option, the program is concerned about students' unequal access to electronic facilities and is considering solutions to that problem.

Regents' programs make up an extensive and complex system that has developed over many years. That complexity has grown greater as the college has enrolled participants at increasingly great distances. Nevertheless, Regents' scale should not deter other institutions' efforts to conduct competence-based programs. Some of Regents' established processes that are generally available may even facilitate others' efforts.

Critical needs are credibility of faculty and the assessment processes they conduct, careful analysis of the elements to be evaluated and the means of carrying out assessments, clear guidance to learners on the means by which they can achieve the desired levels, strong learner support, a comprehensive system to recognize prior learning, and where technical or clinical areas are concerned, resources to give learners experience in those areas.

SIX DOMAINS OF COMPETENCE FOR LIFE

DePaul University—Chicago, Illinois

School for New Learning

Bachelor of Arts Degree Program

Though sharing the Regents College commitment to demonstration of competence, the baccalaureate degree program of DePaul University's School for New Learning (SNL) differs in the population it addresses. Whereas Regents' scope was initially statewide and later national and international, SNL has focused on the Chicago metropolitan area and only recently has reached out further. SNL has conceived its degree in individualized, self-planned terms. It builds on a liberal education base that it seeks to integrate with personal and professional goals and a commitment to lifelong learning.

SNL has offered a competence-based bachelor of arts degree since 1972. The school and the program originated from the concepts of two clergy administrators for better serving Chicago learners whose needs were being poorly met. DePaul had long experience with adult learners through its Evening School, and since 1915, part-time working adults had made up its largest student constituency. Two academic leaders who were well grounded in adult development and experiential learning theory undertook creation of the new initiative, and the competence orientation came from them. They commented, "In the construction of a generic competence framework, the School . . . has sought to achieve a level of specificity that will insure quality and comprehensiveness without undercutting flexibility."

The university provided start-up funding. A 1973 grant from FIPSE enabled the School for New Learning to develop its initial orientation course (the Discovery Workshop) and its competence framework further. Subsequently, the degree program and the school, like most of DePaul's divisions, have been dependent mostly on tuition for ongoing support. However, SNL's success has enabled it to make a significant contribution to institutional overhead also.

DePaul University was established in 1898 to provide individualized higher education in an urban setting, especially to the poor. One hundred years later it has grown to 18,500 students, both residential and commuting, and offers degree programs through the doctoral level. In addition to SNL, it has colleges and schools in liberal arts, education, commerce, law, computer science, technology and information science, and theater and music. A recent aggressive growth strategy has added four suburban campuses to the earlier Lincoln Park and Loop sites. SNL conducts its programs at all sites and will customize programs to workplaces or elsewhere if appropriate.

Two major elements distinguish the SNL bachelor's program for this discussion: its competence-based learning framework and its comprehensive system of academic advising closely linked to the educational program. SNL operates on the premises that individual learners are the primary agents of their own learning, that with assistance learners can discover how to achieve their learning goals, and that curriculum results from the interaction of individual learner experience and goals with significant domains of competence. SNL seeks to provide an individualized learning environment that is supportive and collaborative. Its goal is competent graduates who possess the full range of specified competencies, gained either through experiences prior to SNL or through new learning, that characterize educated adults in contemporary society.

The Competence Framework

SNL's competence formulation has gone through several iterations since 1972. Until recently, each student's degree requirements were expressed in fifty competence statements, divided into five domains of ten competencies each. Some competencies were stated by the program, and others were written by the individual student. Learners demonstrated some competencies by activities the program specified, others by means chosen by the learner.

Following a recent program review, SNL has adopted a revised framework to be implemented in fall 1999. The remainder of this discussion focuses on that revision. SNL concluded that its existing model emphasized individualism at the expense of cooperation and social responsibility. To give greater emphasis to the social dimensions of learning, the school drew on its long-term values but also sought input from task forces and constituents and reviewed adult learning and feminist and critical theory. The outcome is a modified framework that continues to require fifty competencies but now 70 percent of the competence statements are provided by the program and up to 30 percent may be constructed by the individual student.

SNL defines competence as a recognizable level of skill, ability, or knowledge that enables individuals to perform in given contexts and to transfer what they know or can do to other contexts. The competence statements guide students in developing their individualized curricula, guide instructors in designing courses and other learning activities, and guide both students and faculty in assessing learning outcomes. The driving purpose of the competence-based framework is for the student to attain and demonstrate stated outcomes in a direct, self-conscious, and explicit way.

The revised degree structure is organized in six domains requiring varying numbers of competencies (shown in parentheses): lifelong learning (12), integrative learning (6), arts and ideas (7), the human community (7), the scientific world (7), and the focus area (11). The focus area reflects learners' personal and professional goals. Learners specify most of the competencies here themselves, normally organizing them in coherent groups. In the lifelong learning domain, learners participate in an externship, a research seminar, and a final seminar, the Summit Seminar, shortly before graduation.

STUDENT EXPERIENCE OF THE CURRICULUM. Students begin with two courses in the lifelong learning domain that are preliminary to the rest of their programs. The first is the Learning Assessment Seminar (formerly the Discovery Workshop), that the school offers several times a month throughout the year, either on three Saturdays or five evenings. The seminar engages students in an orientation to returning to college, values clarification, and life planning. Seminar leaders, using material from individual interviews and other information provided by the students, assess student competence, including writing skills, for admission to the bachelor's program. Leaders may recommend full or preliminary admission, the latter requiring some additional preparation before students proceed into the degree program. In some cases admission may be denied.

Those who are admitted then take Foundations in Adult Learning, a course offering group and individual advisement as well as instruction.

It introduces learners to competence-based study, assessment practices, the degree design process, and the process of mapping educational goals in a learning plan. Early in this process each student forms an *academic committee* (discussed more fully in the section on advising) that will work with the student throughout the degree program. Students also learn how to assemble evidence of learning from experience to demonstrate competence. With the committee's assistance they develop a plan to achieve their learning goals, including writing some of the competence statements and requirements themselves. They also begin preparation of a reflective portfolio that they will maintain over the duration of the program and submit to their academic committee at the end.

Following the Foundations course, students pursue the competencies of their plans. Some must be demonstrated by successful completion of designated SNL courses. Others may be achieved by a variety of means, such as SNL course offerings, transfer credit, challenge examinations, and assessment by SNL of credit-free courses, essays describing previous learning experiences, work products, or creative works. All SNL courses are designed to address one or more competencies, and SNL has developed a program of experiential learning assessment that has been commended by CAEL. In some cases, learning through direct experience, as in SNL travel-study courses, may be the preferred mode of demonstration.

Students may enter the program any time during the year. SNL describes its program as accelerated in that students may finish in fewer than four years, depending on their previous learning and their rate of satisfying requirements. Self-paced might be a more apt description, because unlike students in accelerated cohort programs, SNL students control the rate of their involvement and can alter the pace as needed. The Weekend College, an evening intensive course, and a cluster mode of coursework offer more intensive cohort-based formats for those who prefer more structure.

The revised curriculum design emphasizes reflection and integration, as evidenced by the new domain of integrative learning. Many competence statements also make connections to other areas and stress relationships and patterns. Three required activities, the externship, the culminating Advanced Project in the focus area, and the Summit Seminar also contribute to these goals.

ADVISING SYSTEM. A comprehensive system of learner advisement is the second distinguishing feature of SNL. The school considers advising an integral rather than supplemental element of its educational program. In an effort to *unlock* students' potential for learning and development, advisement has the goals of enabling timely and individualized interactions between faculty and learners around academic issues, providing accurate and relevant information so learners can make informed decisions, promoting the self-management of learning, and responding proactively to learners' joy and effort in learning. In one sense all interactions of learners with SNL personnel involve advising, and indeed, more persons have an explicit advising role than often is the case in higher education institutions. Faculty receive an extensive handbook and participate in seminars on working with adults. New staff take an orientation workshop and then participate in the Learning Assessment Workshop to gain direct experience of the program.

Advisement begins in the preadmission stage with program literature that reflects SNL's values, and continues in preadmission group orientation sessions, in individual assessments of previous learning that may be applicable, and in the preadmission course, Learning Assessment. After admission and during the Foundations of Adult Learning course, students each form the academic committee mentioned earlier, which they chair and with which they work throughout the rest of their programs. The Foundations instructor becomes the students' individual *faculty mentor* for the remainder of their study. Each student, assisted if necessary by the mentor, also selects a *professional adviser* with a relevant career background, one who is knowledgeable and qualified in the student's focus area. The student also has the option of selecting a *peer adviser* from among students or alumni to offer counsel on issues and provide feedback from the learner perspective. This group, working with the student, develops the initial degree plan, offers continuing advising, and assesses fulfillment of the domain competencies. SNL provides guidelines for first meetings of the academic committee, in which it begins degree planning, and for the final degree completion review meetings, which SNL regards as especially important.

In addition to continuing the relationship with their academic committees as they progress, students interact with others in SNL. An *advising center* staffed with part-time advisers is available at each DePaul center throughout the week, including evenings and weekends. In addition to providing preadmission information, these advisers assist with administrative and registration issues and serve as backup to faculty mentors. Appropriate resident or visiting faculty assist in the development of independent learning options, and they also work with learners in the Summit Seminars. In the Weekend College, peer advising occurs among small groups of students.

A recent university survey of graduates indicated a high level of satisfaction with SNL advising. Staff believe the advising system contributes to a favorable persistence rate among students and a stronger sense among students of belonging to a learning community. The fusion of advising and the learning experience and the linking of academic, professional, and student peer perspectives has given students greater commitment and focus. The inclusion of advisement in tuition-supported credit courses also assists SNL to meet the costs of its commitment to the advising function. In 1996, the National Academic Advising Association recognized SNL for its outstanding advising program.

THE LEARNERS. SNL students, in accord with the university's urban mission, come from the Chicago metropolitan area. The university admissions office conducts general promotion that includes SNL, but the school also provides frequent information sessions and other outreach. It depends heavily on word of mouth as well. Students and graduates employed in Chicago businesses or other organizations tell others of the program, as do visiting faculty. SNL's tuition, though slightly lower than tuition for other DePaul divisions, is high for many students, so employer tuition assistance is important. Seventy-two percent of enrollees are women, many with low incomes. Multiculturalism and diversity are important values for the program, and 29 percent of enrollment comes from people of color.

Future

In pursuing its individualized and competence-based program, SNL relies on several factors. These include a carefully planned initial orientation; an interactive relationship between the learner and the advising committee to develop the curriculum and statements of competencies; a rolling, self-paced calendar; the incorporation of experiential learning; and the inclusion of reflective and integrating experiences such as the reflective portfolio, the externship, the Advanced Project, and the Summit Seminar. To strengthen the critical advising function, the program devotes considerable effort to the development of faculty and staff who reflect the program's philosophy.

SNL has grown rapidly in recent years, as has the university as a whole. In fall 1998, the school enrolled 2,172 degree students, up from about 1,250 in 1990. Of those, 2,042 were in the bachelor's program and 130 in a master of arts program in integrated professional studies. In 1988, DePaul University adopted an aggressive ten-year growth plan to reposition itself as a "high quality, highly visible teaching university." It reaffirmed that vision in 1995, and in 1997, it adopted three centennial goals that included "becoming the dominant provider in greater Chicago of high quality education for part-time working adults" (Meister, 1998, p. 1). To this end it has pursued a *metro-presence strategy* in suburban areas, adding new campuses and delivery methods with the goal of more than doubling suburban credit hours by 2006.

Clearly the School for New Learning and its programs will play a prominent role in this plan. Recent initiatives have included a cooperative degree in computing with another school of the university, which may presage similar linkages with other divisions. SNL is seeking to include more content in ethics, technology, diversity, and global concerns in its curriculum. It is reaching out to provide programs for specific employers in Chicago and beyond, and recently it began international delivery of its program in Hong Kong.

MATCHING EMPLOYER TRAINING TO DEGREE GOALS

Rio Salado College—Tempe, Arizona

Division of Applied Programs

Law Enforcement Technology Program

Rio Salado College works in partnership with Phoenix-area employers to combine employer education and training with college content and curriculum to qualify employees in specialized areas at the associate degree level. The aim is to achieve both employer and learner goals for higher professional competence. The emphasis is behavioral, and the design relates employment-based skills and application of general education competencies while maintaining high academic quality. The cooperative effort gains efficiency by linking training already provided by employers with college resources adapted to employers' needs.

Rio Salado College is a highly innovative institution in one of the most change-oriented community college systems in the country, the Maricopa Community College District. The ten-institution Maricopa system participated in the Pew Higher Education Roundtable's efforts to stimulate change and transformation through dialogue among higher education institutions. During 1994 and 1995, Maricopa carried that dialogue into conversations among its own members with the goal of creating a learner-centered system based on collaboration and positioned for the future (Elsner, 1997). Rio Salado played a key role in generating those discussions and focusing on changed outlooks for the future.

Rio Salado is unique among its sister institutions in several ways. It has no campus but is housed in an office building in a business park in Tempe, on the southeast side of Phoenix. In spring 1998, it had only nineteen full-time faculty members, depending instead on liberal use of adjunct faculty, often practitioners in the fields they teach. The administrative facility has few classrooms because most instruction occurs at well over two hundred sites in the Phoenix metropolitan area and through distance delivery of learning using technology. Most classes do not follow traditional terms, but start as needed and run for periods of differing length. Rio Salado is aggressively market and customer oriented and prides itself on success in competition. Its president has commented, "Our chancellor says to me, if Rio is not controversial, I'm not doing my job" (Healy, 1998, p. A32).

Applied Programs and Educational Service Partnerships

One of the most vigorous parts of Rio Salado is its division of Applied Programs. Applied Programs grew out of the prosperous economy and high employment in the area and accompanying demands from employers for college services to increase workforce skills. The college decided to bring in leadership with both academic qualifications and business experience and orientation. For example, the present dean, who holds a doctorate, has functioned in both higher education and business; the director and faculty chair of the Law Enforcement Technology Program was formerly chief of police in Scottsdale, a Maricopa County community. Faculty are drawn from practitioners closely related to the community. Through hiring practices such as these and close community involvement, Rio Salado creates a seamless relationship between the college and the community.

Applied Programs, which does not shrink from the rhetoric in which students are customers, employers are clients, and the community is an educational market, searches out government and business employers who can use its services. Its basic associate of applied science degree is earned in a framework that allows flexibility and customization of technical requirements while maintaining a strong general education component with study in the humanities; oral and written communication; and natural, social, and behavioral sciences. The goals of both the technical and general education requirements are described as competence outcomes, and general education courses can include applications, exercises, projects, and written assignments related to the technical work. A writing assignment, for example, may be evaluated not only in a communication class but also in other courses whose content it touches on.

Applied Programs has developed the Educational Service Partnership, a model especially attractive to large-scale employers with well-developed, professionally organized internal training programs. These partnerships have the advantage of merging organizational and individual employee goals and connecting them with college educational services. Employers get credibility for their technical training efforts and see them related to broader career path development for their workers. Employees, who may have ignored company tuition reimbursement benefits, now perceive a clear payoff in salary and promotion from participating in employer-endorsed education. The community college fulfills its mission of community responsiveness and increases its service delivery (Van Dyke, 1995; Theibert, 1995, 1996).

The foundational building blocks of the partnerships are the organizational training programs. These often parallel technical college curricula quality in design, facilities, instruction, and evaluation and result in a professional standard of training. If necessary, Rio Salado can add content and instructional resources to them to create college-level courses. Some employer training is equivalent to the specialization requirement of an associate of applied science degree. In other cases, it can be supplemented with content to reach that level. Further, most or all of this learning can take place on the job in the course of normal employment.

Applied Programs provides its contribution to the partnership in three ways. First, in collaboration with the company, it ensures the employer's training courses have college-level content and establishes credit value for them. Second, it provides supplementary technical courses and general education courses necessary to fulfill associate degree requirements. Finally, it organizes delivery of the college-provided courses and supporting services in ways convenient to the students. Delivery may involve instruction on site out of work hours and various distance learning modalities, such as correspondence, audio or videocassettes, and the Internet.

These combinations of effort result in a win-win circumstance for all the parties. Employers benefit from direct application of their resources and gain more qualified workers. Employees receive an extra benefit from training they would experience in any case and may go on to further qualification. The educational provider succeeds in its mission to respond to community needs as it also increases its activity and gains community goodwill.

Rio Salado has worked out several of these partnerships. Among them are agreements with American Express Quality University and America West Airlines. Each year a large number of people participate in American Express training courses, which can lead toward five specialty employment tracks. By recognizing these courses for credit and by adding courses in management and quality, Rio Salado established two new associate degrees, one in Customer Service and one in Quality Process Leadership. American Express pays part or all of the tuition for employees taking the college-provided courses. All the coursework necessary to complete the degree is available on-site at American Express facilities or anywhere in the world by distance learning.

America West Airlines annually sends a large number of staff through a professionally developed training program for customer service representatives (CSRs). Program courses are modeled on college courses, and the company wanted the CSRs to receive degree-level qualification, even though few had any prior college experience. Rio Salado combined the training components, with some modifications, with general education to create an associate specialty in Airline Operations. The entire general studies component is available both at America West training facilities and by distance learning. The latter is an important service for the many personnel who have changing time and location assignments.

In these and other educational partnership agreements, the relationship between Rio Salado and the employer depends on cooperation and shared understandings. Operations are facilitated by oversight committees made up of representatives of the organizations, college faculty, and students. The committees consider program quality control, faculty certification, curriculum development and approval, and future development. At times the college has brokered agreements for sharing facilities among different sponsors.

The Law Enforcement Technology Program

The Law Enforcement Technology (LET) program offers a fuller illustration of the Educational Service Partnership model and of its focus on competence. The LET program arose from a contact the dean of Applied Programs made to the Phoenix chief of police. The police chief described the intensive entry training program for officer recruits but said he saw a need for higher education qualifications if officers were to be eligible for advancement. Together they looked for ways to link Phoenix Regional Police Academy training and associate degree requirements. The result was a program to provide police officer recruits with the technical and academic skills to succeed as police officers and progress to the rank of sergeant.

The Phoenix Regional Police Academy trains approximately 650 persons a year for law enforcement agencies in the Maricopa County area, which encompasses Phoenix, Glendale, Scottsdale, and Tempe. In addition, Rio Salado has formed partnerships with academies of the Mesa police department and the Maricopa County sheriff's office. A growing number of officer recruits from agencies elsewhere in the state attend these programs, and officers from the State Correctional Officers Training Facility also participate. The training at the Phoenix Regional Police Academy is very structured, offering a competence-based curriculum planned to exceed already high Arizona Law Enforcement Officers Advisory Council and national law enforcement standards, and recruits are regularly evaluated. It offers mainly a classroom-based series of courses taken in forty-hour per week schedules over sixteen weeks. Successful trainees are well prepared for their initial assignment as officers, but few have the college background to be eligible for promotion. In addition, variable rotation schedules often prevent most officers from taking traditionally scheduled college courses to acquire this background.

To remedy this problem Rio Salado worked with the academy to review the entry training and to design a program in two phases: academy and postacademy study. After upgrading the academy training sequence to college level, Rio Salado agreed to grant thirty-five semester credits for the academy courses and to award a certificate in *law enforcement technology* on completion. Some newly appointed officers proceed directly into the postacademy study, which consists of general education requirements and leads to an associate of applied science degree, but most defer studies for a period as they take up their jobs. After gaining some experience and beginning to seek promotion and increased salary, many return to complete the general education requirements, with departmental encouragement. The dean and program director describe the program as a stool with three legs, with the Arizona Police Officers Training Board and the academy setting technical standards, the college providing general education standards and content, and the police forces supplying participants and motivation. In a recent twelve-month period, 1,338 persons were enrolled from the various law enforcement authorities participating, with 1,299 completing the certificate and 112 completing the degree program.

The mandated academy curriculum does not allow for individualization of study and concentrates on competence or ability to perform. The postacademy general education allows more flexibility in time, alternative delivery modes, and selection of courses. In addition, instructors endeavor to make connections between the general education and learners' workplace experiences. Performance objectives are stated for all courses required for the degree. Communications courses, for instance, may feature problem-based exercises that involve reading, analyzing, and interpreting written reports; use of graphics; and giving oral presentations that are complementary to the earlier technical instruction. Delivery modes include on-site classes, traditional correspondence or audio- and videocassette courses, and courses offered over the Internet. Degree candidates may transfer in relevant previous college credit and may receive credit based on examinations or recognized by credit-recommending authorities, but no portfolio assessment is available.

The college maintains a strong set of support services for students, largely through interactive communication. Participants can access faculty by e-mail and voice mail. Faculty maintain virtual office hours, communicating with students on-line during specified periods. Students have access to the college library, an electronic library, and other Maricopa system college libraries. On-line tutoring and writing assistance are also available, as is a student chat area in which students help each other. The program reports a dramatic increase in use of electronically delivered courses and services and a need to increase support. It looks ahead to a triage model of technical information support, course information support handled by nonacademic professionals, and academic content support handled by faculty.

Rio Salado worked with the academy at the outset not only to make academy courses eligible for credit but also to assign instructors who meet state standards for community college faculty. Faculty for the college-provided courses are drawn from college adjunct faculty, as in other programs. Rio Salado's Adjunct Faculty Institute prepares new instructors with eight to ten hours of initial orientation and two- to three-hour development seminars each semester. The orientation seeks to convey that employers and students are clients and customers to be served.

Future

Applied Programs staff believe that society's need for progressively better educated personnel will increase demand for responsive services such as the college provides and that service solutions may not be bounded by typical degrees or programs, although familiar mechanisms such as credit courses and degree or certificate credentials will remain relevant. Institutions need to be adaptable, devising new forms of education to meet community needs as they arise.

At the same time, Rio Salado foresees some specific directions of development. Among them are clearer paths to baccalaureate degrees for persons who have technical qualification but need more general education. These paths could include inverted programs, in which associate-level technical preparation supplemented with special study could form a major and be joined with general education in the last two years. The last two years could be accomplished through articulation agreements with four-year colleges or through authorization of community colleges to award baccalaureates in technical fields not offered by four-year colleges. The latter has been discussed in Arizona without any final decision.

Distance learning technology opens the way to offer established programs to wider audiences. Rio Salado is in the process of creating partnerships to offer its Law Enforcement Technology program nationally. Similarly, it is exploring a technology-based program for dental hygienists. Issues of state regulation arise with distance learning, but Rio Salado has worked in other states in partnership with corporations based in Arizona, in some cases using company resources for interactive communication.

Applied Programs has found the Educational Service Partnerships to be effective and efficient. They build on pragmatic motivations of both employers and employees. Over seven years Applied Programs enrollment has grown from 11 percent to 67 percent of the college's full-time equivalent enrollment. Recruitment is facilitated by employers, and employer provision of initial training, meeting space, and other support keeps per student costs low. Individual programs have a multiplier effect, *chaining off* into further activity. Finally, staff express a sense of being on the cutting edge of change and part of a college that is continuously engaged in the community.

COMPETENCE-BASED LEARNING IN SERVICE TO A GRADUATE-LEVEL PROFESSION

Antioch University—Yellow Springs, Ohio

The McGregor School

Master of Arts with Professional Preparation for Teacher Certification

Since January 1995, The McGregor School of Antioch University has offered working adults a Master of Arts with Professional Preparation for Teacher Certification degree program. It is a competence-based graduate program in a highly regulated profession that is strongly oriented to its local environment. It targets persons who already hold baccalaureate degrees and who have significant experience working with children, although not necessarily in teaching. In a two-step process, it qualifies them for Ohio state certification and enables them to complete a master's of arts degree.

The Institutional and Regional Environment

Antioch University is composed of five largely autonomous units. The original unit, Antioch College, chiefly serves traditional age college students. Except for the age of its student population, however, it can hardly be called traditional. From its beginning in 1854, when it enrolled women and African Americans on an equivalent basis with white males, it has led in innovation and has stressed uniting academic learning with direct experience (Clark, 1992; Grant & Riesman, 1978; Pope, 1995; Herr, 1997). The other four divisions are of more recent foundation and provide programs to adult learners at the undergraduate, master's, and doctoral levels. Three are in New England, the Northwest, and Southern California, respectively. The fourth, The McGregor School, is in Yellow Springs, Ohio, along with Antioch College and the Office of University Chancellor. The McGregor School, named after an earlier president and leader in humanist education, Douglas McGregor (McGregor, 1960), began in the late 1980s as a baccalaureate degree completion program. Now it also offers graduate programs.

Yellow Springs is a small city lying in the triangle of southwestern Ohio described by Dayton, Cincinnati, and Columbus. It is a part of

Ohio that has had a long-standing African American population, dating back to the time of the Underground Railroad, before the Civil War. The Dayton region population, for instance, is 40 percent African American. Yellow Springs has been an integrated community for a long time, and Antioch participates in its inclusive culture. Its history of an African American presence and of being hospitable to other ethnic groups has made it a welcoming place for people of color, and both college and McGregor School enrollments have benefited from this. Yet public school systems in the area have been concerned about underrepresentation of African Americans among teachers and have sought to increase those numbers.

Another factor in the region is the presence of Wright-Patterson Air Force Base, situated between Dayton and Yellow Springs. Many of its personnel who are retiring or being downsized have baccalaureate or higher degrees and extensive experience as trainers. Some of them have taken advantage of the Department of Defense Troops to Teachers program to begin second careers in teaching. This program assists personnel with tuition to prepare for teacher certification and offers financial supplements to districts that hire teachers who were formerly military personnel. Participants in Troops to Teachers nationally are 85 percent male and 33 percent people of color, thus program graduates may improve the gender and ethnic balance in the existing teacher cadre (Gantz, 1997). Antioch's program receives a number of participants from Wright-Patterson, and graduates are well received in the nearby school systems.

Professional Preparation Program

The McGregor program is designed to enable midcareer, working adults with bachelor's degrees to complete Ohio state certification in four academic quarters through a program based on expert-defined competencies that the program believes are vital to change and improvement of learning in public education. A second phase of the program allows participants to earn an individualized master's degree. A letter to prospective students states that the program's goals are to develop persons who will be "competent, creative and compassionate teachers who are knowledgeable about current educational research and able to integrate theory and practice in today's diverse classrooms."

The program began in January 1995 with participants from both Antioch College and The McGregor School, but beginning in September 1996, enrollment was limited to graduate students in McGregor.

Students have come mainly from southwestern and central Ohio, some from as far away as Columbus and Cincinnati. The youngest are in their late twenties, but most range from the thirties to mid-fifties in age. About one-third are people of color, many African Americans with ties to Dayton who wish to work in urban schools there. The public schools of Dayton and of Greene County (the county for Yellow Springs), have referred persons to the program as have higher education institutions in the area. The program has received several state grants that have provided scholarships to encourage diversity and partnerships with local schools and funds for a conference, Democracy in Education, that drew attention to the program. A number of applicants are substitute teachers or teacher's aides presently working in the schools.

Admission, which requires transcripts, a résumé, references, and a personal goals statement, seeks evidence of motivation and commitment to work with children. Applicants are assessed through written materials and an interview for their math and writing skills and previous experience with children. Applicants with high motivation and strong skills with children but weak content skills may be accepted, with the provision that they improve their content ability through additional study.

PROGRAM CONCEPT AND IMPLEMENTATION. The program has been shaped by the Ohio state requirements for certification and The McGregor School's philosophy.

The state curriculum requirements for teachers have four elements: forty-five hours of specified general education, forty-five hours of professional education, three hundred hours of preservice clinical and field-based experience, and twelve weeks of full-time student teaching experience. In addition, candidates for certification in some educational areas may have additional course requirements. Students may have completed the general education and some special courses as part of their undergraduate degrees, but if they lack any requirements, they must complete those prior to or concurrently with enrollment in the McGregor program. In particular they must complete subject matter content courses before undertaking instruction in teaching methods for that content.

The philosophy of The McGregor School's program is to integrate theory with practice through interdisciplinary, student-centered learning. It seeks to prepare future teachers by combining the theoretical foundations of the profession with development and mastery of the skills identified by research as best practice. The program is humanist and developmental in its outlook, and it encourages students to assume responsibility for their own learning by taking risks and interacting with their peers. It fosters democratic values in education, a spirit of collaboration and teamwork, a self-reflective attitude, and a receptivity to change. To reinforce the interconnectedness of learning, it arranges its curriculum in four integrated quarter-long blocks, titled Individual and Cultural Diversity, Purpose-Centered Education, Literacy and Competency for All Children, and Demonstrating Professional Competency. These blocks of courses address the substance of the state requirements, including credit in professional education, part of the clinical and field experience requirement, and all the student teaching. Students complete the remaining clinical and field experience requirement individually; they may receive credit for some of it through assessment of previous experience. They also develop skill mastery in ten state-specified professional ability areas in which education students must demonstrate competence.

The articulation between the McGregor curriculum and state requirements illustrates the challenges that often face innovative programs. When the professional preparation curriculum began, the state offered certification to teachers based on a set of guidelines. McGregor was able to demonstrate how the content of its blocks conformed to those guidelines so it could retain its integrated units. Recently, the state has begun to move to a system of licensure instead of certification, stating the requirements in terms of enrollment in specifically identifiable courses. McGregor has responded by revising its block structure and credit hour values to make the required content more visible, although its instructional practice still treats each block as a continuous and interrelated whole. For credit, students must complete the whole block, not just separate parts of it.

Students proceed through the four blocks of the program in cohort groups of twenty-five to thirty. An initial weekend orientation introduces participants to the Antioch culture of value-based, experiential learning and acquaints them with their cohort members. Subsequently, they meet in cohort seminars or subcohort teams two evenings a week and occasionally on Saturdays. Students are challenged to work collaboratively rather than competitively, and staff report that some students with backgrounds in more structured and competitive environments are initially uncomfortable with McGregor's less structured, collaborative, and team-based modes. Because they are required to maintain full and consecutive enrollment with their cohorts, group members become strongly bonded and supportive of one another. A team of McGregor and practitioner faculty is provided for each cohort and plays an intensive role in these meetings, offering ongoing support and mentoring as well as advice to subcohort teams.

COMPETENCE DEFINITION AND ASSESSMENT. In contrast to some other programs, McGregor's approach to competence-based education is humanist rather than behavioral. Staff see competence assessment not as summative and limiting but as formative and developmental and a step on the way to fulfilling human potential. Regarding competence assessment as a tool for growth, they find it consistent with Antioch's humanist outlook.

The competence program design began with an advisory team of school practitioners—teachers, counselors, and principals—who worked with McGregor faculty to describe competence in ways that reflect the reality of K–12 classrooms as well as meet state standards. This effort resulted in the design of the original block curriculum around these competencies. Experience has led to some revision and addition of content. McGregor faculty maintain ongoing communication with certification authorities to review competencies and ensure the school's compliance with state requirements.

Assessment of competence is based on products and team effort in each of the quarter blocks and on two major portfolios prepared in the third and fourth quarters. Study activities in the blocks include seminars, assigned readings, clinical and field participation, preparation of assignments related to modules within the blocks and reflective journals, team projects related to a competence, and preparation of material for the portfolios. Students also prepare journals oriented to various professional ability areas based on classroom experience, reading, and field experience and submit them to team advisers or fellow team members for review and comment. At the end of each quarter, each student's completion of requirements and demonstration of competencies is assessed by faculty for each module and a team adviser according to *exemplary, competent,* or *unsatisfactory* rubrics and the assessment is documented in a narrative record.

The products of each quarter's effort are the *pre–student teaching portfolio* and the *exit portfolio*. The program provides extensive guidelines for portfolio preparation and examples of material to include. Students prepare the pre–student teaching portfolio at the end of the third block, just prior to their student teaching. The portfolio is intended to demonstrate sufficient, although not necessarily full, mastery of the ten abilities identified as the basis for effective teaching. The student's adviser reviews the portfolio in an interview with the student according to the three rubrics. An unacceptable rating indicates insufficient preparation for student teaching.

Participants prepare the exit portfolio at the end of the fourth, or student teaching, block. It is expected to show that candidates have sufficient mastery of the ten ability areas and enough professionalism to begin successful careers in teaching. Portfolios typically contain such materials as transcripts, professional material created by the student, the student's reflections on teaching experiences or teaching strategies, videos demonstrating the student's teaching, supervisors' feedback, and evidence of professional involvement. This portfolio is also reviewed according to the three rubrics. The two portfolios form the basis for review for state licensure. Each student is encouraged to draw upon the exit portfolio for items that will represent him or her well in a *professional showcase portfolio* that can be used in interviews. Ohio also requires candidates for certification to pass the Educational Testing Service PRAXIS II examination. In its forward planning, McGregor is adapting its competence requirements to satisfy the performance assessments that full implementation of state licensure will require after 2002.

The Master's Degree

After completion of the professional preparation program and certification, participants may proceed with twenty credit hours of study to complete a master of arts degree in education through The McGregor School's individualized master of arts degree program. The curriculum for the degree requires completion of ten independently designed credits planned with the advice of faculty and ten thesis credits

Outcomes and Future

Since January 1996, McGregor has had experience with three fully graduate cohorts, and the school finds that former students maintain contact with it. Placement experience has been good. Graduates are competitive and sought out by regional school systems. Some begin as substitute teachers but soon move to regular appointments. Graduates' feedback is positive, although some report a need to adjust to schools unacquainted with Antioch's integrated approach to education. A significant number of professional preparation students have gone on to the master's degree program.

An important element of the McGregor program's success has been its close linkage to the community it serves and to the state regulatory agencies that govern certification and will govern licensure. McGregor's willingness to adapt and align its curriculum to those requirements, despite its distinctive approach, has been critical. The careful definition of competencies in collaboration with experienced professionals from the field and the integration of content has been a program strength, even though that approach has been ironically problematic for graduates in unreceptive job placements. The teamwork and cross-support among cohort members has been important to students, as has the assembly of portfolios to demonstrate their achievement in the program.

Staff are currently exploring the possibility of a similar program for principals who are chiefly interested in working in urban schools. At this stage of its conception the program would place a heavier emphasis on child development and instructional leadership than on management.

However, because of the intense interaction between program administration and faculty and the cohorts, staff are concerned that too much growth at McGregor might affect the close personal relations with students that the program has developed.

CONCLUSION

Each of the four programs discussed here addresses the chief task of competence-based learning, the definition of competence, in a distinctive way that is based on the nature and content of the program's educational goals. Regents College derives its competence standards from prevailing collegiate practice, and in the case of specialized content, from specifications described by well-qualified core faculty. The standards are then developed into measurement instruments by psychometric staff and into criterion-referenced performance assessments by specialists in the fields. DePaul's School for New Learning involves both faculty and learners in joint definition of competence, with faculty specifying several required areas and learners selecting and defining other areas in collaboration with an advising team. Rio Salado cooperates with employers to encompass employer-determined training goals, enhanced if necessary with college content, and then to adapt college general education so it supports job-related goals. The McGregor School formulates competence goals with the assistance of panels of school faculty and practitioner faculty who are acquainted with the school settings in which graduates will teach.

All programs offer considerable flexibility to learners in how they will attain and demonstrate competence. Regents, with its time flexibility and distance learning procedures, and SNL, also with flexible scheduling and numerous learner options in learning modes, perhaps offer the broadest range of options. Yet even Rio Salado and McGregor, which feature tightly prescribed sequences and a cohort model, allow important flexibility, through multiple delivery options for general education at Rio Salado and interaction among peer groups at McGregor.

Of the four, Rio Salado, with its incorporation of outcome-based employer training and adaptation of general education to serve job-related goals, is closest to the behaviorist model that some associate with competence-based learning. At the same time, the program encourages development of broader problem-solving and communication skills. The other programs take a more developmental and humanist approach, even in professional areas, as exemplified by the Regents nursing programs, the McGregor approach to teaching, and the SNL blend of liberal and professional education with life goals. Staff of these programs affirm their intent to expand learners' awareness of their own potential and to encourage integrated and humanist approaches to professions. They also describe the mutual benefit of the programs to learners and their sponsors and the positive social impact.

6

OPPORTUNITIES FOR ADVANCED
PROFESSIONAL DEVELOPMENT

MUCH OF THE ATTENTION in adult higher education—and especially the policy concern—has been focused on increasing access for those formerly excluded. This has led adult educators to concentrate on facilitating entry and success for persons at the associate and baccalaureate degree levels. Far fewer have examined accessibility in graduate and professional education (Jacobs & Allen, 1982; Pelczar & Solmon, 1984). The numbers of graduate adult learners are not as great or as visible as those at undergraduate levels, but because of the immediate contribution advanced professionals with higher degrees can make to social and economic well-being, they may be critical to the nation's future. Yet adult graduate students are likely to encounter even greater disincentives to study than undergraduates because graduate school programs have been less flexible. One of the university presidents who participated in a Commission for a Nation of Lifelong Learners focus group commented that "adult learners coming into master's education face all the same problems that [confront] adult learners elsewhere," and appealed for "ammunition" to open up discussion of graduate policy (Presidents Focus Group, 1997). Despite many innovations in master's degree programs, the statement remains true for many adult learners and is true to an even greater degree for persons seeking doctoral-level education.

This is not to gainsay the extensive efforts to provide recurring continuing education for professionals by colleges and universities, professional associations, and other organizations related to the professions. Continuing professional education has been one of the fastest developing sectors in adult higher education for two decades, driven in part by mandatory requirements for members of professions and in part by professionals' need to keep up with rapid changes in their fields. These continuing education experiences seek to update knowledge, maintain competence, and raise performance standards to new levels. In the process they have spun off the new teaching specialty of professional continuing educator (see Houle, 1980; Stern, 1983; Cervero, 1988; Nowlen, 1988). Yet this work has stood mainly on the margins of the academic enterprise, often without academic credit or credentials even when it is of high quality. Consequently, it does not speak to those who seek degree qualifications.

The growth of an information- and technology-based society has pushed the demand for professional higher education well beyond the traditional goal of a bachelor's degree refreshed through continuing education (Kohl, 1998). Increasingly, persons in professional roles desire or find they must have more advanced qualifications just to maintain their standing in professions, much less advance (Lynton, 1984). The kinds of circumstances that Houle (1980, pp. 101) called "changes in the career line" prompt them to seek new learning. As they mature they discover new interests or want to work at more sophisticated levels than their early study prepared them for. Often changes in their responsibilities prompt them to seek more generalized or more managerial qualifications than their first technical degrees gave them. Or they may wish to combine knowledge in two or more areas for a higher level of capability. Some desire to relate their specialized capability to the broader sociocultural, ethical, or value contexts found in liberal education.

All these factors have contributed to a great increase in graduate degrees awarded in recent years, especially at the master's level but increasingly at the doctoral level as well. Over the latest period for which statistics are available, 1970–71 to 1994–95, degrees awarded increased 72.5 percent at the master's level and 38.4 percent at the doctoral level. That trend has not been linear. A peak in the mid-1970s was not exceeded until 1990–91. But from 1990–91 to 1994–95, master's degrees awarded increased 22.6 percent and doctoral degrees 15.8 percent (National Center for Education Statistics, 1998). The majority of the degree seekers have been part-time adult learners.

Not only have the numbers increased but also the fields in which the degrees are taken. A quarter-century ago, teacher education and educational administration, driven by certification requirements, attracted the heaviest enrollment, much of it at the master's level. Now, education's proportion of the total has declined, and percentages in business, the health professions, psychology, human services, organizational and human resource development, public administration, and information sciences have grown.

The great growth in graduate study has been in professional fields, and it is study intended for application rather than research, a development that has distressed some in the academy but that also has encouraged change. New specialties have arisen in interdisciplinary and applied areas. Among master's degrees awarded, 85 percent are in professional fields, and for most persons, these are the final degrees they seek. Only 15 percent are in liberal arts fields, and these might be considered bridges to doctoral study and research, although some seek them for personal enrichment or because they are the only option available for earning an advanced credential.

Several studies have confirmed these developments, particularly with regard to master's degrees. Master's degrees had declined in esteem by the 1970s, especially in departments that stressed doctoral research and that saw master's degrees merely as stepping-stones to the doctorate or as consolation prizes for unsuccessful doctoral aspirants. The revival started in the 1980s and has continued since, and it has introduced new vitality. Glazier (1986, p. iv) said of master's programs in the mid-1980s that, "it may be that the new paradigm of graduate education is the first professional degree." The Council of Graduate Schools (CGS) commissioned a study of the master's degree in the mid-1980s, and the report gave solid endorsement to the new developments that served mainly advanced professionals. The study found program faculty and administrators, graduates and employers strongly supportive of the master's degree, although accreditation and professional associations were more mixed in their reaction, and institutional administrators were least positive. The report concluded with recommendations for all graduate education sectors to enhance the visibility and vitality of master's education (Conrad, Haworth, & Millar, 1993). In the following year, CGS acknowledged the critical role of the master's degree in professional education and praised the new developments for bringing the university into active relationships with business, professions, industry, and government (Council of Graduate Schools, 1994). Earlier CGS had also embraced alternative models for providing master's and doctoral programs in off-campus settings (Council of Graduate Schools, 1989).

Despite the growth in graduate programs accessible to adult learners, many practices remain that discourage adults from participating. Admission processes linked to records of earlier undergraduate performance such as grade averages or test scores rather than to assessment of adult performance or maturity of goals can exclude adults. Requirements for full-time residence and continuous attendance (with the goal of professional socialization) often are not feasible for fully employed persons. Calendars and schedules may be incompatible with adult responsibilities. Some graduate schools and disciplinary cultures are resistant to the professional applications and interdisciplinary problem solving that adults need to conduct. In its recommendations the Commission for a Nation of Lifelong Learners (1997) urged state education authorities and regional and professional accreditation groups to reexamine policies that penalized adult learners.

Many new models that address these barriers offer useful solutions. Discriminating but individually flexible admission procedures and programs that have minimal or no in-person residence requirements are being offered at many institutions. Technology is enabling distance learning. Approaches to learning are being turned upside down, not only in delivery but also in conceptions of education. The Weatherhead School of Management at Case Western Reserve University totally reconceived its program to concentrate on learning by adults rather than teaching (Boyatzis, Cowen, Kolb, & Associates, 1994). Other management programs have also adapted to the needs of specific groups of learners through customization of content and delivery mode (Svetcov, 1995). Some institutions have instituted highly selective executive master's and doctoral programs in which cohort members meet intensively for short periods and then disperse for independent work while maintaining contact electronically. Duke University's Global Executive MBA and the Weatherhead School's Executive Doctorate in Management are examples.

The one doctoral and three master's programs that follow are only a sample from among many. They demonstrate how high-quality graduate programs can provide adult learners with necessary flexibility, maintain currency of knowledge and technological delivery, and relate to individual needs for professional growth. Rensselaer Polytechnic Institute responded to requests from its long-time corporate supporters for programs to develop professionals without taking them away from the workplace for long periods. The Fielding Institute recognized a need in the rapidly changing electronic environment for persons with management and organizational skills who could work as members of an electronic community, both within an organization and across organizations. Duke University, although not explicitly pursuing professional goals through its Master of Arts in Liberal Studies program, nevertheless often fulfills professional needs. Nova Southeastern University pioneered doctoral-level education at a distance, employing local clusters and short, intensive seminars. Three of the examples depend heavily on technology for delivery and communication, and the fourth, Duke University, finds itself being led in that direction by learners at great distance from the university.

USING TECHNOLOGY TO RESPOND TO PATRONS

Rensselaer Polytechnic Institute—Troy, New York

RSVP Program

Satellite-Delivered Master's Degree Programs

The RSVP program at Rensselaer Polytechnic Institute (RPI) illustrates the commitment of a major research and technical institution to reach out and respond to its constituency in business and industry. When long-standing corporate supporters of its degree and research programs called for assistance in preparing their advanced-level professionals, RPI responded with an in-house, on-site, technology-based delivery system that in ten years has grown to global proportions.

RPI is the oldest engineering university in the country and proudly claims leadership in technological innovation. It was established in 1824 for the purpose, in the words of its founder, Stephen Van Rensselaer, "of instructing persons . . . in the application of science to the common purposes of life." Located in Troy, New York, part of the state's capital district, it has become a Carnegie Research II classification institution, offering degrees through the doctorate in engineering, science, management, architecture, and liberal arts. It currently enrolls nearly seven thousand students. Although several large-scale, local industrial facilities have downsized in recent years, RPI still maintains strong ties to national and international companies (Gilley, Fulmer, & Reithlingshoefer, 1986).

The RSVP Program

In 1987, RPI began RSVP in response to requests from client companies for graduate-level courses for their technical and professional employees. The companies wanted to keep specialists current in their fields, to upgrade their professional capability, and to enable some to move into new and different roles such as management. They saw a benefit in associating with an institution whose quality and technological leadership they knew from past experience. In making its response, RPI acknowledges borrowing concepts from the National Technological University in Fort Collins, Colorado, of which it is a participant. It built the RSVP program, however, on its own curriculum for clients with special ties to the institution. RSVP is the acronym for the name of the institute's original delivery system, the Rensselaer Satellite Video Program.

DELIVERY MECHANISMS. The main goal of the program design was to provide campus-equivalent instruction to employees of corporate partners with as little interruption of their accustomed schedules and as little additional travel expense as possible. The solution was to deliver courses through live transmission by satellite or telephone to receiving facilities at company sites. The courses are taught in real time to resident student classes on RPI's Troy and Hartford campuses. In some cases they are sent through telephone line relay to company videoconferencing facilities, which provide for two-way video and audio signals and replicate participation in the actual class. In other cases the video and audio signals are sent one way by satellite, and the distance students interact with the RPI instructor and class by telephone connection. Some courses are rebroadcast by RPI at later times or are recorded at the company site for delayed viewing. For sites with substantial enrollment, RPI also delivers videotapes of previously broadcast courses. An increasing number of courses are also offered over the Internet, with faculty-student communication conducted by e-mail or through the World Wide Web.

The delivery system depends on client cooperation. Companies provide reception facilities, meeting space, computing facilities, and site administrators to work with the program. Site administrators coordinate application and registration procedures, develop site schedules, review course syllabi, maintain libraries of video materials, and monitor examinations. They also distribute materials sent to the site by RSVP, including syllabi, notes, assignments, and examinations. The site administrators return the assignments and examinations to RSVP by overnight delivery service when completed. RSVP arranges with a textbook vendor to distribute texts and supplementary materials on individual student order.

CURRICULA AND FACULTY. The RSVP program offers seven master's degrees: Master of Science in Computer Science, Master of Science in Management and Technology, Master of Science in Manufacturing Systems, Master of Science in Microelectronics Manufacturing Engineering,

Master of Engineering in Management Engineering for Service Systems, Master of Engineering in Mechanical Engineering, and Master of Business Administration in Management and Technology. Requirements for these degree programs are identical to on-campus departmental requirements. Programs vary with the specialty in prerequisites, required credit hours, and capstone experiences.

RSVP also offers a number of four-course certificate sequences intended for nondegree students, although these courses may be applied toward degree qualifications. These courses, like the degree courses, maintain the campus equivalency goal of the program.

Faculty normally are regular departmental faculty. Departments sometimes employ adjuncts to supplement regular faculty in the campus courses but not solely for the RSVP program. To date over eighty full-time faculty have taught in the program. Faculty working with RSVP receive orientation to teaching in the program through a videotape and an annual class for faculty. Staff counsel both experienced and new faculty in the predelivery stage. RSVP supervisors monitor courses at midterm in a formative evaluation process and are beginning to include a performance in distance learning factor in standard end-of-course evaluations. Excellent faculty performance is recognized through general campus processes, and some client companies recognize faculty through their own evaluations.

LEARNER SERVICES. RSVP provides a variety of supports to learners in the field. Specific faculty advisers for each degree program are identified in student information material, and students may talk to them by telephone and e-mail. Faculty and teaching assistants in courses are regularly available by e-mail and telephone. The program believes some synchronous engagement of learners with each other and with program faculty is important. RSVP can arrange videoconferences between faculty and learners at specific sites and faculty visits. RSVP staff travel to field sites frequently. Turnaround time on student assignments is critical, and staff work with faculty to assure responsiveness. The program publishes a tentative schedule of course offerings one year in advance to assist students with their schedule planning. Students depend heavily on contacts with program office staff, who are oriented to work with adult learners by their supervisors.

THE LEARNERS AND RECRUITMENT. The corporate sites are the gateways to the program and the venues through which study takes place. Enrollment in RSVP pivots on the site relationships the program has developed with participating companies. Beginning with five sites in the northeastern United States with a total of sixty registrations a term in 1987, RSVP had grown to over fifty sites and a total of more than nine hundred registrations a term from around the globe in 1997. Representative partners, some with multiple sites, are Allied Signal, American Electric Power, DuPont, Ford, General Dynamics, General Motors, IBM, Lotus Development, Lucent Technologies, Pitney Bowes, United Technologies, and Xerox.

Students fall into two categories. The first consists of groups of technical and professional employees whose companies wish to develop their capability. These companies often already have relationships with other parts of RPI and want education for their employees from the same institution. Many have become linked to international enterprises and can benefit from a delivery system with global capabilities. The second group comprises individual learners whom RPI has identified with the help of company organizations but who are not part of a company group effort to increase education. Because RSVP believes that synchronous contact and cross-support among participants is a necessary complement to mediated learning, it prefers to form learning groups with at least ten members who can meet at a given site. Students have ranged widely in age, from twenty-two to seventy.

Many in both categories are technical personnel and professionals who want to maintain a sharp edge in their technical fields or gain new technical competence. Others are making career shifts into management and need preparation for new roles. Some participants want only a specific course or two for updating or can meet their goals through the shorter certificate programs. Students may apply for a master's degree either on a matriculated or nonmatriculated basis. Application requires a bachelor's degree and is relatively simple, paralleling campus procedures. Standardized test scores are not required, although applicants are advised to submit them if available. Some accommodation may be made, for instance, for poor early academic work, but all applicants are expected to demonstrate capability for graduate study. Matriculated students may transfer up to six credits of relevant work from other institutions.

FUNDING AND ADMINISTRATION. RPI lent funds for the program's start-up from its general institutional sources. These funds were later repaid from program income, and the program is now self-supporting from tuition income. Initially, a surcharge was assessed on standard tuition rates to assist with the start-up, but as the program developed, the surcharge was eliminated, and participants pay the same tuition as campus students. Companies participating in the program provide support through the on-site facilities described earlier. RSVP is administered by a director, who in turn reports to the dean of the Division of Continuing Education. This division is a provost-direct unit. The program believes that it benefits from this central administration access and concern.

Summary and Future

The continuing growth of participation among corporate affiliates convinces the RSVP staff that the program serves the purpose for which it was intended. Strengths that contribute to this success are direct access to campus-based instruction, flexibility in admission, prompt responses to assignments and inquiries submitted by learners in the field, and the face-to-face contact among small groups of learners that RSVP encourages.

The program graduated over six hundred master's degree candidates during its first ten years, and it was twice recognized by the U.S. Distance Learning Association. Attrition among enrollees has been low, and corporate sponsors have maintained their support. The program is encouraged with current participation and anticipates expansion to serve more international partners. It also is examining the possibility of offering undergraduate programs delivered to individual learners through personal computers.

CREATING COMMUNITY IN CYBERSPACE

The Fielding Institute—Santa Barbara, California

Master of Arts in Organizational Design and Effectiveness

This relatively new program seeks to cope with issues of organizational turbulence and the isolation of people separated by physical distance by developing electronic communities.

Change and turbulence, rather than stability and predictability, have become the constants that confront many present-day professionals operating in a global, interconnected environment. Leaders and managers may be challenged by alterations brought about by distant forces over which they have no control, by failures of systems overburdened by demands, or by unforeseen consequences of their own deliberate actions. Corporate reorganization, technological innovation, shifts in public taste, imposition of new regulations, political unrest, unanticipated reactions to management decisions—all create urgent and new demands that professionals must meet in order to maintain equilibrium. As Vaill (1996) suggests, we live in a world of permanent white water in which survival depends on our ability to learn as we go. And learning often requires connecting and networking with others, even at great distance.

The Master of Organizational Design and Effectiveness (ODE) degree of the Fielding Institute responds to this need for active, *just-in-time* learning. It brings hard theory and research together with soft skills in group process and development to address current learner-identified issues in an electronic environment. Program participants not only work on problem solutions but observe processes of learning that they can apply to other settings. They also gain skills in electronic collaboration and community building that are becoming essential within and among organizations. The ODE program mission states that the program is "dedicated to transcending the boundaries among academic disciplines, sectors of the economy, national borders, and human differences" (Fielding Institute, n.d., p. 4).

The Fielding Institute is a free-standing, external degree institution offering both master's and doctoral degrees in clinical psychology and an interdisciplinary concentration, human and organization development (HOD). The institute was founded in 1974, one in the wave of new special-purpose graduate institutions of that period. It is accredited by the Western Association of Schools and Colleges, and its clinical psychology program was the first external program to be accredited by the American Psychological Association. Fielding's administrative offices are in Santa Barbara, California, but its students and faculty reside throughout the country, and some students are abroad. Fielding adopted electronic networking technology early, establishing its own network in 1986. It now requires that all administrative, faculty, and student communication be conducted electronically.

The Need for a New Degree

The ODE program arose from the convergence of several complementary factors. In the mid-1990s, Fielding considered increasing the range of its master's offerings in HOD. Some faculty members were interested in extending work related to management. Others wanted to build on experience they had developed in electronically delivered doctoral seminars and in use of electronic communication generally. The HOD program had great strength in group process, which it wanted to take into another medium. Previous internal faculty discussion had identified new core concepts for a program in organizational development. Finally, Fielding's leaders noted critical discussions of existing MBA degrees in management literature, critiques that coincided with ideas emerging among Fielding faculty. These ideas suggested less emphasis on finance and marketing content and more emphasis on management, organizational development, global orientation, capability with computer learning, awareness of process within systems, and guided practice related to immediate experience of participants (Evangelauf, 1990; Linder & Smith, 1992).

A group of core faculty worked with these concepts to create a new degree curriculum, structure, and process. They designed a cohort-based master's degree sequence of five eleven-week terms that extends over nineteen months. Cohort cycles begin twice a year, in January in Santa Fe, New Mexico, and in September in the San Francisco Bay Area. The program includes two short residential sessions of three or four days at the beginning and midway points of the sequence, although participants may optionally attend more sessions. The balance of the program, conducted electronically, consists of three core courses, four event-based seminars, an integrative capstone seminar, and a master's project. The ODE program enrolled its first participants in January 1997 and graduated that group in September 1998. Start-up costs were supported by a grant from a program development fund contributed by a previous Fielding graduate, but the ongoing program operates on tuition income.

Curriculum

Participants move through the program in cohorts of approximately thirty-five members. Their group experience, both face to face and in electronic exchanges, is central to the program's goal of building community. About a month prior to its first residential meeting, the Orientation and Planning Session (OPS), each incoming cohort is formed into small groups of six to eight people, each group led by a faculty member who also will teach one of the later *core courses*. In each group, participants discuss norms of confidentiality, feedback, and on-line etiquette as well as the assignments for the core courses that they will take as a group. The OPS also orients participants to the ODE learning model, develops rapport among the cohort members, begins the study of group dynamics, and provides technical training in the program's on-line delivery system.

Participants enroll in two courses per term. They first take three core courses that introduce theory and research at the level of individual, group, and societal development: Human Development and Leadership, Group Process and Development, and Organizational Structures and Sociocultural Systems. Students remain in their OPS groups for these courses but course faculty will change. In each course, students explore four content modules—theory; multiplicity or differences; the impact of electronic communication; and skill building for work at the individual, group, organizational, and societal levels. Faculty lead group members through materials provided by the program and set assignments for regular and timely responses.

In the second term, participants enroll in their first event-based seminar. During the seminars their contacts expand to other professors and students in the program. Students have a broad choice of seminar themes, but the work of all the seminars grows out of actual cases or problems illustrating the themes that students present at the beginning of the term. Examples of themes are virtual leadership, organizational change and consulting, knowledge management, and virtual team building, but over time others may develop from faculty perceptions or student suggestions. Through assignments, faculty demonstrate systematic methods to define, describe, and analyze the problems, as group participants apply their experience, new study, and creativity to developing solutions collaboratively. Students take two more such seminars in the third term and another in the fourth, with the goals of developing ability to discern general patterns of response and design creative interventions.

At the beginning of the fourth term, participants attend their second residential session. By this time they have prepared a preliminary draft of their *master's project,* which ultimately will become a professional product such as a training curriculum, an organizational intervention, a new instrument, a set of educational materials, or other contribution. At this session, they return to their initial small groups to participate in *project critiques,* in which they receive feedback on their initial plans. Concurrently, they receive training in advanced group process and help design a group process for on-line discussion and review of their developing master's projects.

Work on the projects continues during the fourth and fifth terms. In the fifth term, students also enroll in a *capstone seminar* that integrates the learning and professional experiences they have gained in the program and builds a framework for application. At the end of the fifth term, students receive their degrees on completion of their master's projects. They may optionally enroll for a sixth term and earn an additional certificate in the development, management, and facilitation of electronic learning environments.

The ODE program offers two opportunities for recognition of exceptional participant performance. At the completion of the core courses, a small number—up to 10 percent of the cohort—may be selected to participate in *grand rounds*. This is an opportunity, with expenses paid by the program, for the selected students to shadow faculty who are distinguished organizational consultants as they carry out their work over a three-day period. Alternatively, recipients may invite the faculty member to their own organizations for a consultation or use the funds in other ways for their own professional development. The second recognition is an invitation to selected students to present their completed master's projects at an annual exposition in conjunction with a San Francisco Bay Area residential session. Invitees make both poster demonstrations and more formal presentations.

Electronic Technology and Networking

One of the ODE program's chief goals is to build community in an electronic environment. It also depends on electronic communication to deliver the greater portion of learning in the program. To these ends, it devotes major effort to developing electronic participation and accustoming learners to a cyberspace environment. Entering students must be computer literate and have adequate computer hardware available to them. About a month before the OPS, the program forms small groups within the new cohort, and previous students begin working with newcomers to familiarize them with the Fielding electronic system and to assist with problems. At the OPS, a large portion of time is devoted to developing electronic communication skills. A computer laboratory staffed by expert instructors is available, and students are trained especially in advanced applications such as using graphics and conducting on-line research.

After the OPS, this momentum is maintained by a system of rules that defines expectations for the means and intervals of participation and the significance of membership in the group. Students are required to contact members in their group electronically at least twice a week, initially in response to faculty assignments. Staff and faculty monitor contacts for the first ten days or two weeks to ensure students are becoming involved, and they contact students who are not connecting. Later the rules requiring students to post materials on time and to keep in touch continue to provide support and goals. Faculty comment that students cannot get lost for lack of attention.

The electronic system has been conceived to provide a learning *architecture* that is functionally analogous to site-based facilities. The ODE program uses AltaVista Forum software, which enables asynchronous message board discussions. Using the message board, students enter a Web page, or *classroom,* where faculty can lead them through discussion of topics in a *class.* All group members may observe and comment on material posted to this class. When extended or ancillary discussions arise, students can pursue them concurrently in *café,* or *bar,* space on the board, without interrupting the flow of the class. When a topic is of broader interest, it can be posted in a *community hall* for comment by anyone in the program. When students have individual questions for the faculty member, they can address them to an *office* space on the board. Unique or strictly personal communications can be sent by e-mail. Students may communicate with the program only electronically. Program staff believe there is an egalitarianism in this requirement that flattens other characteristics of identity, such as age, ethnicity, and gender, that may affect exchanges.

Community hall communications are open to all ODE program participants. Class communications, because they reflect the intense working relationship of the group, are confidential to class members. Others must have permission from the faculty member to enter the discussion. This transparency and ability to respond within the group contributes to the program's *horizontal* learning, in which students learn from and stimulate each other as well as interact with the instructor. It enables a cadre of operating professionals from a diversity of organizations to pool past backgrounds and new knowledge. Over time, the interactions contribute to an electronic community that the ODE program hopes will endure beyond the degree experience.

Recruitment and the Learners

The ODE program recruits participants largely through direct-mail materials sent to members of groups such as the American Society of Training and Development, ODNet, and the Society for Human Resource Management. Staff also attend meetings of such organizations, among whom Fielding has a positive reputation based on its other programs. The program also maintains a Web page targeted to its key market.

Minimum requirements for admission are a baccalaureate degree; professional employment experience in a technical, management, or service delivery position; and fluency in English. Critical additional factors are computer literacy, access to necessary electronic hardware, ability in writing and critical thinking, and the ability for self-direction in learning. With their applications candidates submit a statement of purpose and an autobiographical essay that demonstrate these characteristics.

Current enrollment is approximately one hundred. The large majority have human resource and organizational development experience. Some are nonprofit administrators. Thirty percent already have master's degrees, mainly MBAs, and another 10 percent have doctoral degrees. Fifteen percent reside outside the United States, the largest number in Canada, but South Africa, Belgium, Hong Kong, Japan, and Australia are also represented. Retention is good, with only one withdrawal from the first cohort and an approximately 10 percent rate among the later groups.

Summary and Future

Central to the program is a plan of progressive, integrated steps that lead to both an individually oriented learning product and immersion in an electronic community. Beginning with their first contact before the opening session, participants are led through a series of experiences that develop their acquaintance with course content and their understanding of how to work mutually at a distance. The initial pacing and structure prepare them for ever widening initiative and cooperation. Further, through reflection and feedback, they learn means of collaboration and problem solving in the future.

Reactions from the first group, which graduated in September 1998, have been very positive. Graduates showed great interest in each other's project presentations at the final session, and in one case this led to the hiring of one graduate by another as a consultant. Interest in the ODE program from the field has been strong (Phillips, 1998), and recruitment seems promising. Response to the program so far has led faculty to plan a group of postbaccalaureate certificate sequences that could serve as building blocks toward a full master's program in areas such as knowledge management, designing electronic environments, change agency, and conflict resolution. Faculty are also considering a group of customized certificate sequences in the study of leadership that could be made available to groups of six to twelve persons from either single corporations or groups of corporations. The program also wants to build on its existing electronic communities by encouraging continuing networking among graduates and offering continuing education experiences such as seminars or book clubs reflecting graduates' developing interests.

EXPANDING MIDCAREER HORIZONS

Duke University—Durham, North Carolina

Master of Arts in Liberal Studies Program

Increased professional advancement or competence is the strongest motive for graduate study among most postbaccalaureate professionals. They may want deeper specialization or understanding in a particular field to advance their careers, or they may have become attracted to research in a field after many years of practice. Often their employers have identified them as candidates for a shift from a technical or specialist role to a managerial position that requires different capabilities. These are the persons who populate the enormously expanded professional master's and doctoral programs that have arisen in recent years.

Alongside them, in graduate programs of a different sort, are a much smaller number of persons who seek advanced study for personal enrichment or intellectual growth. Private, rather than career, goals have prompted them to resume education at this later stage of life. The study programs they select may reflect long-deferred interests or ambitions or newly developed curiosity about ideas or questions of meaning. These persons are often the midlife participants in degree programs in the creative arts, community and human services, and graduate liberal studies.

Yet this latter choice may not be the divergence from strictly professional goals that it seems. There may very well be a complementarity between personal enrichment and professional life. Moreover, the future leadership of many of our organizations may depend on this junction. Such is the argument of Kolb and his colleagues, based on studies of adult development at midlife and related inquiries (Kolb & Wolfe, 1981; Kolb, 1991). They found midlife transition to involve changes in personal, family, and work life that challenged individuals and stimulated them to move away from specialization and toward integration and valuing. Echoes of this perspective appear in such various recent works as Tennant and Pogson (1995), Boyatzis, Cowen, Kolb, and Associates (1996), and Vaill (1996). Many "midlife professionals," Kolb (1991) remarks, "reach this transition point relatively unprepared for the integrative life challenges that lie ahead" (p. 112). Thus college and university liberal education has a special role to play in the lifelong learning of advanced professionals. More specifically, "A college for forty-year-olds would have to address the knowledge infrastructure neglected by vocational professional education—the arts and sciences, literature, philosophy and history—for the wisdom of these fields bears directly on the challenges of adult development" (pp. 120–121).

Graduate Liberal Studies at Duke

The Duke University Master of Arts in Liberal Studies (MALS) offers such a program. The MALS program describes itself as extending liberal education beyond the undergraduate degree. Its mission is "to provide motivated adults with opportunities to explore new subjects and to apply fresh perspectives from a variety of disciplines" (Duke University, n.d.). Like most of the graduate liberal studies (GLS) programs described in Chapter Nine, the Duke MALS program does not claim to provide professional preparation. Nor do its applicants cite career-related development as their goal, although nearly half have professional undergraduate backgrounds and 95 percent are currently employed. Yet MALS graduates consistently report they have made professional application of their MALS learning. And the program acknowledges that its interdisciplinary approach is flexible enough that it "extends students' intellectual resources and ranges, . . . stimulates students to find connection between their learning and their personal and professional lives, and encourages a lifelong commitment to learning, free inquiry, and the life of the mind" (Duke University, n.d.).

The MALS program benefits from a rich intellectual and professional setting. The university is a leading research institution with distinction in many liberal arts disciplines. It is one of the anchor institutions in the North Carolina Research Triangle defined by Durham, Chapel Hill, and Raleigh. It is surrounded by leading high-technology and information-intensive corporations that employ highly educated professional staff. The MALS program draws much of its enrollment from these and other professionals in the area, some of whom are supported by employer tuition assistance. Although most students come from the immediate region, Duke's reputation also attracts learners who commute several hours' distance from elsewhere in the state.

The origins of the program lie close to the intellectual heart of the university. The Graduate School of Arts and Sciences is the host for all

Duke Ph.D. and master's degrees in liberal arts. Support from the school dean was essential at the outset and has remained so since. In the early 1980s, he initiated an exploration of the GLS concept. He convened a group of distinguished faculty from across liberal education disciplines to inquire into the growing number of GLS programs then appearing in the country. After reviewing and visiting a number of GLS programs, the committee proposed the new Duke degree of Master of Arts in Liberal Studies. Approval at all levels soon followed, and enrollment began in fall 1984.

Start-up costs were met by the Duke Endowment Fund and an early grant from the Fund for the Improvement of Post-Secondary Education. A turning point came in 1987 when grant funds ran out, and the university asked the program to become self-supporting gradually. MALS survived this transition, and now it supports itself and contributes to Graduate School of Arts and Sciences overhead.

CURRICULUM. The MALS program is squarely in the liberal education camp, although it includes unique interdisciplinary and integrative elements. It draws content equally from the humanities, social sciences, and natural sciences, in contrast to many GLS programs that focus solely on the humanities or on relationships between the humanities and social sciences. The degree structure follows the standard Duke master's degree pattern of ten three-credit courses, or thirty semester hours. Students take three MALS program seminars. They also select, in cooperation with an adviser, an additional six courses chosen from additional MALS seminars, other graduate school courses, and no more than one independent study. They have an alternative option to choose from several planned certificate sequences to build their programs. They complete the degree with a final written project that is integrative and may expand previous interests.

Each semester the MALS program offers five to seven interdisciplinary seminars designed by the program for MALS students only. Recent seminar titles have been Envisioning America; Culture, Education and Identity; and Madness and Society. Students begin the program by taking two liberal studies seminars before proceeding to other choices in the curriculum. Seminars enroll small groups of fifteen or fewer students. They normally meet one evening a week or Saturday mornings during fall and spring semesters and have a somewhat variable calendar during the summer term when travel-study seminars and other options are offered. Participation involves heavy reading and writing assignments. The seminar ethos is participatory, interactive, and exploratory, and faculty seek active contributions from all members. Following the first two liberal studies seminars, students, with the assistance of program and faculty advisers, develop individualized plans of study for their remaining courses. The program director and faculty facilitate contacts to faculty throughout the university who may be helpful to the students' study planning and *final projects*.

The final project is the culminating activity of the program, helping the student integrate the entire study experience. Students begin consultations with their advisers and choice of relevant courses half to two-thirds of the way through their courses. Subsequently, they participate in workshops to develop skills for the project, and by the next-to-last semester, they submit a project proposal to the MALS office for approval. Students enroll in a final project course during their last semester, and they present the project in an *exit interview* with two graduate school faculty members. Projects typically explore interdisciplinary topics, often with policy or professional implications. Some project titles have been "Animal Rights, Legal Rites," "The Culture of Care: The Cultural Perception of the Aged and Its Relationship to Ethical Standards in Long-Term Care," and "Avenues to Community Policing: An Ethnography of Contemporary Police Culture."

LEARNER SERVICES. Students are supported by an intensive group of services. The program director is the primary adviser and knows all students well. She tries to fit Duke resources to student goals and encourages students to engage with faculty who share their interests and may ultimately guide them in their final projects. The program's six-member Faculty Advisory Committee, drawn from the various liberal education areas, also assists in advising and acts as liaison to other university faculty, who are usually generous with counsel to students.

The MALS program offers extensive writing support to participants, many of whom have been away from academic writing for some time. A continuing doctoral-level staff member offers the New Student Writing Workshop several times each term, which is required for beginning students. This staff member is also available for individual face-to-face writing consultations and can also be consulted by e-mail, fax, or telephone. He also devotes much of his time to assisting students with their final projects. Each term the program offers optional research seminars to improve students' research and library skills, and it recently introduced seminars in technology to help students with using the Internet and conducting electronic library research.

Financial aid services play an indispensable role in the program's success. Students pay tuition at regular Duke graduate rates, which are comparatively high for working adults. Between 15 and 20 percent of them, including some Duke employees, receive employer tuition support, but the number of employers offering that benefit has declined during recent corporate budget tightening. The MALS program is allowed to devote some of its income to scholarship support, and 57 percent of students receive tuition scholarships ranging from 30 to 70 percent per course. Some scholarships are available from contributed funds, and the program also offers a deferred payment plan. Student loan programs are also available for those who qualify.

FACULTY. From its beginning, the MALS program has benefited from strong support among senior faculty in the university. It draws mainly on regular university graduate faculty for teaching courses and advising on final projects, although occasionally exceptions are made. New faculty participate in half-day orientation workshops led by experienced faculty, following which the program director provides individual mentoring. The Faculty Advisory Committee provides academic guidance on admissions policy, standards, choice of faculty, and liberal studies course offerings. The program recognizes exceptional faculty performance through periodic celebrations and nominations for external awards such as those of the Association of Graduate Liberal Studies Programs.

RECRUITMENT AND THE LEARNERS. The MALS program does a great deal of its recruiting through paid advertising in local media. It places notices in regional newspapers several times a year, keyed to admission and enrollment cycles. Radio announcements have proved valuable in reaching an interested audience. The program holds six public information sessions a year, on campus and elsewhere. A number of local bookstores have hosted sessions that attract persons with the interest in reading and inquiry the program requires. And students are encouraged to carry program information back to their workplaces.

Recently, the MALS program has experienced increasing response to its Web page, including inquiries from out of state and around the world that present new challenges because the program has not previously worked with students at a distance.

Currently, the program enrolls just under 150 students. New intake is about 40 to 45 students each year. Ages range from twenty-three to sixty, and average age has remained consistent at thirty-eight to thirty-nine.

More women than men enroll, and the proportion of women has increased recently. MALS students have significant ethnic diversity; 14 percent identify themselves as ethnic minorities: 9 percent African American, 3 percent Hispanic, and 2 percent Asian. Although most students have liberal arts undergraduate degrees, a very large number have professional backgrounds. Fifteen to 20 percent have other graduate degrees, including doctorates, many of them in professional fields.

Admission requirements reflect the general standards of the Graduate School of Arts and Sciences, although with some variations. For instance, no standardized tests are required. Each applicant is interviewed individually by the program director and a member of the Faculty Advisory Committee. They seek indications of maturity of purpose, intellectual curiosity and flexibility, and adult experiences that suggest compatibility with the program. Both motivation and writing ability are assessed from writing samples. The recent increase in applications from out-of-state and international candidates has led the program to experiment with telephone interviews.

OUTCOMES AND EVALUATION. Since the program's beginning, over two hundred graduates have completed the Master of Arts in Liberal Studies degree. Between twenty-five and thirty graduate each year, maintaining a completion rate of about two-thirds. Students normally take about four years to complete the program. Each year the program conducts a detailed survey of graduates, of whom two-thirds consistently respond. Respondents praise the program for its rigor and compliment the staff on their service. They express satisfaction with the faculty and their sensitivity to adult learners, and they suggest additions to the curriculum. Few report career changes, although some have advanced in their jobs and nearly all report they do their jobs better and enjoy them more since completing the program. In general they describe personal development that enhances their overall personal satisfaction and job performance. The program is well regarded on campus and in the local press.

Future

The MALS program appears to meet a continuing need in its region and has growing potential for distance learning. However, because it succeeds in large part through the flexibility it offers individuals and the high degree of personal attention staff and faculty give to students, it is concerned that growth much beyond its present level may jeopardize its character.

One unanticipated but desirable future event may be interaction with other arts and sciences departments in interdisciplinary efforts. Currently, the MALS program is Duke's largest arts and sciences graduate program; some other departments are even experiencing graduate enrollment decline. The MALS program may serve as a catalyst for interdisciplinary efforts that will allow departments to support each other's enrollments and future program development.

BUILDING LEADERSHIP AT A DISTANCE

Nova Southeastern University—Fort Lauderdale, Florida

National Doctor of Education Program for Educational Leaders

As the Council of Graduate Schools recognized in its policy statement on off-campus graduate education (Council of Graduate Schools, 1989), there is an increasing demand for doctoral and master's degrees offered by means and in settings readily accessible to busy midcareer professionals. The need appeared earliest in fields such as education and clinical psychology, but it has spread to many other professions including management, organization and human resource development, engineering, and public health.

Various doctoral models have developed since the early 1970s in response to the demand. Some, such as the California School of Professional Psychology, are free-standing, special-purpose institutions with calendars and delivery formats convenient for adult learners. Others are cohort programs that alternate sessions of recurring intensive study on campus with periods of independent study off campus. The Adult Education Guided Independent Study (AEGIS) program of Teachers College at Columbia University, to which participants from around the country travel one weekend a month for two years, is an example.

Among other doctoral models for adult learners are the distance learning, external degree programs, many of them also dating from the early 1970s. They include programs at Union, Fielding, and Saybrook Institutes and Walden University, and more recently the Graduate School of America. Although the programs differ in detail, they share many characteristics, such as relatively brief and sometimes optional attendance at program seminars, considerable independent study and individual design of learning, and participation with other students in clusters or similar groups, usually with the guidance of a faculty member. Increasingly, such programs are binding students, faculty, and administration together with electronic communication. One of the pioneers of this methodology was Nova University, later Nova Southeastern University, following its 1994 union with Southeastern University of the Health Sciences. Nova Southeastern's flagship degree program is the National EdD Program for Educational Leaders, begun in 1972.

Nova University was chartered in 1964 on the initiative of a group of Fort Lauderdale, Florida, civic leaders who saw an opportunity to found an educational complex on the property of a local military base that was being closed. The spirit of the start-up was entrepreneurial and has remained so. In its early years Nova University worked in collaboration with an outside for-profit group, but by the late 1980s, it bought out that interest, and it currently has independent nonprofit status. It has grown to be a large and diverse multicampus institution, offering both residential and external programs, and in some cases the opportunity for learners to move among them. The Abraham Fischler Graduate School of Education and Human Services, which houses the EdD program, is in North Miami Beach. The university's 227-acre main campus is west of Fort Lauderdale. There and at other facilities in the Miami–Fort Lauderdale area, Nova offers campus-based degrees in a variety of fields.

The National Doctor of Education Program

The National EdD Program for Educational Leaders, which began in 1972, is geared to practicing leaders in schools and related environments. It is a field-based, accessible program that seeks to develop participants' skills and leadership by engaging their formal study with existing problems and conditions they confront in their environments. Participants study in cohorts made up of local colleagues, whose experience and insight provide an additional working resource. The educational systems to which learners belong become laboratories for the design, testing, and implementation of interventions. Entrants to the program must have master's degrees and administrative certification; they must also be currently employed in administrative positions where they have authority and latitude to carry out an action research project of educational improvement that will demonstrate their leadership skills.

DELIVERY MECHANISMS. Nova conducts the National EdD Program through a combination of regional cluster meetings and annual *summer institutes. Participants,* a term used by Nova to reflect the cooperative spirit of learning between enrollees and the program, join the program in groups of about twenty individuals who live in proximity to each other. They commit to working together and with Nova national lecturers and staff over a three-year period. The clusters meet at scheduled times, usually all day on a Saturday once a month; participants are required to attend these sessions and to make up missed sessions. In between meetings they study independently and engage in a study group with assigned responsibilities. Enrollees must have daily access to computers with modems to receive information on the program, communicate with fellow participants, and access library facilities. Technology training is provided, and each cluster has a designated facilitator of technology.

A *cluster coordinator,* who is a doctoral-level Nova staff member, directs each cluster, providing overall leadership and guidance. In addition to monitoring individual participation, the coordinator serves as a liaison to program staff and faculty, identifier of local resources to assist the cluster, advocate and supporter for participants, and academic counselor.

Clusters can be formed as interest warrants. Recently, fifty clusters functioned at twenty-seven sites. At some sites continuing clusters operate, taking in twelve to fifteen new members each fall or winter to replace members who have completed the program. An international format is available for participants outside the United States. It employs a combination of field-based delivery, supervised study, electronic communication, and seminar participation at the Nova campus.

In addition to cluster attendance, participants must attend two seven-day summer institutes, usually held in Fort Lauderdale. The institutes present national and international perspectives to supplement the clusters' local orientation. Attendees join in presentations, discussions, and individual exchanges with scholars and other participants. Each institute is organized around a theme of current significance in education, and leading experts are invited for lectures and discussions. To receive credit for the institute, participants are required to complete an institute-related activity in their local settings, such as preparing a proposal for an application, writing a paper to be submitted for publication, or presenting training sessions on the institute content for their local colleagues.

CURRICULUM AND FACULTY. Curriculum content for the EdD program is organized in nine study areas, which participants pursue through cluster meetings, group projects, and individual study. Nova planned the content to equip school administrators with the information and conceptual resources to improve schools, so it advises persons inter-

ested in basic research or specialized technologies to seek other programs. Content deals with leadership, current issues, curriculum, policy, human resources, management, evaluation, and research. One goal
is that each participant will develop a personal leadership plan.

Nova faculty who are *senior national lecturers* design the program of
study for each study area, select associate lecturers to assist in presentation, and evaluate student performance. Each study area extends over
three cluster meetings, and students complete three areas each year for
three years. A senior national lecturer usually conducts the first all-day
intensive meeting; associate lecturers may conduct later sessions.
Students work on assignments individually or in groups during the
month following each meeting, including the last one. National senior
lecturers evaluate cluster participants based on examinations, projects,
or papers, using a pass/no pass grading system, and participants must
pass all nine study areas to complete the program.

Concurrently with work in the study areas, participants also undertake a practicum in which they conduct an individual action research
project to bring about change in a school or work site. Work on the
practicum begins early in the program through the *practicum research*
study area, in which each participant writes a concept paper. After the
study area leader accepts the concept formulation, the participant is
assigned a *practicum committee* composed of a chair and reader.
Guided by the practicum committee, the participant conducts preliminary investigations for about six months. In the second year, using
results from these investigations and continuing to work with the committee, the participant expands the concept into a practicum action
research proposal. Once the proposal is approved by the committee,
the participant puts the proposal into action. During the yearlong
implementation the committee and participant discuss the work and
modify activities if needed. At the conclusion the participant prepares a
report on the project and its outcomes.

The EdD program is designed to be completed in three years, and
participants must pay tuition for that whole period. Tuition, which is
payable quarterly, is charged as an annual amount for comprehensive
services, including cluster and summer institute participation. There
are some additional one-time charges, such as practicum editing fee,
and participants are responsible for book purchases and travel and accommodation expenses at the summer institutes. Some students require part of a fourth year to complete all their requirements, but they
must complete their work within five years from their cluster start
date. Reduced tuition is charged for the fourth and fifth years. The

program is funded from tuition income, and it contributes significantly to university overhead.

Award of the degree is based on sixty-six credits of post–master's degree work: twenty-four credits in eight study areas, thirty-six in the practicum research study area and practicum, and six in the two summer institutes.

Some faculty are full-time program professors and practicum faculty, mainly based in Fort Lauderdale. They are joined by the national lecturers and by practicum faculty who hold academic positions at other academic institutions or professional positions, usually elsewhere in the country, and who work with clusters as needed. They are assisted by full-time education faculty and staff at the Fort Lauderdale headquarters. The program also has a national advisory board composed of educational leaders in school systems and higher education in the United States and Canada.

Future

Enrollment in all Nova education programs was 7,814 in 1998, and in the National EdD Program for Educational Leaders it was 1,100. Nova has produced 3,200 National EdD Program graduates since it began in 1972, and its division of education as a whole, 20,000. The Abraham Fischler Center offers several other programs at the master's and doctoral level, including a higher education EdD that follows a cluster model similar to the educational leadership EdD. At the same time, Nova's approach is no longer unique, and it faces competition from other programs addressing the same market. Consequently, Nova is looking at possible programs for its doctoral graduates and credit-free activities for new audiences, such as human resource development professionals. The Abraham Fischler Center (named after Nova's first president) recently moved to new facilities that have enabled it to offer health service programs at the same site. In a plan that replicates the concept of *wraparound,* or full community service, schools, it hopes to bring faculty expertise in education and in other human service fields together to work on issues of children and families and to model that practice.

CONCLUSION

Demands of society and of adult learners are pushing more institutions to adapt or create graduate programs for highly talented postbaccalaureate professionals. Clearly the programs described here demonstrate that a capacity for creative and high-quality innovation exists that can open up graduate study to meet the demand. They also show that such responses can come from very different settings if the will is present to undertake them. The fields these programs address cover a wide range, from engineering and management to organization and human resource development to education to liberal studies. Two of the programs are in long-standing research-oriented institutions for whom such efforts are a significant departure from accustomed processes. Two others are in organizations specially created to respond to adult needs, and they have carried out this response with state-of-the art methods. Three of the four programs use technology as a central part of their delivery systems, and one has made communication and the creation of relationships through technology an integral part of the curriculum. Technology has made it possible for those first three to extend their reach abroad, and the fourth program, at Duke, finds that its Web page puts it in touch with a wider world than it anticipated.

Admission to the programs, although selective, employs individualized and autobiographical procedures to assess the appropriateness of the learners to each other and the program, rather than formal measures such as standardized test scores or grade averages. Each of the programs, in its own way, provides students with strong advising and a supportive relationship. Nova creates a close-knit unit through its cluster system and cluster coordinators. RPI provides easy access to campus faculty and staff, reinforced by site representatives who also assist students. Fielding begins building cyberspace cohorts even before the first group meeting, and it fosters the group sense with seminars and electronic contact throughout the program. Duke's small classes and the openness of faculty and staff to frequent contact with students create a bonding among program participants.

The programs are strengthened by other characteristics that they all share. Each involves faculty deeply in curriculum design and interaction with students, although with a different pattern in each instance. All offer students opportunities to engage with real-life professional and experiential settings in their study or to reflect on them, although such application is not always required. Each asks for the production of some individual product that serves to integrate the experience of the degree sequence.

These are only a few of many possible examples, but I hope they will stimulate inquiry about further potential for advanced professional study.

PART THREE

STRATEGIES AND APPROACHES TO PROGRAM IMPLEMENTATION

7

COLLABORATIVE RELATIONSHIPS
AMONG PROVIDERS

ONE OF THE EARLY recommendations of the Commission on Non-Traditional Study (1973) was that "increased collaboration among existing institutions should be encouraged, including that among public and private institutions" (p. 53). Later in the same report, the commission made a similar recommendation for collaboration in educational technology among institutions that were geographically disparate but shared common academic interests. Although the period since those recommendations has seen many instances of collaboration among institutions, the commission's exhortation remains valid. This chapter examines several recent examples of joint efforts on behalf of adult learning and illustrates their benefits. Several of these examples have also adopted technological communication as a central method of delivery.

First, it is important to distinguish two different meanings of the terms *collaboration* and *collaborative*. Research and direct application increasingly demonstrate how effective it is for people to learn in groups or communities through a joint effort, and this has raised doubts about the older ideal of the solitary scholar working in isolation. The terms *community* and *collaborative* have been applied to learning partnerships and to the mutual processes of individuals engaged in such special learning relationships, and this collaborative, or community, approach has strong support among adult educators (O'Banion, 1997; Saltiel, Sgroi, & Brockett, 1998; see the latter for a review of the literature on such partnerships, pp. 5–11).

In this discussion, however, I use the terms *collaboration* and *collaborative* to describe cooperative, or partnership, relationships that educational providers engage in to serve their learners better and achieve a societal benefit. The degree of collaboration can vary widely, from simple agreements that facilitate transfer of course credit from one institution to another to near fusion of programs. Sometimes collaboration may involve third parties who provide the impetus for connections among higher education institutions. State systems have sometimes mandated cooperation among their members, as in the case of articulation agreements to ensure transfer of course credit among institutions or such multi-institution higher education centers as are found in Denver or Tulsa. At other times, large clients of higher education, such as employers, request services that can be provided only through institutional cooperation. In still other instances institutions themselves have recognized a shared mission and common benefit that they might accomplish through joint voluntary action.

The benefits of collaboration can be considerable, both to learners and to institutions. Bureaucratic hurdles for learners moving from one educational institution to another can be smoothed out by agreements to share information, jointly offer programs, and accept one another's credit. Duplication of effort and more efficient use of resources, especially in public systems, can be achieved by decisions to cooperate in offering programs. Where they would be unfeasible for a single institution, large-scale efforts extending over broad geographical areas, sometimes for highly mobile populations, can be accomplished by groups of institutions working in cooperation. Offerman (1997) describes a five-institution collaboration in Wisconsin to provide opportunities to earn bachelor of science degrees in nursing, from which he posits a model of collaboration. Alternatively, the provision of a group of services at a particular site may require cooperative action by several providers. Apps (1988) has pointed out that the needs for and gains from such combined effort are multidimensional and increasingly demanded by public sponsors and clients of higher education.

Adult learners in particular have benefited from collaborative relationships among institutions. One of the most effective has been the cooperation between community colleges that have large enrollments of adult students and four-year colleges that can facilitate these students' continuation to baccalaureate degrees. Another has occurred in states where resources of all public institutions are shared. Empire State College in New York, for example, was created with the understanding that its students could use learning resources from any institutions in the SUNY system (Hall, 1991). This cooperative effort has been enhanced by increased exchange among the SUNY institutions through technology.

The four programs described in this chapter, although they differ in their circumstances and scale, demonstrate some of the possibilities of collaboration. They originated from a variety of motivations, and each had to overcome obstacles to its implementation as it developed. Yet persistence and shared goodwill among the designers brought these programs to completion. Harry S. Truman College, a Chicago community college, and DePaul University's School for New Learning recognized a common goal to serve disadvantaged adult learners, and they devised a public-private program to facilitate the learners' transition into bachelor's degree programs. With encouragement, but not a mandate, from state system leadership, University College at the University of Minnesota and Twin Cities community colleges have developed a series of cooperative applied bachelor's degrees that support regional workforce development. At the request of Toyota Motor Manufacturing of Kentucky, a group of public and private institutions have formed a consortium to provide higher education opportunities for Toyota employees, whom Toyota calls *team members,* who had limited higher education opportunities at their site. In response to a bargained agreement on education between a regional communications company and two major labor unions, twenty-four institutions in New York and New England have entered into a cooperative agreement for the entire region. All these partnerships are relatively new ventures and offer interesting models for future collaborative efforts.

FACILITATING TRANSITION AND SUCCESS

Harry S. Truman College and DePaul University—Chicago, Illinois

The Truman/DePaul Bridge Program

Associate Degree to Baccalaureate Degree Transition

The Truman/DePaul Bridge exemplifies collaboration on a small scale. Yet the purposes and intent of this program are qualitatively important. The Truman/DePaul Bridge is a partnership between two institutions that are dissimilar in many ways although each has a central mission to the people of Chicago. The program's mission is to facilitate and ease the transition of economically and educationally disadvantaged students from two-year associate degree to four-year baccalaureate degree programs. Often students in the program are people of color, and all are adult learners. By working together the two institutions encourage and sustain persons who otherwise might not even attempt the higher qualification or who might become casualties of the stresses of transfer or the differences in culture between two-year and four-year programs.

Two Distinct Cultures

Harry S. Truman College is a two-year institution in the City Colleges of Chicago system. The college is located in the northeast Uptown district of Chicago, an area of mixed population, including blue-collar and professional persons, diverse racial and ethnic groups long resident in Chicago, many recent immigrants to the city, and some international students. The college grew out of early efforts to serve the community through programs offered in local school facilities. It was reconstituted as Truman College in 1976, and its opening was greeted by a community-created mural proclaiming, "This College must be for everyone." By the late 1990s, it had grown to 4,500 students enrolled for credit and over 30,000 enrollments in various outreach programs, mainly for adults. Its programs include associate degrees in the liberal arts and sciences and career fields, developmental skills programs, lifelong learning opportunities, and services to the community.

DePaul University is a large private university with two large and four small campuses in the Chicago area and an enrollment of about 18,500 students at all levels through the doctorate. The university was founded in 1898 with a twofold mission that staff describe as "urban" and "Vincentian." The former refers to service and concern for social justice among the people of the metropolitan area. The second alludes to the beliefs of the seventeenth-century founder of the Vincentian religious order, St. Vincent de Paul, that people should be worked with individually, one at a time. DePaul's adult learning programs have long had high visibility in the city. Its principal vehicle for serving adults is the School for New Learning (SNL), which was discussed in greater detail in Chapter Five. SNL offers a baccalaureate program, entry to which is preceded by an exploratory and planning experience called the Learning Assessment Seminar.

Truman and SNL contrast in a number of significant ways. Truman is on the semester system, offers program sequences by a traditional approach, is limited to a set of course offerings designed to prevent duplication in the City College system, and has a hierarchical governing structure. SNL functions on the quarter system; is self-contained, with course planning taking place within the college; offers competence-based, individualized curricula; and has an interdisciplinary structure without departments. The Bridge not only assists students to progress from a two-year to four-year level but also connects the two academic cultures and facilitates learners' movement between them.

Early in 1990, Truman initiated a conversation with SNL to develop a model that would support Truman's Weekend College students who wished to transfer to SNL's weekend degree program. Shared values of diversity and student access provided a good basis for cooperation and led to a successful request for Illinois Board of Higher Education (HECA) funding in fiscal year 1991. The program received an additional grant, called Strengthening the Bridge, in 1992 from the Philip Morris Companies to augment the program's advising component and help meet its administrative and faculty needs. The goals of the latter grant were to "ease the transition from an associate degree to a baccalaureate program for economically and educationally . . . disadvantaged students," and to smooth for them "the tough bureaucratic task" of moving from a traditional framework to a competence-based, individualized program (Holton, 1997, p. 6). The program focused on three areas of collaboration: curricular content, interinstitutional faculty development, and recruitment and retention. Its measure of success was to be students' persistence to graduation, and students were to be sustained by consistent and intensive advising.

The Bridge System

From these initial efforts and support, a system emerged to facilitate *transition* rather than *transfer* between the two-year and the four-year institution. Many articulation agreements exist to ease application of credit and learner movement between these two types of college, but they do not provide support that aids assimilation and promotes success as students go from one environment to another. The Bridge addresses this gap by mutual collaboration between the institutions, an intensely personal support system for vulnerable students, and ongoing aid until degree completion.

The system includes these specific elements: a strong and continuing advising system; administration of the program from both institutional sites; jointly offered, team-taught courses combining faculty and students from both institutions and using locations at both; development of student peer advising and study groups, or clusters; facilitation of movement from a mandated to an individualized curriculum; use of prior learning assessment to complete degree plan requirements; and critical support for students working on individual final projects. The program has also opened up opportunities for school-to-work transition and careers in teaching with an emphasis on diversity.

RECRUITMENT AND THE LEARNERS. The Bridge seeks adult Truman students who are at sophomore level and who are considered economically or educationally disadvantaged. It is not necessary for Truman students to complete their associate degrees before moving to DePaul, but they may do so. Prospects receive information through orientation sessions, the college catalogue, brochures, notices, and word of mouth and also through the direct efforts of the Bridge coordinator-adviser, who holds a DePaul appointment and works at both campuses. The Bridge has a good reputation at Truman, and it has generally good success in attracting highly motivated applicants. The coordinator-adviser interviews applicants and serves as an educational broker who shows students how to become involved in the next stage of education and leads them to the necessary financial aid resources. Despite their motivation many of these students are tentative about their prospects and face both educational and personal problems in undertaking the program. Staff try to convey hope and to support the learners' intrinsic motivation. The Bridge coordinator-adviser and the Truman assistant dean who work with the program, both of whom have high educational and professional achievement despite obstacles they faced, serve as role models for many of the students.

In 1996, the first year in which some students completed the full cycle from entry to the Bridge to graduation, 127 students were identified as Bridge students. Women predominated, but 27 percent were male. Almost all, 98 percent, were people of color. A little more than half of the students were still taking courses at Truman, and the other half were at various stages at SNL. The first two students graduated in 1996 and another six in 1997 (Holton, 1997).

ADVISING AND CURRICULUM. Supportive advising is crucial to enlisting students and moving them through a successful transition. The Bridge coordinator-adviser administers an eight-step preadmission process that requires an average of five visits prior to the SNL Learning Assessment Seminar. The process involves orientation sessions, transcript review, preparation for the seminar, identification of areas for skills development, and financial aid orientation. Students step onto the Bridge by completing the seminar and they remain there until they are admitted to SNL and enroll in its initial Foundations course.

After attending the seminar students receive further assessment, academic preparation, and emotional support. Advisers help students complete SNL admission and financial aid applications and discuss with students the differences between the Truman and SNL learning approaches. Once admitted to SNL, students continue to receive Bridge advising but on a diminished basis as SNL's strongly supportive advisement and student services assume primary responsibility for carrying the student through degree planning, additional prior learning assessment if appropriate, and enrollments or activities to fulfill the educational plan. Additional support is made available in the concluding individual project stages.

The process of transition from Truman to SNL progresses in four phases after students are accepted to the Bridge. Phase I of the Bridge includes further orientation to the program, assessment of applicability of Truman coursework, enrollment in special Bridge courses, and completion of students' applications to DePaul's SNL. Phase II involves development of planning strategies for a DePaul education, attendance at the SNL Learning Assessment Seminar, and submission of applications to SNL. Phase III marks the initial engagement with SNL through acceptance into the SNL program, enrollment in its Foundations in Adult Learning course, development of clear educational and professional goals, and preparation of learning plan drafts. This phase is accompanied by transfer of relevant work from Truman, identification of SNL faculty mentors and professional advisers, and the organization of degree committee meetings, following which students pursue their individual SNL degree plans. Phase IV offers support during the concluding SNL externships and major pieces of work, individual learning steps that previously have proved obstacles for many students.

The Bridge courses offer liberal arts and sciences content and are part of the regular Truman curriculum. They are taught by teams made up of resident faculty from each institution and are adapted to help students reach transition goals. The faculty make a commitment of extra effort to work with the program. Their motivation is sustained by encouragement and faculty development from their institutions and by the mutual respect that has developed among Bridge faculty.

Bridge courses follow a semester calendar, thus exposing DePaul students to that mode and supporting Truman students in their accustomed academic terms. Half of the courses are presented at Truman and the others are presented at DePaul's downtown Loop campus. Students from both campuses enroll in the courses, approximately 60 percent from Truman and 40 percent from DePaul (the non-Bridge students are attracted by the content, format, team teaching, diversity of membership, and possibility for advising). The original class concept called for small groups of about thirty, but demand has pushed class numbers higher. Truman students may register for up to two SNL competencies in each course as well as Truman credit, which acquaints them with SNL's mode of measuring academic progress. All students pay tuition at the rate of their home institution, an anomaly that DePaul students appear to accept. Faculty are open to discussing the Bridge program, educational planning, and course choices. Team teaching is popular with the students, who develop close relationships, especially in the weekend format. Since 1996, these courses have offered peer advising for new students by experienced students and have helped students form small study and discussion groups.

OUTCOMES AND EVALUATION. By spring 1997, 127 students were in the pipeline toward degree completion, and 8 had earned degrees. Bridge students have done well at DePaul, some earning scholarships. Early experience with graduate placement has been successful. A new element is a school-to-work component to connect upcoming graduates to employers and to inform employers about nontraditional education. One result of early experience with the program has been the development for Bridge students of a separately administered concentration, Careers in Teaching Multi-Cultural Education, in DePaul's School of Education.

In 1997, the program undertook an internal self-evaluation that was fundamentally positive, but at the same time, experience revealed some areas for concern and improvement. The underlying theme of these concerns was the magnitude of human effort, communication, administrative support, and tangible resources necessary for a service-intensive undertaking such as the Bridge to succeed. This was especially apparent when the Philip Morris grant ended. Continual communication at all levels is required to resolve differences of outlook, procedure, and perceptions of partner capability in institutions of contrasting cultures. Strong leadership and clearly identified responsibility for the cooperative program are essential. As the Bridge grew in numbers, it came to need a more articulated administrative staff, appropriately placed in the institutional hierarchy, to deal with the burdens of advising, collaboration, and faculty development. Both students and staff expressed concern about the heavy demands of the advising role. Close and continuing support of students in the transitional phases and the final degree steps is essential to the program's effectiveness. Adequate financial aid for students, most of whom have meager resources, is a constant need. Internal observers of the program believe these issues are remediable and regard the self-analysis as a positive step.

Morale in the program appears high, and faculty and staff express a considerable degree of satisfaction with their work. The Bridge depends heavily on the dedication of those working with it, especially those serving in advisory roles at Truman College. These advisers acknowledge the potential for burnout as a result of the intensely personal relations they maintain with students during the transition phases. Replicability of the program may depend on finding similarly dedicated personnel.

That possibility will be tested by the decision in late 1996 of the City Colleges of Chicago chancellor and the SNL administration to extend the program to other colleges in the system, beginning currently with Malcolm X College, on the near west side.

PARTNERSHIP FOR APPLICATIONS

University of Minnesota and Twin Cities Community Colleges—Minneapolis–St. Paul, Minnesota

University College Partnership Programs

Bachelor of Applied Business

Over the last several years, University College, the outreach division of the University of Minnesota, has launched several applied baccalaureate degree programs in collaboration with local community colleges, businesses, and other community interests. The joint effort also involves cooperation between two-year colleges and a graduate-level research university—all public institutions. Programs are designed to develop necessary workforce capability in the region and expand the community roles of all program participants.

The *partnership programs,* as they are called, demonstrate the positive results that can arise when a group of institutions and their constituencies work together to develop programs for needs they have identified jointly. The programs are based on cooperative relationships among University College and the other colleges of the university, community colleges in Minneapolis and St. Paul, and business and community groups, and they have the goal of helping students earn bachelor's degrees with a combination of community college lower-division credit and university upper-division credit. The model is readily transferable to other public systems.

The partnership concept arose in the early 1990s from conversations among the presidents of the four branches of the Minnesota higher education system: the technical colleges, the community colleges, the state colleges and universities, and the University of Minnesota. Their discussion of how better to work together resulted in the Twin Cities Higher Education Partnership (TCHEP), a vehicle for cooperation between regional community colleges and the university. Subsequently, the first three sets of institutions were joined together as the Minnesota State College and University System, but their cooperative relation with the University of Minnesota has continued. The partnership agreement was reaffirmed and expanded in January 1998 to include potential partnership agreements between the university and any of the other institutions in the state system. Early in the TCHEP relationship, various institutional presidents suggested areas for program development, and two were selected for initial exploration: the Bachelor of Applied Business (BAB) degree and the Bachelor of Information Networking (BIN) degree. Later, bachelor's programs in Construction Management and Emergency Health Services were added.

The Partnership Model

Over several years of partnership experience a pattern of program development has emerged. Ideas for programs may come from anywhere in the community—higher education institutions, business or industry interests, or community organizations, for example—although most have originated from recognition of a need by the community colleges or the program staff of University College (UC). Because the potential outcome is a degree program at the University of Minnesota, UC takes the lead in evaluating the idea, using staff consultation and market research and alerting the Office of the Vice President for Academic Affairs that discussions that could lead to a new degree proposal are under way. A major feature of the evaluation is discussion with focus groups convened by UC that may include university and community college faculty and administrators and business and community representatives with an interest in the content area. The latter may come from the community at large, leading local companies, interested trade associations, or other business or community organizations. In one case discussions involved management and union representatives from the same sector of the economy, although they did not result in a program.

If the explorations indicate that the program idea is promising, UC requests the academic affairs vice president to appoint an initial focus group, with other members added as necessary, to serve as a planning committee. The committee undertakes curriculum development and remains in being until a degree proposal, often presented by the committee chair, is submitted to the university board of regents. Following board approval of the program, the committee, or some of its members, may continue as an advisory group for ongoing program operation.

CURRICULUM. The curriculum for each program is likely to grow from offerings, including current associate degrees, that already exist in the participating community colleges, although community colleges may modify these offerings to better support a new program's overall goals. The colleges maintain academic responsibility for the courses and any associate degrees they offer. The university, as awarder of the bachelor's degree, approves the overall degree curriculum, including the community college components, and is ultimately responsible for the courses it offers. These may be UC courses, which UC supervises, or courses from other university colleges, which those colleges supervise, although UC may advise departments on adaptations that would make courses more suitable for a program. Because these partnership programs offer applied degrees, the university has adopted more flexible general education requirements for these programs than for other programs. Program curricula are heavily prescribed, both at the community colleges and the university, although students may make their coursework more individualized and applicable to their jobs through electives and project and practicum assignments.

THE LEARNERS. Entrants to the bachelor's degree programs must have a minimum of fifty semester credits that are transferable to the program, including general prerequisite courses and possibly other specific requirements depending on the program. Many applicants have planned their previous college study with entry to the university program in mind. Lower-division courses are offered at the community college. Upper-division courses may meet either at the colleges or on the university campus; this varies with the program. Applied business courses are largely taught at community college sites, and information networking courses, which require specialized computer laboratories, usually meet at the university campus. Meetings occur mainly in the evenings, but some programs also use Saturdays and Sundays. The applied business program is developing some on-line courses, and such courses are expected to increase. One course is available by correspondence.

FACULTY. Faculty for the university's upper-division courses may be either adjunct or regular. Courses drawn from university departments are likely to be taught by departmental faculty. However, some of the necessary courses for some partnership programs do not exist in the departments and must be offered through UC, using adjunct faculty.

Bachelor of Applied Business

The Bachelor of Applied Business (BAB) degree piloted the partnership model for UC, offering its first course in spring 1993. An associate dean from the School of Management at the university chaired the curriculum development committee, which included faculty and administrators from the university and several Twin Cities community colleges and representatives of several large businesses that had worked previously with the community colleges. The university central administration supported the start-up with a program development fund grant to UC, which the administration anticipated would be recovered from program income and recycled to future programs. UC now works with six area community colleges to carry out the program.

CURRICULUM. The curriculum plan for the 120-semester-credit degree states lower-division requirements in general business and management topics to which various courses could apply, and it recommends additional areas in general education. A transfer guide explains which community college courses apply to the requirements. The upper-division curriculum requires specified courses in four areas: Perspectives on Business Problem Solving, Communication and Interpersonal Effectiveness in Contemporary Organizations, Information in Organizations, and Leadership and Ethics in a Changing Workplace. In addition, students complete fifteen credits in *functional area applications,* and they may select several electives.

RECRUITMENT AND THE LEARNERS. The program recruits students through advertising in general print media and local area newspapers, especially those circulated in neighborhoods near the cooperating community colleges. BAB is also getting an increasing response to notices on UC's Web page. UC conducts information sessions for persons interested in the program. The heaviest advising occurs at the time of admission, when applicants consider the appropriateness of the degree to their goals and review how much of their previous credit may be usable. Following that, faculty in courses provide guidance, and the program director works with students nearing completion to ensure they fulfill requirements. UC provides convenient and supportive services to all its students through extended student services hours, its own financial aid staff member, and communication by phone and e-mail as well as in person.

Since it began, BAB has admitted 168 students, and about 150 are currently active. It has had twenty graduates. Entrants have been 61 percent female and 39 percent male. Median age has been thirty-one years, with a range of twenty-one to fifty-five years. Median work experience has been nine years, with a range of two to twenty-nine years. Students have brought considerable previously earned credit, with a median of about seventy-five semester hours. In addition, other students enrolled at the university have elected BAB courses. One program graduate has been admitted for graduate study to the university's selective Curtis L. Carlson School of Management. Anecdotal reports from graduates indicate satisfaction with the program's results and significant job improvement.

Summary and Future

BAB and its sister programs have added important options to the university's service to its constituency in the Twin Cities metropolitan area. The partnership concept enhances the resources of both the community colleges and the major university in the state and strengthens the institutions' cooperation, and the concept has the potential for growth if the Minnesota State College and University System institutions become program partners in the future. These present partnership programs make a useful contribution to the workforce capability in a region that depends on highly educated personnel. The BIN program, for instance, experiences difficulty in bringing its students to degree completion because so many are hired for well-paying jobs in electronic networking before they finish their last requirements.

Although the applied degrees prompted some initial skepticism within the university, traditionally a research institution, they have become more accepted and are now recognized through guidelines approved by the university senate. These guidelines affirm the value of the partnership degree model in the current knowledge environment and

approve of it as an effective pooling of state resources. They also call
for avoidance of duplication of programs, maintenance of academic
standards, assurance that cooperation is leading to cost-effectiveness,
and provision for regular program review and evaluation.

Finally, collaborative applied programs such as these may point a
new direction for institutions, especially those within a state comprehensive higher education system, encouraging them toward innovative
and interdisciplinary responses to their base constituencies.

COOPERATION BETWEEN A COMPANY AND A COLLEGE CONSORTIUM

*Toyota Motor Manufacturing, Kentucky, and Participating
Institutions—Georgetown, Kentucky*

TMMK Reach for the Stars! Consortium

Associate, Bachelor's, and Master's Degree Programs

Sometimes an initiative from outside higher education prompts interinstitutional cooperation. In February 1996 Toyota Motor Manufacturing, Kentucky, convened a meeting with six higher education
institutions to initiate a cost-effective cooperative venture to offer degree
programs at the factory for Toyota employees, or team members. Two
months later Toyota held a press conference to announce Reach for the
Stars! The briefing was attended by Kentucky governor Paul Patton,
who praised the effort for building Kentucky's "mental capital," and by
the presidents and directors of the consortium of participating institutions: the University of Kentucky, Kentucky State University, Midway
College, Eastern Kentucky University, Northwood University, and
Georgetown College. The first course in the program, offered by Midway College, began on June 8, and the regular fall semester began on
August 26, with twenty-three courses offered on site.

The Consortium

It was Toyota's location that recommended a consortium approach.
The factory is situated in Georgetown, a small city of about thirteen
thousand that is about twenty miles from Lexington. Georgetown
College, a small Baptist liberal arts college, is the only higher education

institution right in the town; however, additional higher education institutions are located within a fifty-mile radius. Bringing resources for different programs and various degree levels to workers on site necessitated cooperation among these institutions.

The rapid development and launch of Reach for the Stars! was due to the energy and determination of the representatives from Toyota and the six partner institutions. Toyota's goals were to offer an educational benefit to its team members and to support the company's desire for a well-qualified workforce. It sought to accomplish these ends by calling on nearby institutions to offer existing degree programs on site and to control costs and optimize resources by cooperating. The institutions saw a sizable new population to serve among the 7,500 workers in Toyota's Georgetown plant, and the public institutions in particular recognized a service responsibility to a major employer.

The six colleges and universities represent a significant range of institutional types. Three are public state institutions; three are independent. They represent five Carnegie classifications: Baccalaureate I and II, Master's I and II, and Research I, and one is a Specialized Institution of Business and Management. Five are in state; one is out of state although it previously operated a site in Kentucky. They vary in enrollment from about 1,000 to more than 23,000. One of their early challenges was to establish an effective operating relationship given their diversity.

Toyota convened a College Day in April 1996 for team members to meet with institutional representatives for exchange of information about programs available and student program preferences. Over six hundred persons attended this initial session. A second College Day was held in May, and similar information sessions just prior to term registration have become a regular part of the Reach for the Stars! academic cycle. An interest survey during the spring elicited 1,170 responses, which also facilitated planning.

START-UP AND COORDINATION. Each institution designated a representative, and they along with company representatives became an ongoing committee for program development and management. The associate vice president for academic affairs of Georgetown College was designated chair and continues to play a critical role in facilitating the committee's work. Initially, the committee met weekly to iron out operational details, but meetings have now been reduced, to monthly or six-week intervals, and they emphasize planning as much as operations. Members maintain ongoing communication between meetings by telephone, e-mail, and electronic bulletin board, and company representatives no longer attend all meetings.

The main issues of coordinating the offerings were resolved between June and August 1996. Toyota wanted a set of complementary degree programs oriented to its general educational needs. It also wanted to avoid duplication and to plan course offerings that would cross-support the institutions. The planning process required give-and-take among the participants. The early meetings identified equivalent courses and reached agreements to apply them to multiple programs, regardless of where offered. Details of requirements, rules for transfer, responsibility for specific courses, and overall administration were worked out. Georgetown College, a liberal arts institution, assumed responsibility for all general education courses, but did not offer a degree. The other five institutions offered various occupational or professional degrees from the associate through master's, depending on their institutional specializations. Often the public and private institutions held different perspectives that required reconciliation. Most had previous experience with off-campus classes, but some to only a limited degree. Some had previous experience in cooperative relationships; others did not. The committee chair has commented on the effectiveness of their cooperation and consortial relations during an intense period, but he has also acknowledged the energy and "grunt work" necessary to get started. The cost in human energy was high, but the financial cost was and continues to be minimal, limited mainly to the time of the various representatives.

Although the committee chair has recorded the minutes of meetings since their beginning, no written agreements have been made among the institutions. They function as a loose consortium, based on the relationships among the representatives. Because Reach for the Stars! depends heavily on these continuing relationships and people's memory of processes, it is vulnerable to changes in membership. When such changes have occurred occasionally, new representatives have had to be assimilated into the committee and oriented to ongoing activities, and the committee members revisit the base assumptions annually to be sure they still have agreement. These assumptions are expressed, and periodically revised, in a handbook that Toyota (1997) issues to team members.

CURRICULUM. Toyota's primary perspective on Reach for the Stars! is that it is an employment benefit to individuals and that responsibility for the academic programs lies with the separate institutions. Secondarily, the company wants to support education that will contribute to team members' capability as workers, and it provides logistical support for all the courses required for a degree. However, it offers tuition reimbursement only for study that has job applicability, and it does not directly link job advancement to educational achievement in the program. The company therefore serves as a facilitator, making adult learning programs available to workers that serve its human resource needs and enlisting institutions to provide those programs. It does not guide the student's choice of what to study, or seek to mediate the content and procedures of the providing institutions, each of which adheres to its own academic guidelines.

The degree programs include quality assurance management, manufacturing, electronic technology and computer science, management, and engineering. Admission requirements follow the policy of the institution offering each degree. For undergraduate programs admission is generally open. Kentucky is an American College Test (ACT) state, and some institutions may ask Toyota team members for the test after admission to complete students' records. Graduate admissions require Graduate Record Examination (GRE) scores and fulfillment of graduate admission requirements of the particular institution. When the program was beginning, the University of Kentucky sent a staff group to provide all team members with information on returning to college, but low rates of interest discouraged repetition.

Once admitted, students in good standing may enroll in courses offered by any of the institutions without further admission approval, although they are expected to verify the applicability of courses to their specific programs. Students sign a waiver giving all the consortium institutions access to their student records, and the consortium maintains a unified database of records for all program participants. Various forms of transfer credit and prior learning assessment are available, depending on specific institutional policy. Record-keeping and transfer of credit among the institutions is fluid and transparent.

Consortium members cooperate to plan course offerings in timely sequences and schedules. Most course schedules follow shift patterns, with day-shift workers attending following their shifts and evening-shift workers going before their shifts. Instruction is normally offered in one-and-a-half-hour blocks two days a week, although some learners may take several classes on a Saturday. Some institutions offer accelerated formats and group students in cohorts, practices favorably received by students who have heavy overtime schedules or wish to safeguard personal time. Method of presentation varies with institutions and courses, from traditional lecture classes to group discussions and experiential exercises. Engineering and technology courses often involve real projects or applications related to the work site, a practice the company appreciates although it does not ask for specific customization of the curriculum. Some experimentation is beginning with asynchronous video presentation and interactive television.

FACULTY. Faculty are drawn from the regular faculty and adjuncts of the consortium institutions. A high proportion are regular faculty engaged on an overload basis. New faculty receive an orientation to working with adult learners and a guideline pamphlet the consortium has developed. Because the Toyota plant is located in an International Trade Zone with limited access, faculty must be informed about access and security procedures. Also, some faculty must pass through a work area to reach their meeting rooms, so Toyota provides a safety orientation for them.

LEARNER SERVICES. Just as class meetings take place at the work site, most learner services are provided there also. Prior to each new term, the company holds the College Days at which new prospects can receive information and current enrollees can seek advice, plan their course schedules, and receive counseling. Representatives of the consortium institutions are regularly available at the plant for consultation, and a good deal of communication occurs by telephone and e-mail. Often company education and training personnel can provide information, although they do not undertake the institutional advisement role. The consortium publishes a newsletter prior to each new term with the institutions assuming production costs and the company the mailing costs. Reach for the Stars! students have library privileges at all consortium institutions and access to a small library at the company's training center. An arrangement with a local Georgetown bank enables students to get short-term loans while they wait for tuition reimbursement.

LEARNING RESOURCES. Toyota provides on-site logistical support for the program with meeting rooms and office space for institutional representatives. Representatives also have access to voice mail and computers, and the company provides file space and electronic storage for student records. Company-supported staff are assigned to the program and represent Toyota in meetings. Learning aids and computers can be made available for instruction on request. Graduation ceremonies also are held at the company.

The company's main contribution comes through its tuition assistance program. Reimbursement for tuition and some laboratory fees is available to all team members up to a defined maximum per term if the course is preapproved for reimbursement through an application process and if the student earns a grade of C or better. The main factor in course approval is course content that contains "a substantial amount of material that is transferable to Toyota." Lists of preapproved courses are included in the students' handbook, but students may apply for additional courses, either with consortium institutions or elsewhere, if they believe they are job related. Some general education courses required for degrees and some electives are not approved, but Toyota estimates that with careful selection among approved options, team members can cover between 66 and 75 percent of degree cost.

THE LEARNERS. High wages and a strong benefits program have attracted an already well-educated workforce to Toyota. Forty percent have the equivalent of two years of college, and some persons working on assembly lines have bachelor's and master's degrees. Early surveys indicated a high degree of interest in Reach for the Stars! and rates of application for tuition reimbursement have increased significantly during the program's operation.

At the same time, participation rates of 125 to 150 persons per term have been lower than consortium partners initially expected. Various observers have suggested explanations. The plant has gone through two model changes over the first two years of the program, strongly affecting team members' work demands and work schedules. Team members have faced heavy overtime demands, especially on Saturdays, so discretionary time for educational participation has been limited. Motivation for education may be reduced by two factors. Good employment conditions and a sense of well-being may lead team members to give priority to personal time, family recreation, and other involvements over the rigors of study. Also, the company's decision to offer the benefit but not to relate education more directly to job advancement reduces the incentive for education.

Summary and Future

Company and institutional representatives express positive judgments about Reach for the Stars! A critical factor has been the cooperation and partnership among the consortium members, which in large degree relies on informal, personal relationships rather than formal structures.

Good communication and regular reaffirmation of basic operating principles enables the partners to maintain both their collaboration and distinctive program characteristics. Because so much of the consortium's effectiveness depends on collective memory, a point of vulnerability is turnover in either company or institutional personnel. Continuing consortium members strive to acquaint newcomers with the informal processes and assumptions, but each change of members involves the risk of misunderstanding.

Despite the strenuous effort needed to begin the program and lower enrollment than anticipated, most involved believe it has been a success, and they value their participation. Toyota had not set specific goals for participation when it initiated the program and is satisfied that the service is available to its team members. One or two institutions may reevaluate their participation because of low enrollment. Participation might improve if work schedules become more stable and if the company decides to relate education more explicitly to job progression.

A new factor is the increase in educational technology available, which has excited considerable interest, and several institutions foresee evolving methods of presentation and content. Because of the consortium connection, some institutions have increased their degree of cooperation and sharing of facilities in ventures beyond the Toyota program. All express satisfaction with the results of their common effort and exhibit high morale in a collaboration they believe is unique. Further, they believe the model has valuable implications for similar settings because it maximizes resources, eliminates duplication among the partners, and promotes cooperation.

PREPARING WORKERS FOR THE INFORMATION AGE

Bell Atlantic, Communication Workers of America, International Brotherhood of Electrical Workers, and Twenty-Four New York and New England Community and Technical Colleges

The Next Step Program

Bell Atlantic Human Resources—Marlboro, Massachusetts

New York City Technical College—Brooklyn

Associate of Arts Degree in Telecommunications Technology

Next Step is an ambitious program with a large number of players in a multistate region. It brings together three very different groups of partners—a major regional communications company, two national labor unions, and twenty-four higher education institutions in the northeastern United States. Their goal is to address the rapidly changing and in some instances unforeseeable workforce needs in a high-technology industry. The scale of the partners, their geographical spread, their engagement across differences in organizational culture, the complexity of the undertaking, and the degree of interinstitutional collaboration make Next Step a model for partnerships among higher education institutions and business and labor.

The program grew out of a March 1994 labor contract agreement among the NYNEX Corporation, the Communication Workers of America (CWA), and the International Brotherhood of Electrical Workers (IBEW) local that dealt with New York State. The importance of the agreement was recognized by then Secretary of Labor Robert Reich, who called a press conference to single out the settlement as a "path-breaking . . . critically important agreement" that would set a pattern for high-technology industry ("Reich Singles Out NYNEX Pact," 1994; Smith, 1995). A few months later, NYNEX and IBEW agreed to extend the program to New England. In 1997, NYNEX merged with Bell Atlantic, but Next Step continued unchanged in the northern, formerly NYNEX, region of Bell Atlantic.

The Next Step Program

Next Step grew out of a mutual recognition by the company, the unions, and the workers that the changing technological and business environment required a new approach to workforce development.

ORIGIN. As the 1994 bargaining round approached, NYNEX foresaw an environment in which advanced technology and customer demands would outstrip the capability of technical workers. Effective, one-stop customer service required technicians with broad education, problem-solving ability, flexibility, and the ability to educate themselves to keep up with change. The unions saw the potential to preserve employability of their members through increased education and adaptability. Workers recognized an opportunity, perhaps a one-time event, to position themselves for employment and improvement. Leadership committed to education on both sides played an essential role in the bargaining. This convergence of interests, along with many colleges' willingness to provide educational services, enabled the collaboration to work. Indeed, collaboration became a central program goal (CWA/NYNEX/IBEW, 1995, p. 5).

The company had emphasized worker development previously through a training mode that had developed skills as needed to perform current tasks. Now, in place of this incremental approach, the collaboration partners sought to "catapult" the workforce toward the future (CWA/NYNEX/IBEW, 1995, p. 4). They created a new job classification of telecommunications technology associate (TTA), or informally, *super tech,* that would be based in a deeper conceptual grasp of technology combined with broader customer-oriented abilities in problem solving, communication, and teamwork. Ideally, the super techs would be self-learners and together would form learning communities able to move to new levels as needs changed. Next Step's conception moved beyond training to education and a higher education credential.

SYSTEM IMPLEMENTATION. The contract agreement established a group of three Next Step codirectors, one each from the company and the two unions. The codirectors have equal weight in decision making, and they are backed up by the Employee Development Board, which can arbitrate otherwise irresolvable differences. So far, the triumvirate has worked out differences through discussion. The company carries out decisions of the codirectors.

The company's outsourcing division took the lead in implementing a system, following guidelines from the codirectors. It issued a request for proposals to several New York colleges. Hudson Valley Community College in Troy, New York, which had previously organized a customized program for the automobile industry, was selected as the lead institution and primary contractor for the program. In turn, it enlisted other colleges located near concentrations of company workers as partners and subcontractors. Initially six and eventually fourteen institutions joined (including New York City Technical College, which I discuss later as an example of a member institution). A contract spelled out relationships and accountability. Hudson Valley handled administrative and financial management of the program and maintained coordination among the consortium members through program coordinators at each institution.

After the NYNEX-IBEW contract for New England was concluded, a parallel system was instituted there, with Springfield Technical Community College, in Massachusetts, as the lead institution. Springfield formed agreements with nine comparable institutions in New England. After the first year of experience, the New York and New

England systems were linked in one continuous program, although Hudson Valley and Springfield continued to play their respective administrative roles.

CURRICULUM. Company human resource personnel played a central role in developing the educational program for TTAs. They reviewed existing company job descriptions, researched trends in the industry and technology, collected input from interviews and focus groups, and searched educational and training literature, all with a view to describing the abilities future super techs would need. The inquiry resulted in the following mission statement: "Our mission is to provide an innovative, educational, skills-based program that will enable employees to stay apace with advancing technology, to understand changing marketplace realities, and to enhance customer service skills through the acquisition of an Associate Degree in Applied Science with a focus on Telecommunications Technology. The result will be an empowered, technologically competent, customer-accountable workforce that is committed to the value of lifelong learning" (CWA/NYNEX/IBEW, 1995, p. 9).

Further background research, in which college faculties participated, resulted in a proposal for a sixty-credit associate degree program that is about two-thirds required technical and electronics courses and one-third liberal arts and sciences courses and that ends with a capstone social science course to integrate the previous learning. Overlying the degree curriculum is a set of *umbrella competencies* for the workplace, which are introduced into courses through assignments, experiential activities, team projects, and modeling by the instructors. The umbrella competencies are quality, interpersonal focus on customers, teamwork and team building, project leadership, problem solving and critical thinking, and technology and service delivery. Faculty are expected to introduce, develop, and assess the competencies in their courses and to integrate them in the capstone experience. These goals are stated in the 1995–96 strategic plan that still guides the program (CWA/NYNEX/IBEW, 1995).

The plan required all the consortium institutions to customize their existing offerings. Only three colleges had a preexisting associate degree in telecommunications technology on which the program could be based, and even those programs required adaptation. Some institutions had to strengthen their capabilities, especially in technical areas, to offer the program. Working groups of faculty and company and union representatives developed templates for specific courses as the program proceeded. Faculty base their instruction on the templates but may adapt activities and sequence within courses to local and individual choices. The need for interinstitutional consistency in such areas as use of the modular templates, incorporation of the umbrella competencies into courses, and extensive computer use has required faculty to change accustomed practices and generated some initial resistance. Experience over time appears to have resolved those issues.

The curriculum extends over four years in a predetermined sequence, with students taking two courses per semester. The company supports students by releasing them from work one day a week with pay. This enables them to attend two three- to four-hour classes on one day rather than hourly periods several times a week. Students are formed into cohorts of up to thirty persons and are expected to remain with their cohorts throughout the program. They may leave and reenter under special circumstances, but other interruptions of cohort participation or failure in a course results in dismissal from Next Step. The uniformity of course content, texts, and sequencing makes transfer to other consortium institutions easy and transparent for participants whose job assignments or locations change.

ELECTRONIC LEARNING. Cultivation of computer proficiency among both students and faculty and stimulation of an electronically based community of learners are additional program goals. To facilitate them the company issues each student a laptop computer for use during the program. As students use computers in their assignments, they become more computer proficient for their jobs. The computers come with LotusNotes, a software program that enables students and faculty to access information and communicate through company servers. Students form peer support groups through the network and access and exchange information through an electronic bulletin board. *Knowledge depots* have been set up to store short- and long-term program information to which all program participants have access. Staff believe this communication has broadened the learning platform and contributed to a pattern of self-directed learning among participants. They also believe that the four-year duration of the program is necessary to embed the habit of community learning. Finally, faculty and administration use the network to communicate not only with students but with each other about the program, curriculum, teaching issues, problem solving, and additional knowledge they may be seeking. This faculty interchange takes place both within and among institutions, and Next Step encourages use of computers and the network for this purpose.

FACULTY DEVELOPMENT AND CURRICULUM MAINTENANCE. Next Step recognized that its distinctive model would require continuing interaction and development among institutional faculty. Further, because the customization has evolved as the program proceeds, faculty need ongoing means to create the curriculum.

To accomplish this, Next Step invites all faculty to annual faculty institutes. Institutes normally occur in early June over two and one-half to five days, with three and one-half days seen as optimal. Most faculty come, although some who are preparing for summer teaching find some difficulty in attending.

The institute activities are matched to perceived faculty development needs. Meetings largely focus on learning process topics, such as adult learning theory, learner-centered education, new teaching methodologies, and improved computer skills. The institutes also offer an opportunity for faculty to discuss curriculum within and across disciplines. They are vehicles for development and documentation of new courses and for description of specific activities and practices faculty have found useful. Results of these discussions are posted in the knowledge depots to be available to all faculty.

Next Step sometimes needs to enhance faculty capability, typically in technology areas, and the program provides experts for special sessions on these topics.

In addition to continuing faculty input, currency of curriculum is maintained through introduction of new technology, review of course evaluations, and recurring external reviews of the program.

THE LEARNERS. The 1994 labor contracts specified employee eligibility for the Next Step program, with a slight variation between the New York and New England regions.

In New York, all bargained-for employees may apply, with priority in selection based on seniority. In New England, priority is given to rated technicians; among these technicians priority is given on the basis of rating date seniority. This has resulted in a greater number of New York entrants with little or no technical background and less experience with the sometimes physically demanding and outdoor conditions of technician assignments. This lack of experience may have contributed to some early attrition.

Benefits associated with the program make Next Step extremely attractive to applicants. The company pays full tuition and textbook expenses for an associate degree. Those accepted receive an upgrade in job classification, and a pay increase, which can be considerable if they move from a nontechnical classification. In addition, they receive one day a week of release time with pay to attend classes, the use of a computer, and the prospect of new job roles in the future. The New York program opened an 800 number to take inquiries at the beginning of the program, and it received 9,250 calls (Smith, 1995).

Initially, New York began with a pilot group of 130. Subsequently, it has started two sets of cohorts a year, and New England one set. Enrollment targets were set at 400 to 600 per year in New York and 200 to 300 in New England. Actual enrollment has leveled off at 400 and 200 respectively. The company expects Next Step to continue at this level through 1999, when its future will be evaluated. Applicants take the SUNY-required Assessment of Skills for Successful Entry and Transfer (ASSET) test to screen their preparedness. A number of remedial courses are available through company-sponsored programs. New York City Technical College (NYCTC) experience illustrates program demographic trends. Ages at NYCTC have ranged from thirty-five to sixty-three, and the mean age has declined from 50.2 to 44.9 since the program began. About 30 percent of enrollees are from nontechnical backgrounds. Female participation increased from 11.5 percent in the first cohort to 33.3 percent in the fifth. Retention was high for the first cohort, dropped for the second, and has now gradually improved to an overall rate of 66.6 percent (New York City Technical College, 1997, p. 26).

New York City Technical College

New York City Technical College, as one of the original consortium members, has experienced the program throughout its history, including all the phases of development, the creation of institutional mechanisms to manage the program, the challenges and stresses of institutional change, and the evolution of an approach that can be transferred to other partnerships. NYCTC is a division of the City University of New York, offering associate, baccalaureate, and credit-free study in the liberal arts and a variety of technical areas. The college, which enrolls about eleven thousand credit students, was founded in 1946 and is located near the Brooklyn end of the Brooklyn Bridge. A few months after joining the consortium, NYCTC received a grant from the National Science Foundation (NSF) to develop a model of industry-education collaboration for workforce development based on the Next Step program. The NYCTC reports to NSF detail the college's Next Step start-up phases (New York City Technical College, 1996, 1997).

MANAGEMENT. The college early discovered that the scope of Next Step required wider college participation in program operation than the college had experienced with other programs. The Division of Technology assumed initial administrative responsibility, but a year's experience demonstrated the need for broader involvement. Management was transferred to the Division of Continuing Education and External Partnerships, and two cross-college teams were created to work with Next Step. A *coordination committee,* composed of members from administrative, academic, and technology departments, meets monthly to facilitate administrative, program, and liaison issues. A second group, the *partnership committee,* includes representatives of twenty academic and administrative departments related to the program. The partnership committee meets twice a semester to plan, implement, evaluate, and improve program delivery. This committee infrastructure has enabled the college to foster collaboration, maintain communication, facilitate internal change, and model the umbrella competencies through its own activities.

CURRICULUM. NYCTC participated with consortium, company, and union members in the development of the Next Step curriculum. When the overall curriculum was determined, each college examined how to apply its existing offerings to it. Although NYCTC had previous experience with telecommunications technology degrees, Next Step customization required creation of a new track. The college found that given sixteen Next Step courses, four existing NYCTC courses matched Next Step courses, five existing courses could be modified to match, and seven courses needed to be newly developed. The complexity of adapting and creating courses was increased by the need to maintain uniformity among consortium institution courses and also gain college and CUNY system approval for the degree program. The uniformity goal was achieved through curriculum team meetings at the first and later faculty institutes. A special curriculum coordinator facilitated internal college approval, and a company appeal to CUNY's administration expedited approval there, shortening the approval process to eight months from the normal two years.

As the program proceeded, faculty and staff worked to link telecommunications technology theory and field practices, to integrate the umbrella competencies into course content, to create exercises and projects related to students' work environment and adult experience, and to make interdisciplinary connections among the courses. To accomplish this they depended on communication among themselves, with company field experts, and with other consortium faculty and on exchanges of best practices.

Meanwhile, the partnership committee designed a new daylong orientation program for beginning and returning students in spring 1996. Although both company and union representatives participate in the orientation, NYCTC emphasizes that students' academic responsibilities are to the college alone. The orientation provides information on program process, academic policies, support and development services, and advice on effective strategies for success.

INSTITUTIONAL CHALLENGES. Inevitably, the introduction of a new program that required adaptations by many people in a short time gave rise to issues and challenges. Because of the different cultures of the company, the unions, and the college, the demands for change contrasted with more familiar external interventions such as accreditation or program review. A facilitating factor was like-minded agreement and communication among the partners, even though they were external to the college.

Internally, issues and resistance arose that reflected the differences between academic and other points of view. The one-day teaching model. with courses presented in three- or four-hour blocks conflicted with faculty habit and faculty union agreements. Use of uniform course templates, incorporation of the umbrella competencies and field experience content, and interdisciplinary linkages among courses challenged individual faculty members' autonomy. Some faculty were slow to take up use of computers. Others felt the company and union roles in the program were intrusive. Variations from other college courses raised questions about the equivalency of Next Step courses. As the program proceeded, anomalies arose in the cohort sequencing, and the college expressed concern for students who were dropped from the program but who might be able to participate in other college curricula. A system problem emerged over the use of the SUNY-required ASSET test as opposed to the CUNY-required Skills and Assessment Test (SKATS) for admission.

Solutions to most, if not all, of these issues have been negotiated or resolved through experience. As the first cohort approaches its final term, both college and Next Step administrators believe all parties have come to share common goals and practices. Even the test issue has been alleviated, by administering the SKATS in the early stages of the program after using the ASSET test for initial admission. Some college concern remains that higher entry thresholds should be set for students' technical and mathematics backgrounds.

OUTCOMES AND EVALUATION. The first cohort is approaching completion as this is being written, and it is early to see conclusive results of the program. Both central Next Step staff and NYCTC have closely monitored participants through evaluation surveys and focus groups, and they express satisfaction with outcomes so far. Persistence rates have been good, and motivation has remained high. NYCTC staff comment that participants describe personal as well as job proficiency changes in themselves. Some anticipate further education, and some of those are thinking of earning the NYCTC baccalaureate degree in telecommunications technology.

Central Next Step staff conducted a series of evaluation interviews in February 1998, inquiring for reactions on four levels: general reaction to the program, effect on competency, reflection of competencies in job behavior, and impact of behaviors on the business. Overwhelmingly, the comments were positive and specific about changes that had occurred to individuals. Respondents expressed greater confidence in themselves and the breadth of their understanding of their work. They believed they could work more independently and efficiently to handle problems without calling for assistance. They could anticipate customer needs and thought customers had more confidence in them. They also thought they gave more value to the company.

The one area of negative comment was concern that the company had not anticipated how it would put learners' new capability to use. TTAs felt they were in a zone between a new, not fully defined role on the one hand and on the other their supervisors and the persons they had worked with previously who did not understand or even resented their new capability. Some expressed confusion about their futures. One comment summed up these attitudes: "You gave us the skills, now have the confidence in us that we can use them to benefit the company, because we can."

Both the company's human resource staff and NYCTC acknowledge this frustration and see that integration of the new TTA competence into field operations should have begun sooner. Efforts are now under way with supervisors and other field personnel to assimilate the newly trained people into one-stop customer service and customer advocate roles. Coaching and peer tutoring are among the strategies being used.

Future

Despite issues and differences that have arisen over the short life of Next Step, representatives of the company, the unions, and the colleges all express satisfaction with the program. Relations among the partners have been good, and all have learned more about collaboration. All comment on the importance of leadership commitment to an effort such as this. Workers have welcomed the opportunity and see value in it for themselves and their jobs. The company believes the TTAs are a valuable asset who will want to remain with the company as a result of their education.

NYCTC has experienced major institutional change and has learned concrete lessons that can be applied elsewhere. Faculty and staff have learned how to work across internal boundaries. Service department faculty, such as English faculty, who previously saw students only in a single course, now have the satisfaction of following their progress through the whole program. The college borrowed the Next Step model of multiple office coordination for an immersion program for students with limited English skills. It is also developing a college-to-work transition program, using its experience in industry partnerships and cross-college cooperation. Perhaps most significant is the acknowledgment, by at least some in leadership roles, of the constancy of change in today's world and the need to make innovation systemic.

CONCLUSION

In each of the examples in this chapter, collaboration has increased the effectiveness of what the separate institutions could do. Most important, adult learners in these programs find their paths smoothed and supported by the relationships among the partners. Judging from student demographics, the University of Minnesota's applied bachelor's degrees have proved in just a few years to be a useful model that found a ready audience with previous credit and experience. The degrees open a new role for the university that may lead to additional cooperation with a broader range of partners. Despite their very different institutional cultures, Truman College and DePaul University came together to help less fortunate adults in Chicago. Together they provide valuable assistance to otherwise vulnerable students. Neither the Reach for the Stars! nor the Next Step program would have been undertaken without an external stimulus, the company in the case of Toyota's Reach for the

Stars! the company and the unions in the case of Next Step. The willingness of the educational institutions to work together now provides an array of educational choices in a relatively isolated location for Toyota and a transparent, fluid regional system for eligible Bell Atlantic employees in the northeast.

Creating the programs was not without obstacles, as evidenced by different operating perspectives among corporate, union, and higher education representatives and by initial interactions among Truman and DePaul faculty and professionals who were accustomed to different academic calendars, organizational structures, and institutional styles. Yet in each case, a combination of persistence among the players and strong positive leadership kept the programs developing. Each developed its own mechanisms for communication, negotiation of relationships, and decision making that served its purposes well.

8

CUSTOMIZING PROGRAMS
TO SPONSORS' NEEDS

MUCH OF THE ATTENTION given to adult education theory and practice has been directed to individual adult learners and their specific needs, goals, and requirements. Although program planning has sought to accommodate learner roles within individuals' family, work, and community responsibilities, plans have tended to assume that learners are the primary and voluntary clients for programs that they freely chose. There are, however, many exceptions to this assumption.

In fact learners may attend programs because some other agency or condition provided the impetus that created the learning program and provided the motivation to participate, whether voluntarily or by requirement. Many programs come into being at the request of some sponsor of adult learners who perceives a need or a value that a program can satisfy. When programs conceived under these circumstances are designed and executed, adult learning principles sensitive to the individual learner may very well guide their plan and delivery, but it would be a mistake to focus on the roles of the learner and the educational provider and to disregard the role of the third, or external, party in producing the experience.

The sponsors of programs for learners are probably most often businesses that need to develop specific employee capability or want to provide a beneficial enrichment to their workers. Or the initiative may come from an agreement between a company and a labor union who foresee joint benefit from the program. Two programs that began this way are Bell Atlantic's Next Step and Toyota's Reach for the Stars! discussed in the preceding chapter. Such corporate–higher education partnerships are on the rise and take many different forms (Meister, 1994).

A provider-sponsor relationship can arise from other interactions as well. An institution's well-established reputation for service to businesses may form the base for employer-responsive program offerings in a whole region. Market research may reveal a formerly unrecognized need for a program and lead to collaboration with new clients to establish the offering. The military services sponsor many service personnel in voluntary education through tuition assistance for credit programs offered through contracts with higher education institutions. The willingness of the institutions to meet specific conditions may determine whether they are eligible to compete for the contracts and whether their military students can receive assistance. Or a perceptive adult education program may recognize an unmet community need, and through exploration of it, elicit a community definition of and request for a program. Examples of all these cases are represented in the descriptions that follow.

Overall, higher education adult practitioners have responded well to requests from sponsors, and in some cases sponsored programs form the foundation of their adult, or continuing education, operations. Community colleges, with their strong sense of responsibility to their service areas, also are very active, although some suggest they could do more (Grubb, 1996; O'Banion, 1997). Johnson (1996) describes fourteen examples of such cooperation.

Yet sometimes a college or university is unwilling or lacks the understanding to engage with an external partner from business or labor or with a public agency, or the institution sees such a relationship as inappropriate to its mission. This occurs frequently enough to produce a widespread dissatisfaction among many potential clients of higher education. The result is missed opportunity and lost benefit for both. *Spanning the Chasm,* a Business-Higher Education Forum report (1997), describes this breakdown in communication and misunderstanding between business and higher education. A survey of small to midsize businesses has uncovered their confusion about how to approach education providers and their frustration with the quality of the program responses (Chisman, 1992). The Modernization Forum (1992) has found that "education and training institutions have not focused on developing learning systems within foundation firms" (p. 9). The Council for Adult and Experiential Learning (CAEL) (1992) has identified a number of barriers to employer implementation of educational programs, several of them based on educational institution resistance. In its publications the National Alliance of Business offers a litany of what business expects both from schools and higher education, with an emphasis on inculcating in students expectations of lifelong learning ("What Business Expects from Education," 1996; "K–12 Reform?" 1997; "Knowledge Supply Chain," 1998).

These complaints describe a challenge, but even more, an opportunity for higher education institutions to undertake or increase collaborations with sponsors of learners. Verville (1995) has surveyed the implications for higher education of business sponsors' needs and concludes that colleges and universities "who see opportunities surely will be the winners in the global competition of the next century" (p. 50). All indications point to increasing demands for an increasingly well educated workforce and citizenry. Personal well-being and economic stability are tied to higher levels of educational accomplishment, as are effective participation in citizenship and the community.

The programs described in this chapter illustrate five different instances of program origin and institutional response. Empire State College reacted to a direct request from a previous client. Dallas Baptist University extended an earlier reputation for services to businesses into a regional system. The Alfred North Whitehead College at the University of Redlands discovered a need through market research and in the process connected with sponsors of learners. Thomas Edison State College found and remedied anomalies in its procedures and opened up greater military participation. The University of Minnesota followed the lead of one of its programmers and found community support for a new certificate program.

EXPANDING EMPLOYEE CAPABILITY

SUNY-Empire State College—Brooklyn, New York

The Bell Atlantic Corporate/College Program

Individualized Associate and Bachelor's Degree Programs

The Corporate/College partnership of Empire State College and Bell Atlantic is an excellent example of how a higher education institution and a major corporation that share compatible characteristics can work together in a successful application of their resources. Each is a large organization of its type, with personnel and activity extending over a broad geographical area. Each is capable of flexibility and adaptability to new and challenging circumstances. Each exhibits persistence and patience that have enabled it to overcome initial issues in this collaboration. Their cooperation enabled them to adapt the program as they gained experience in its operation.

Addressing a Workforce Development Need

The cooperation began in 1991 at the initiative of the New York Telephone Company, at that time a division of NYNEX, which subsequently merged with Bell Atlantic. New York Telephone faced the need to recruit and develop customer service representatives (CSRs) in the New York City area. These representatives are the focal point of the company's relations with its customers, dealing with questions, complaints, and problems, often from persons who have limited English and are experiencing stress. CSRs must be able to maintain calmness and courtesy, articulate ideas clearly, and engage in extemporaneous problem solving. The company found it had to screen numerous candidates to find persons qualified for employment, and it sought a means to reduce recruitment costs and improve retention. It also had the twin social goals of supporting education for persons who might otherwise not be able to afford it and of increasing diversity in its workforce.

The company chose to meet its goals by linking recruitment to relevant higher education that would increase CSR capability. It invited ESC to join with it in a cooperative program to offer new CSR recruits free college enrollment. New York Telephone had already had positive experience with ESC because many of its personnel had participated in degree study in other ESC programs. The new relationship promised to bring new employees into a beneficial educational program and to enable current employees to acquire more education to grow into new, well-paid job classifications. The company and college fitted their employment and academic goals together and launched the program in September 1991. Johnstone (1994) describes the early stages of the program.

The Initial Learners and Curriculum

The initial student group, assembled over the summer of 1991, included 100 graduating high school seniors recruited with assistance of the New York City Public Schools. In addition, another 20 persons from outside the company and 30 current employees selected by lottery joined the group. Along with employment in positions with good salaries, all 150 were offered full four-year college tuition and books at company expense. Participants who had completed the company's entry training were awarded seven semester credits, as recommended by American Council on Education PONSI (Program on Noncollegiate Sponsored Instruction) review.

The program design for both the associate and the bachelor's degree continues to follow the basic structure of ESC's individualized programs described in Chapter Three. Each person begins working with a faculty mentor to develop an individualized degree plan, selecting from among the areas of study ESC offers. If the student's background warrants it, he or she may seek credit for previous learning by examination, review, and portfolio assessment and then fulfill the remainder of the requirements through the term-by-term learning plan worked out in cooperation with the mentor. Most study occurs in individualized units or small-group courses from ESC. Students may cross-register in other institutions if necessary, but the program has preferred that the bulk of the enrollment be with ESC. The full range of the student services and learning resources of the ESC system are available to the Corporate/College students.

Prior to the opening of the program an ESC planning team, chaired by a senior college administrator, worked to apply the institution's extensive experience in working with adults to this new group. The team sought maximum flexibility and adapted program processes to the large number of younger persons being admitted with little or no higher education experience. Classes or small-group meetings are scheduled after work hours at New York Telephone company sites convenient for workers around the city. The program responds flexibly to such job factors as changes in shift schedules, forced overtime, and job reassignments. Initially, most students began with light academic loads; the older students generally progressed more rapidly. A *collegiate seminar* was established to accustom younger participants to college study and give them support. One unanticipated benefit of the program arose from the use of credentialed professionals in the company as individual tutors or seminar leaders. A call for such assistance produced a large response, and in some cases the experience has led the new helpers into new career paths or advanced study of their own.

As the program has progressed, consideration has been given to customizing a curriculum track especially for the company's needs, but ESC and the company have decided not to pursue that option. The ESC individualized model allows sufficient flexibility for students to include job-related content if they wish. Moreover, the company supports the strong liberal education content of the ESC curriculum, believing it valuable to the CSR role. Participants frequently select concentration areas such as business, economics, and communications that have significant applicability to their employment.

Changes in the Learners

After several years of program operation, the makeup of the student population has changed from the initial group. Early retention and success among the younger Corporate/College students was high compared to that of other young people enrolled in New York City community colleges. Job performance among the new young recruits was also excellent, and the company achieved its goal of adding valuable new employees. Yet many young Corporate/College students expressed disappointment with the differences between their Corporate/College experience and "real college" with its more traditional patterns of courses and activities, such as they had experienced in high school. At the same time, the company's need for new CSRs was lessening. In spring 1996, recruitment shifted to community college graduates, but many of them also expressed discomfort with ESC's individualized and alternative procedures. In contrast, acceptance and success of the program among current company employees has remained high. Consequently, new admissions now come entirely from within the company, although some of the previous entrants from high schools and community colleges are still pursuing their degrees. The program has also been extended to employees in the Buffalo area.

With the shift to in-house recruitment, many new enrollees have considerable earlier college credit or noninstitutional learning that they can apply to their degrees. Associate degree students average 18.2 previous credits, and baccalaureate degree students average 54.1. Assessment processes add an average of 7.1 credits for associate candidates and 9.7 credits for bachelor's degree seekers. The preponderance of students—approximately five-sixths—enroll at the associate level, although many of these plan to proceed to the four-year level. Current enrollment is approximately 260 students per term, almost all part time, with an annual graduation rate of 15 percent.

Company and College Cooperation

Administration and liaison is very important in a cooperative relationship such as this. The company and ESC have worked together with confidence and trust since the beginning, and that goodwill has continued into the merger of NYNEX and Bell Atlantic. Corporate/College has a distinct status within ESC. It reports to the vice president for academic affairs and has status parallel to that of a regional ESC center. The program is administered on a day-to-day basis by a statewide director based in Brooklyn. The director works with a Bell Atlantic counterpart who handles such company matters as administration of employee educational benefits. ESC maintains a staff of seven full-time and four part-time faculty mentors for the program who work at fourteen sites in four New York City boroughs and on Long Island. They are supported by professional and clerical staff. When the program began, a joint liaison advisory board was established, composed of two vice presidents and the representative from the company and two vice presidents and the director from ESC. The board met annually in the early years, but now a smaller group maintains continuing communication.

Outcomes and Future Development

Staff have commented on major benefits of the program, both to the participants and to the organizations offering it (Johnstone, 1994). For many participants, it has opened a way to higher education that otherwise would have been unaffordable. It has brought education to the workplace and has integrated training and workplace skills as legitimate aspects of education. The emphasis on competence and individualization accommodates the life circumstances of a majority of the present students even though it seemed inappropriate to the first, younger population. For the company the program contributes to a growing body of more qualified persons in one of its most important job assignments and helps ensure an adequate supply of personnel. The company especially values the liberal education content as a contribution to the CSRs' effectiveness. An unplanned benefit is the stimulation the program has given to the employees who have served as tutors and teachers. ESC has had the satisfaction of applying its model in a new and creative way, and its staff have had their confidence in flexible programs reaffirmed.

The future of the program looks promising. The method of payment is being shifted from a direct payment by the company to ESC to individual tuition reimbursements to students. Further, eligibility for the program may be broadened from the CSR job classification, thus enabling employees across the company to participate. The prospects are that the program will grow significantly.

REACHING OUT TO EMPLOYERS

Dallas Baptist University—Dallas, Texas

College of Adult Education

Baccalaureate Degree Completion

Rather than building a relation with a single employer, Dallas Baptist University (DBU) has developed a system to support a variety of employer and employee clients in a large metropolitan area. DBU is a private denominational institution with strong roots in its community. For over two decades it has sought to serve adult learners, and it now explicitly includes adults in its mission statement. It has moved aggressively to offer degree opportunities in the Dallas–Fort Worth metropolitan area, particularly for learners who are employed in regional area businesses. Fourteen hundred employers are represented by the enrollees of the university's College of Adult Education, many of them offering programs and courses on site and others offering tuition reimbursement programs.

The university is located in a metropolitan area of over 4.7 million persons, with a vibrant and growing economy, low rates of unemployment, and high demand for well-educated workers. After a period of recession in the early 1980s, the Dallas–Fort Worth economy has recovered and diversified, as insurance against future downturns. It now is one of the most prosperous urban complexes in the country. The metropolitan concentration and the need for highly qualified workers presented a challenge to which the university has responded.

DBU was founded in 1897 as Decatur Baptist College, the first junior college in Texas, in the small town of Decatur northwest of Fort Worth. In 1965, it moved to Dallas at the invitation of the Dallas Baptist Association and became Dallas Baptist College. From its beginning it received strong support from the Dallas business community, initially through grants of land for a campus. In 1968, it began offering bachelor's degree programs, and subsequently master's degrees, with a strong Christian orientation. By 1985, it had changed its name to Dallas Baptist University.

DBU College of Adult Education

DBU added an adult degree completion program in 1974. That program since has grown into the College of Adult Education. The college is an integrated unit dedicated to serving adult learners and focused on the Dallas–Fort Worth region. It offers two baccalaureate degree completion sequences, the Bachelor of Applied Arts and Sciences and the Bachelor of Applied Business Administration, with a choice of sixteen majors. Key elements of its effectiveness are a highly recognized program of prior learning assessment; great flexibility in course times, locations, and formats; a comprehensive system of learner services available at many sites; and close working relationships among the academic departments in which faculty and academic control reside. The college collaborates with corporate clients to provide services ranging from facilitation of tuition reimbursements to offering entire degree programs on site.

Corporate Relations

The college maintains a special staff group that works on corporate relations and recruitment. These staff identify potential business clients and contact decision makers there with information about programs the college can offer. After initial contact they maintain follow-up relations for up to a year, exploring each client's needs and DBU's ability to meet them. These overtures may lead to a variety of relationships, from cooperation on individual tuition reimbursement programs to agreements to offer courses or whole programs on site. Agreements to cooperate are based on an informal and personal understanding rather than formal written documents, and the terms differ with specific cases. Often the company will provide on-site classroom space, audiovisual support, and meeting space for counselors or advisers, and the college will provide agreed-upon courses in a sequence that enables students to complete their coursework in a timely fashion. Companies also assist with recruitment by making e-mail and fax announcements and supplying mailing lists. The college carries out initial advising, registration, and book services on site and also provides regular advising support. At some larger clients, advisers may be present several days a week.

The college has several clients among the many aviation industry employers in the area, including Bell Helicopter and Lockheed Martin. Its most fully developed program is with Northrup Grumman, where a full business-related degree program is offered. College staff work with a company planning team to develop such offerings. Although the college does not adapt the degree curriculum to specific employers, frequent opportunities arise to use work-related experiences in the coursework. Students have complete services available at the Northrup Grumman work site, including advising, registration, complete course offerings, tutorial labs, and book sales. Participation at the work site is limited to employees, but the employees may supplement the work site courses with offerings at other locations more convenient to them. Other major regional employers with whom the college works are Southwestern Bell Telephone, American Telephone and Telegraph, and General Telephone.

Degree Program Operation

Enrollees in the College of Adult Education, regardless of the site at which they participate, follow similar programs and procedures.

RECOGNITION OF PRIOR LEARNING. Entrants to the adult degree completion program may have no previous college credit, but they must have four years of full-time work experience in other than casual jobs and preferably be twenty-five years old or older. In fact many do have previous college credit, both in academic and technical subjects, and their work experience often includes academically equivalent learning through training or experience. DBU has articulation agreements with regional community colleges, who inform them of students with 48 or more credit hours, and many applicants already have associate degrees. The university has a generous transfer policy allowing all but 30 credits of the 126 required to be applied from sources other than the university. The transferred credits may include up to 66 hours from two-year colleges, and there is no limit on four-year institution credit. Credit may also be applied based on recommendations from authorized sources such as ACE or examination programs such as CLEP (College-Level Examination Program) and DANTES (Defense Activity for Non-Traditional Educational Support).

In addition, students may petition for up to 30 hours credit based on portfolio assessment by the college's prior learning assessment program. New entrants to this program enroll in Foundations of Lifelong Learning, a course with three elements: portfolio development and preparation, reflection on one's life orientation in relation to various worldviews and perspectives, and consideration of the goals and purpose of education and the skills necessary for it. College faculty present the course and guide the portfolio preparation, which includes writing an autobiography and degree planning. Upon completion the portfolios are reviewed by two trained evaluators, one from the appropriate university department and another from the field. If necessary a third evaluator may be called in to resolve differences. After the review, petitioners pay a flat fee for transcription, regardless of the amount of credit awarded, and then receive a degree plan indicating the requirements they have fulfilled. The college's prior learning assessment process was cited for outstanding quality by the Council for Adult and Experiential Learning in 1992.

Younger enrollees with primarily technical backgrounds enroll in

Perspectives, a course in which their technical learning is evaluated for its potential application to elective requirements.

CURRICULUM AND FACULTY. Except for the Foundations and Perspectives courses, all aspects of the curriculum are overseen by the appropriate major departments of the university and are taught by their faculty. All majors consist of a thirty-nine- to forty-eight-credit general education component, chosen from a menu of designated courses; a major block of twenty-four to thirty-six credits; and electives to make up the balance. The general education includes a religious requirement, which, in keeping with the college's character, is oriented toward Christianity. When sponsors of on-site programs have requested it, the content has been modified to a broader religious studies approach. The majors include an interdisciplinary major that can be individually designed. The college also offers an inverted degree program for persons with credit toward or completion of technical specialty associate degrees and fewer than four years full-time work experience. The work they have already completed is supplemented with general education, elective, and major course content to reach the baccalaureate degree level.

Major departments staff a majority of the program courses with regular full-time faculty and the balance with adjunct faculty. All faculty receive orientation to working with adult learners through faculty workshops, a monthly faculty information letter, and periodic retreats. Faculty performance is regularly evaluated, and outstanding service is recognized at college ceremonies. Because of the institution-wide support for the adult program, close cooperation exists between the departments and the College of Adult Education.

LEARNING RESOURCES. The College of Adult Education is able to serve its large and diverse student body because it has created a comprehensive and widely distributed service system. As Vice President Blair Blackburn (1997) testified before the CNLL, "To meet [student] needs, DBU has designed our programs to provide adult students the flexibility and convenience necessary for educational access and effective learning."

The distances alone in the Dallas–Fort Worth metroplex would deter participation if instruction occurred at a single or only a few sites. In fall 1998, the college offered courses at thirty-eight extension sites throughout the area. Nine were at corporate sites and open only to employees of the sponsors. Twenty-nine, however, were available to any enrollee in the program, so students could choose a site with maximum convenience for them, or if they needed a course not being offered immediately at a site close by, they had multiple options elsewhere. The university has close relations with denominational churches in the area, and some provide meeting space for classes and learner services and also run recruitment notices in their bulletins.

Flexibility is available in scheduling as well as location. The college provides courses in nineteen time formats, ranging from the traditional fifteen-week semester to shorter variants of ten, five, four, two, and one weeks. Some of the shorter ones are intensive courses that require pre-assigned reading before the course begins. The college monitors the comparative performance of students in the various formats, and a recent accreditation review approved the scheduling procedures. Two complete degree programs are available in a weekend college format; courses meet at times from Friday evening through midday on Sunday over a series of weekends. Normally, students may select among the various time formats, and this too allows them considerable adaptability to the demands on their personal schedules.

Learner services are also widely distributed. As mentioned, advising, registration, and book sales take place at the extension sites. In addition, the college maintains two *service centers* with full-time staff in strategic locations on the north and east sides of Dallas. All program services are available there at convenient times. The main campus is on the southwest side of Dallas, between Dallas and Fort Worth, and adult students are eligible to use all facilities there. Offices providing learner services are open for extended hours two days a week, and all day one Saturday a month.

Summary and Future

Leading features of College of Adult Education programs are a staff experienced in corporate relations, access to degree specializations and faculty throughout the university, unusual flexibility in course times and learner services, a comprehensive system of prior learning assessment, and distribution of courses throughout the region, including total on-site delivery. The system provides breadth of content, convenience of service at whatever level it is desired, and responsiveness to needs of both learners and employers.

College of Adult Education enrollment has grown 88 percent over the last decade, and its enrollment currently is approximately half that of the university. It averages six to seven hundred graduates per year, a high proportion of whom proceed on to graduate-level study. Hitherto the college has limited its program efforts to the Dallas–Fort Worth metropolitan region. Now, using the facilities of some of its corporate clients, the college is exploring the application of distance technology to its programs and is reaching company employees at sites outside the Dallas–Fort Worth area. With Southwestern Bell it is offering courses via the company's interactive TV facilities at various distant locations. It is piloting an experiment to offer the initial Foundations course online over the Internet, and if that proves successful, it may proceed to offering a whole degree. The college expects that adult offerings of various sorts will continue to be a central aspect of the DBU's offerings but in proportion with other traditional and graduate programs.

FACILITATING MILITARY PARTICIPATION

Thomas Edison State College—Trenton, New Jersey

Military Degree Completion Program

Associate and Baccalaureate Degree Completion

Providing voluntary degree programs for military personnel is a major part of the effort of many adult-oriented institutions. Sometimes, however, innovative programs confront difficulties in serving military audiences because military regulations presume more traditional practices. Thomas Edison State University (TESC), a leading assessment institution with flexible programs that would be beneficial to service persons, faced such a mismatch with military requirements. It responded with adjustments in its own procedures that overcame the barriers and made its programs even more sensitive to service members' needs.

Thomas Edison State College (TESC) in New Jersey, like Regents College in New York, has been a leader in awarding degrees based on assessment of college-equivalent learning. As such, it illustrates aspects of the early assessment or examination external degree models described by Valley (1972) and Houle (1973). TESC was founded in 1972, as college publications state, "for the purpose of providing diverse and alternative methods of achieving a collegiate education of the highest quality for mature adults." To this end it has mobilized a range of strategies for the attainment of coherent degrees, including acknowledgment of previous collegiate and noncollegiate instruction, the accreditation of experiential and extracollegiate learning based on various forms of assessment, and provision of learning opportunities as alternatives to formal classroom study.

TESC has a current annual enrollment of 8,600 students, who pursue twelve different degrees in the arts, sciences, and applied sciences at the associate, baccalaureate, and master's levels. Under these degree rubrics, over one hundred specializations are available. TESC's campus-free model enables its students, whose average age is thirty-nine, to study at a distance, and the college draws students nationally and internationally as well as from its state.

Military Clients

Recently TESC has responded to one of its major constituencies, the U.S. military services, by adapting its services to make its programs more accessible to military personnel, who depend on sponsorship through military tuition assistance programs. TESC has long served military personnel and is a member of the Servicemen's Opportunity College (SOC) Network. It also has a memorandum of understanding with Defense Activity for Nontraditional Education Services as an external degree provider. In spite of this long history, TESC discovered procedural problems in its system for service personnel, which it addressed through its new Military Degree Completion Program, instituted in March 1997. The program guides military personnel to effective use of TESC's exceptional flexibility to reach their degree goals, and it facilitates administrative, calendar, and tuition procedures that enable students to receive military tuition assistance until completion.

THE LEARNERS. It is well recognized that U.S. military services are among the largest sponsors of adult education in the country. Through both their ongoing training efforts and their development of specialist capabilities in an increasingly technical profession, the services impart learning that is frequently college equivalent and is formally recognized as such. In addition, the voluntary education program of tuition assistance and Veteran's Administration benefits encourages active personnel to pursue degree goals through off-duty college enrollment. Many institutions have responded by offering their programs both within the United States and abroad under contract agreements with the services.

At the same time, military personnel often experience conflicting responsibilities that exceed those of ordinarily busy adults. They are subject to relocation after two- or three-year periods of assignment and sometimes even more frequently. Unexpected exercises, emergency situations, and special assignments often interrupt their schedules. They may be located where the specific courses they need are not available. Despite having accumulated considerable previous course credit or creditable training and experience, they may find difficulty in applying this background to the specific requirements of a single institution.

TESC's assessment and credentialing model offers solutions to many of these problems. TESC accepts transfer credit from other accredited institutions up to the total required for a degree. Through various processes and authorized recommendations, it awards credit for training and education sponsored by the military or other noncollegiate sources. It also assigns credit on the basis of standardized examinations or the examinations it has developed in special areas. In some cases credit is awarded to holders of licenses and certificates on the basis of a review. TESC is a standard-setting leader in assessment of prior learning documented by student portfolios. It also offers course learning opportunities through various flexible distance procedures. The range of specializations possible in TESC's several degree programs also is attractive to military learners, because service training can apply to many of them. All of these processes ease the bureaucratic or procedural barriers that many military personnel face on their way to degrees.

PROBLEMS THAT REMAINED. Discussions with military education service officers (ESOs) revealed that although TESC's flexibility was useful to military personnel, the college's program still presented two problems. First, service persons' mobility made long-range educational planning difficult. How could they see that the varied backgrounds they brought, the unpredictable schedules they followed, and the uncertain course offerings available to them would result in a degree? They needed to be able to see clearly how a particular course enrollment would contribute to eventual fulfillment of a degree plan.

Second, there was a mismatch between TESC's fee system and guidelines for military tuition assistance. Much of TESC's program was based on a fee-for-service pricing policy. Instead of charging a basic tuition for term enrollment, TESC assessed an annual enrollment fee. Although it provided continuing advising, degree planning, and credit recording services, it also charged separate fees for such special services as credit transfer and prior learning assessment and examinations. None of these charges qualified for military tuition assistance, which is based on course enrollment in defined academic periods. In addition, the college often referred students to other institutions for courses and they paid tuition to those institutions. In the eyes of military education administrators, their personnel were being charged TESC service fees, which tuition assistance did not cover, and enrollment fees in other institutions for the course credit to fulfill their TESC degree programs.

MDCP: THE SOLUTION. TESC staff responded to these observations by proposing the Military Degree Completion Program (MDCP). MDCP addressed the problem of degree planning through an admission and evaluation process that assessed the applicant's previous learning and then offered the applicant a choice among degree options that could be completed by clearly specified enrollment within TESC's own offerings. MDCP also linked its enrollment periods and pricing to tuition assistance regulations that required courses to be completed within eighteen weeks or less. MDCP students now enroll in sixteen-week terms, during which they may earn up to six credit hours in courses or qualify for credit in specific courses through portfolio assessment or TESC examinations.

ENTRY AND DEGREE PLANNING. The college works through ESOs at military installations to implement the Military Degree Completion Program. Military applicants prepare a relatively simple admissions form and submit it through their ESO, along with application and credit evaluation fees. These fees are not eligible for tuition assistance and are borne by the applicant. The application includes basic personal and military information and the applicant's choice of degree level and specialization. The ESO compiles and attaches documentation for the applicant's possible sources of credit, including college transcripts, college-level examination results, military documents, certificates and licenses, and American Council on Education credit recommendations. Once TESC receives a completed file, the admissions office responds with evaluations of the credentials and produces an individual degree plan. The plan shows templates of the options for completing a degree related to the applicant's choice by using various TESC credit avenues. The templates also show which requirements have already been fulfilled by previously earned or assessed credit or creditable experiences. The applicant selects whichever option best fits his or her needs and registers for it. Upon enrollment the plan is registered as an SOC agreement, and applicants proceed to fulfill their individual options through successive enrollments.

LEARNING RESOURCES. As described earlier, MDCP students register for six-credit sixteen-week blocks. The tuition fee, eligible for military tuition assistance, covers enrollment in guided study courses, on-line computer classroom courses, contract learning courses, portfolio assessment for specific TESC courses, and credit by examination. To provide maximum flexibility, TESC begins sixteen-week sequences every two months, and registration is ongoing. As students complete one block, they may proceed to another virtually without interruption until they complete their degree requirements.

Once a degree plan is established, TESC assumes that students will exercise individual initiative to fulfill its provisions and to monitor its requirements. Various services, including communicating with administrative offices and consulting advisers, are accessible through a computer-assisted, Web-based lifelong learning (CALL) network. Students may also contact the college's Student Service Center by telephone or mail.

Because MDCP enrollees, like many other TESC students, usually bring considerable amounts of credit or creditable experience with them, they typically have the equivalent of junior status when they enter the program. They may have already completed many of their general education and elective requirements and portions of their specialization work. The possibility of completing their remaining degree work through a program that is accessible from any location, has an adaptable calendar, and has no minimum institutional residence requirement is very attractive.

The change from a fee-for-service model to tuition-based pricing has necessitated administrative adjustment within the institution. During the first eighteen months of MDCP, its record-keeping was handled manually because the existing computer could not accommodate the requirements. Staff used that start-up period to analyze and pilot a new record-keeping system that will accommodate MDCP and be available to the entire college in the future.

Summary and Future

TESC's basic degree model is an unbundled system: it disaggregates the various functions of a traditional higher education institution and provides the ones that are still required separately from one another (for unbundling in general, see Wang, 1975). The college's assessment process enables it to accredit learning however achieved, to provide alternate paths to learning, and to limit services to the specific function that the learner elects to use. It does not attempt student socialization in the sense that a traditional campus does.

However, the military system with which TESC works does not recognize this degree model. In response to this anomaly, TESC effectively *rebundled* its services to meet the military's required descriptions of academic terms and rates of progression. At the same time, by facilitating individual learner choice through the admission and degree planning process and by assembling academic services as a menu of courses, assessments, and examinations that can be completed term by term, TESC preserved much of the flexibility that characterized its programs from the outset.

The MDCP program is still young, but it has found increasing acceptance, and some students have already completed their degrees. Enrollment from across the services has grown at TESC as a result; an end-of-pilot-year review indicated enrollment from all service branches. MDCP was recognized by the military with the Ray Ehrensberger Award in 1997, and it has been described in the *Military Educator* (Martini, 1997). TESC has received contracts to apply the MDCP planning process to map training and education activities to degree level for a group of military specialists and a group of civilians in areas where degrees will eventually be required. Using this model, the Servicemen's Opportunity College is working with the U.S. Army to advance personnel to associate degrees in occupational specialties.

COLLABORATING WITH CORPORATE CLIENTS TO CREATE NEW PROGRAMS

University of Redlands—Redlands, California

Alfred North Whitehead College

Bachelor of Science in Information Systems

The University of Redlands' Bachelor of Science in Information Systems (BSIS) arose from a recognition by the university of a need and close collaboration with employers in its service area to create and maintain the program. In the mid-1980s, Redlands' division for adult learner programs, the Alfred North Whitehead College (ANWC), undertook a needs assessment with the assistance of the College Board. Results indicated strong interest in a curriculum in information systems. To respond, ANWC convened the first of several employer and professional advisory boards that have given ongoing advice and support. Together they planned a program, launching it in September 1986. Since then, the BSIS program has gone through several iterations to reach its present form of seventeen courses and fifty-seven semester credits, offered in a cohort-, or cluster-based, program over 114 weeks.

Redlands, mainly through the earlier work of ANWC, brought extensive experience with a cluster, or cohesive group, model of instruction to the new program. The university was one of a small group of institutional leaders that began offering accelerated degree programs in the early 1970s. In May 1976, the university's trustees established the Alfred North Whitehead College to serve adult learners, taking inspiration from Whitehead's work with adult learners at the University of London from 1911 to 1924. The evolution of the college through many changes of environment is discussed more fully in Chapter Nine. A commitment to liberal education is carried through in ANWC by means of requirements in philosophy and ethics in addition to basic general education requirements. Since its foundation, ANWC has expanded program services from the main campus to its own learning centers and to on-site facilities of employers throughout southern California, extending from the Los Angeles area south to San Diego and east to the so-called Inland Empire in the vicinity of Redlands and San Bernardino. It is a region replete with high-technology businesses and government agencies that generate continuing demand for programs such as this.

Employer Collaboration

Currently, the BSIS is administered through the ANWC Department of Management and Business. From its initial planning, the BSIS program has maintained close ties to employers and professionals in the field. At the outset, ANWC convened a *corporate advisory board* made up of a director, managers of information systems, and a professional consultant to assist in planning. The advisory body met regularly to develop curriculum and monitor the start-up, and it continued to function in this role to 1989. A successor corporate advisory board met twice a year from 1991 to 1995 to provide ongoing advice and ideas for program direction. This board had twelve members in senior positions, seven from corporations and the rest from government agencies. During the academic year 1996–97, a third group met on an ad hoc basis to assist in overall curriculum revision. Recently, a newly appointed program director has continued the advisory relationship by reconstituting a board for the BSIS and forming an additional board for a new degree, the Master of Science in Interactive Telecommunications Management. Start-up costs for BSIS were borne by ANWC, after which the program has supported itself from tuition income.

Curriculum

The BSIS is a degree completion program that builds on a minimum of 40 semester hours of previous college work that students transfer into the program. Participants may apply up to 66 credits earned by previous courses or ANWC-assessed prior learning credit to the 120 required for the degree. Prior credit applies mainly to degree general education requirements and electives. Previous courses may be accepted toward BSIS core concentration requirements if they are equivalent, although in practice this is rarely done. Students complete the 57-credit BSIS concentration in cluster groups that stay together over the 114-week program. The seventeen courses in the curriculum vary from 2 to 5 credits each, earned by attendance at two weekly four-hour classes per credit, accompanied by sixteen hours of out-of-class study per week. The BSIS program divides the coursework into four semesters of differing length and credit value. Participants proceed directly from completion of one course to the beginning of another in the following week. Tuition is based on a credit hour rate and is guaranteed for the duration of the program so long as the student maintains continuous enrollment.

The content of the BSIS concentration reflects the judgment of faculty, the recommendation of successive advisory groups, and conformity to joint national standards set by the Association of Information Technology Professionals and the Association for Computing Machinery. The program closely monitors developments in the field and is flexible enough to adjust quickly to emerging needs and to update its courses as professional guidelines change. During a program redesign in 1997, the program conducted a survey of graduates and over one hundred information system directors in the area.

The course sequence, although focusing on information systems, is interdisciplinary, drawing also on courses in management and business administration. A course in information technology fundamentals and the course Philosophical Foundations of Management introduce the program and screen for those for whom the program is inappropriate. During Philosophical Foundations, students develop *experiential learning* portfolios. Subsequent courses are linked in ways that achieve deliberate integration of elements from one course to another. Faculty coordinate their course planning so that students revisit material as they proceed through the sequence. Courses incorporate hands-on assignments that can be carried out in the work setting, and students may individualize their learning by independent application of class work to job situations during out-of-class study periods. The sequence strives to develop students' technical and managerial capability by giving them an understanding of human factors that can support decision making in organizations. The sequence also includes courses in computer ethics and geographical information systems (GIS) that exceed usual national standards and give the BSIS program an enhanced curriculum and competitive edge. GIS content reflects ANWC and campuswide strength in that area.

During the last seven months of the concentration, students enroll in two *applied software development project* courses, where they carry out a senior project that integrates their previous learning as they produce an information system. Each student identifies a problem, conducts a feasibility study, designs and constructs a system, and implements it within an organization. The student then writes up the work in a document and presents the system to the other cluster members. The BSIS program offers an honors program option for project students. In addition to meeting university-wide grade standards for honors, honors candidates must include an expanded literature review and creative elements in their projects, which are then evaluated in terms of a university-wide standard by a panel of three faculty.

BSIS courses may involve various instructional modes: lecture components, evaluation quizzes and discussion of outside study, guest speakers and field trips, videotapes, practical experience in computer labs, and use of computer facilities for exercises out of class. The program is offered only where a computer lab is available. ANWC has labs at the Redlands main campus and its regional centers. When a cluster meets at a work site, the employer must demonstrate to ANWC staff that cluster members have access to adequate facilities. Even with this provision, students will need to travel to a college site for exercises requiring specialized software.

The Learners

Presently about two hundred students are enrolled in the program, and more seek admission. The main constraint on enrollment is availability of computer laboratory facilities. Many participants come from regional corporations that offer tuition assistance, such as IBM, Southern

California Gas Company, Toyota, GTE, Unisys, and Boeing, and from government agencies. Pacific Bell has sponsored employees since the program began. Some students are self-employed or independent consultants. Entrants usually are already working in information systems and want to move up in that field.

The BSIS program describes itself as essentially an open admission program although it does have some general requirements. In addition to the forty hours of previous college credit mentioned earlier, students are expected to have a minimum grade point average of 2.0; five years of full-time work experience, including work in the home; and facility with the English language. Applicants also must have learned beginning computer programming or an equivalent and have access to a computer system at home or work that can run current software packages.

Learner Services

When a new cluster begins, the BSIS director attends the initial meeting, along with representatives of the various ANWC student supports and services who introduce and orient students to the program and the administrative and student services. Cluster students also attend semi-annual orientation days convened on the Redlands campus. Each cluster adjourns one of its evening sessions so students can attend these all-day Saturday meetings, during which the normal cluster session is held and students also become acquainted with the campus, participate in program activities, and observe senior project demonstrations. ANWC staff believe the campus experience raises student morale, cultivates awareness of academic goals and standards, and helps students identify with the institution.

ANWC has a centralized advising system that serves all its programs, including the BSIS. Advisers are located at the main campus and ANWC's regional learning centers and are available for individual advising. At the beginning of the first course in a cluster sequence and again in the last course, advisers attend cluster meetings to explain degree requirements and how they can be met through ANWC's system. ANWC maintains its own financial aid office through which a variety of aid programs are available to eligible students.

In addition, a computer adviser, a member of the adjunct faculty, is available at each regional center and the main campus. Advisers hold workshops on evenings and Saturdays and can also be reached by telephone and e-mail. The centers also provide CD-ROM tutorials that students may borrow and advice on helpful Internet resources.

Faculty

The BSIS program is staffed by both full-time regular ANWC faculty and part-time adjunct faculty who are engaged by the program and are practitioners in the field. New full-time faculty receive extended orientation in their departments through a six-month process that may involve eighteen to twenty hours of formal meetings.

ANWC follows a careful assessment process to select adjunct faculty. Full-time faculty review applications and conduct telephone interviews. Three or four times a year, attractive applicants are invited to an assessment day on campus during which they engage in various activities that enable faculty to evaluate their suitability. Those chosen to be hired are invited back to the campus for an orientation to working with Redlands, following which they observe an experienced faculty member conduct classes. Later, the new faculty member also is observed teaching a class. In addition, since the early 1990s, the information systems division has offered optional workshops focusing on teaching issues several times a year.

Outcomes

The BSIS program has had about six hundred graduates since it began. The program has not attempted to follow its graduates systematically, but it reports a variety of contacts with them. During the recent curriculum revision, graduates responded well to a survey questionnaire on the program. Graduates often refer applicants to the program, and graduates have accepted invitations to the campus to meet current students and to present their senior projects at campus orientation sessions. Some graduates who have risen in their organizations have served on the program advisory boards. The program also receives frequent requests from graduates for letters of recommendation to support applications to graduate schools, and some graduates continue in various master's degree programs offered at ANWC.

Summary and Future

The BSIS program's history demonstrates the value of using continuing needs assessment to identify whether sufficient potential demand exists to warrant undertaking as complex an effort as creating a new degree offering. ANWC followed its positive finding with direct interaction with the anticipated employer sponsors of program participants. The various advisory bodies have kept the program in close contact with its constituency and with the rapid change in a dynamic field. These contacts have been supplemented with surveys of graduates and liaison with related professional associations. The cohort model affords predictability coupled with individualization of student work in the field, especially the senior project. The university honors its historical liberal education commitment through courses specially designed for the program. Faculty, many of them adjunct, are carefully recruited and trained, and learner services are comprehensive.

Program staff are optimistic about the future of the BSIS in their region. After economic difficulties in the early 1980s, information- and technology-based companies are growing and are initiating requests for program clusters. The Inland Empire in the vicinity of Redlands is developing rapidly and has prospects for becoming an electronic technology center with a need for BSIS graduates. A prospective Master's Degree in Interactive Telecommunications Management program is also attracting favorable attention from both corporations and government agencies.

RESPONDING TO COMMUNITY EXPRESSED NEED

University of Minnesota—Minneapolis, Minnesota

University College

Certificate in Child Abuse Prevention Studies

Some programs are a response to a perception of community need rather than to an employer's or other sponsor's initiative. Such is the case with the Child Abuse Prevention Studies (CAPS) program at the University of Minnesota, an interdisciplinary, credit-based certificate sequence offered throughout the state. Creators of the program, who had close community connections, recognized an emerging crisis in the care and protection of children and families. They addressed the need with a graduate-level program to prepare persons for professional work in preventing child mistreatment, either as employees or as volunteers.

The CAPS program is located administratively in University College (UC), the outreach division of the University of Minnesota. UC and the School of Social Work jointly sponsor the program. The commitment of School of Social Work faculty to serve professionals in the field and the faculty's spirit of collaboration have been critical to the CAPS program's development and operation. The School of Social Work oversees faculty, courses, and program development, and UC implements the program.

Collaboration in Design

A UC staff member who had worked with an earlier program in early childhood development and who had strong community links first detected the need for development of professional capability in child abuse prevention. She set up a round-table session to bring faculty and others from the university together with statewide community professionals. Their discussion identified major issues and benefited from strong community professional input. Subsequently the School of Social Work and UC cooperated to establish a planning committee, which in turn sought broader input through faculty connections to the community. Participation of community members, many of whom later became community faculty, strengthened the interdisciplinary content, which addressed multicultural, legal, and other concerns as well as social work methods.

The interdisciplinary approach was reflected in the learners the program targeted: social service professionals, early childhood educators, child-care workers, guardians ad litem, community health professionals, mental health practitioners, law enforcement and legal professionals, advocates, human service personnel, and school teachers and administrators.

Program development continued into the first course offerings of the program. Both social work and community faculty had extensive involvement with the first group of students, meeting with them to gain feedback and elicit recommendations, some of which influenced curriculum changes.

Curriculum

The CAPS program stresses that its content is graduate level; however, a baccalaureate degree is the only specific requirement for admission. This opens access for persons from diverse educational backgrounds. In special cases an exception may be made to the degree requirement. The curriculum requires two nine-month sequences, each with one course a quarter for three terms, resulting in nine credits for each sequence. All entrants begin with a required social work course, Child Abuse, Neglect and Violence: Research and Theory. A Level I Certificate in Child Abuse Prevention Studies is awarded at the end of the first sequence and a

Level II Certificate at the end of the second. The Level II track prepares students for public or private service in advocacy, program development, and leadership in change. It also provides students with a foundation for understanding the *risk and resilience framework* in direct work with children and families. In addition, the Level II track explores child maltreatment and the law, and risk assessment and interviewing. It offers one course on working with communities of color.

The program is flexible in that students may enroll in individual courses for professional development without taking the entire sequence, and graduate students in social work may elect CAPS courses. Certificate graduates also may use their courses toward the Master of Social Work degree. CAPS courses are applicable to other related graduate degree programs, although students are advised to confirm the acceptability of CAPS courses in other programs before they enroll.

In fall 1999, the university will shift from a quarter to a semester calendar system. The CAPS program has plans to adapt its courses and titling to the new calendar while retaining its current content. Students will take one three-credit course each semester and will need six semester credits for each certificate level.

Program Delivery

CAPS classes are conducted on the main campus of the University, in Minneapolis, and may also be transmitted by interactive television (ITV) to receiving sites throughout the state when there is sufficient enrollment. Remote delivery so far has been supplied chiefly in Duluth, Morehead, and Rochester. Site facilitators, often local professionals, work with groups at the ITV sites and preserve videotapes of the classes for students to consult later. Classes are usually held in the late afternoons, from 4 to 7 P.M., to accommodate adult learners. Students receive course packets at the beginning of each term with text materials, instructions, and assignments, and they return assignments to the Minneapolis campus for review. Classes employ a variety of approaches, including lecture and discussion, small-group work, presentation of student projects or applications, and problem solving of current issues. Site facilitators often continue small-group discussions beyond the class meeting times. Some groups continue to meet spontaneously after the end of the course and sometimes even beyond completion of the certificate sequence.

Faculty for the program come mainly from the School of Social Work. One full-time faculty member has a professional, nontenured appointment with UC but is integrated into a working relationship with the school. The program also uses community faculty, usually professionals working on child abuse prevention. Most faculty have had previous experience teaching adults, so there is no formal program of faculty preparation, although the program director works informally to orient faculty. There is explicit orientation for ITV site facilitators.

Learner and Community Services

The program office at UC is a one-stop service resource for students, and it facilitates other contacts they may need to make. Application and registration processes are simplified and can be accomplished by mail and fax. The program office has extended hours in the evenings. University financial aid services are available, but the program acknowledges a need for a broader range of financial support to assist low-income students. Participants pay tuition at the UC rate, which is somewhat higher than resident university tuition, but UC students do not pay the additional fees that campus students are charged.

One innovative program feature is a series of afternoon workshops held around the state each spring in anticipation of new fall enrollment. The workshops serve as both recruiting events and opportunities to deliver service to members of the community. Lasting about one and a half hours, they present information on the certificate programs, and CAPS faculty explore issues of child prevention with the professionals who attend, engaging them through discussion in critical analysis of their previous experiences. Staff believe this content related to the field benefits those who attend and demonstrates the program's effectiveness.

Outcomes

The program began in 1992, with internal funds from its host, then the Continuing Education and Extension Division, and some additional allocation from the division dean to support the extra cost of distance delivery. Its goal is financial self-sufficiency, which it is approaching but has not reached. So far, CAPS graduates total 105. Enrollment in fall 1998 was fifty-eight.

Summary

The identification of potential learners for the CAPS program demonstrates the importance and value of formal or informal work by sensitive adult education professionals to recognize needs that have not yet surfaced. Persons with broad contacts can sometimes discern patterns not yet visible to others. In this case, fortunately, a related academic unit had a strong commitment to developing professional capability in the field, and it cooperated willingly in discussions with community professionals to initiate and develop the certificate sequence. Links between the CAPS certificate content and the social work graduate program enable CAPS courses to draw campus graduate students and enable certificate program participants to progress to full degree programs. Because the participant population is dispersed, the program has also benefited from an existing university distance learning system.

No systematic effort has been made to track graduates, although staff recognize the desirability of doing this. One unanticipated development was that the first graduate group continued to meet voluntarily for mutual support following the demanding and sometimes stressful recollections of their own experiences that the program elicited. Some certificate graduates have continued on into the Master of Social Work degree program, having apparently used the certificate experience as a means to test their viability for graduate work.

The program has attracted positive attention within the state, and the director has been invited to participate in numerous statewide conferences in the field and to supply information to local radio and television stations. The program was awarded a grant to evaluate a county child protection system, and it was commended as a nationally innovative and critical program by an official of the National Committee on Child Abuse Prevention.

CONCLUSION

The programs discussed here illustrate several ways in which institutions can be sensitive to employer and community needs and can work with sponsors of learners. In two of the cases, the colleges responded to requests or issues raised directly by potential sponsors. In three others, the institutions identified particular needs through their own perceptiveness, or they positioned themselves to receive requests for assistance from the sponsors. Empire State responded to a direct request for a program intended to prepare people for a particular job role. Thomas Edison had a model well suited to military personnel except for some technical barriers, which it removed once it recognized them. Dallas Baptist, building on its community reputation for service to business, made itself available for regional learners supported by their employers, all the way from individuals on tuition assistance to workers needing in-house, on-site programs in specific fields requested by the employers. Alfred North Whitehead College discovered an emerging need from its market research, and it engaged its potential employer clients from the beginning in creating, maintaining, and developing further a program that continues to lead. The University of Minnesota, through an adult learning staff member, perceived a statewide need in communities. By brokering a relationship between relevant faculty and community representatives, it created an advanced-level certificate it could distribute widely using the technology available to it.

Programs such as these become more than instances of delivery of training or education to a client on demand. Running through these interactions is a sense of what Johnson (1996) called "common ground," as colleges and sponsors build close relationships, a sense of shared purpose that benefits both, and the potential for more extensive cooperation. Both sides learn to understand their differences of culture, outlook, and goals, and they gain mutual respect for each other. Faculty and administrators in colleges on the one hand and human resource and other corporate personnel and community leaders on the other learn how to cooperate.

A central element in such cooperation is some mechanism of partnership that all members subscribe to. It may be similar to the advisory committees or other ongoing structures created by ANWC and Empire State or like the less formal planning committee process used by Minnesota. It may be exchanges among persons who routinely work together and who can exchange frank observations and suggestions, as occurs at Thomas Edison. It may also depend on institutional initiative as at Dallas Baptist. In all these instances, a means existed for exchange of information, negotiation of problems, and receipt of continuing feedback.

An important step for higher education to consider taking at this time is to extend partnership or sponsorship relations beyond large-scale organizations to small and midsize business, which taken together have large numbers but individually have thin resources. Their representatives issue appeals for such help and look to higher education to provide it.

9

SUSTAINING AND RENEWING
SUCCESSFUL PROGRAMS

ADULT EDUCATORS OFTEN experience precariousness in their work. Many institutions regard work with adults, whether called extension, continuing education, outreach, or other euphemistic names, to be ancillary to their main missions. Correspondingly, they may give adult learning little or no support, either moral or financial, and they may even assess heavy burdens of overhead on successful adult programs to finance activities in other sectors. Despite some examples where new programs have had generous administrative or philanthropic support to get started, most new ventures have to self-fund their start-up costs and ongoing operations from other adult program surpluses or their own income. Adult education professionals take courageous risks when they attempt activities for new learners or customize programs for different learner sponsors. They may invest extensive creative and financial resources only to have a new initiative fail. It is not surprising that a persisting question for programmers—one that often occurs in the small hours of the night—is, Will the class make it? Or having made it once, will it run again?

These anxieties most frequently arise about the broad range of credit-free activities and special events and sequences in continuing education, especially those offered to the general public. Degree programs are more complex and may be less exposed to failure at the beginning. Once authorized, they may have more generous start-up funding and institutional support, although that is not always the case. Over time, however, they too may become vulnerable and may begin to cause the adult educator's chronic angst.

A useful analysis of program failures and the lessons that can be learned from them is provided by T. J. Sork and his colleagues (Sork, 1991). From several years of observation Sork delineated four situations of program failure: (1) planning is undertaken but is terminated before implementation; (2) the program is planned and publicized but canceled for lack of participation; (3) the program is planned, publicized, and recruited successfully, but the participants are dissatisfied at the end; and (4) the program is offered to the satisfaction of participants, but it does not achieve the objectives the planners intended. Sork suggested various program flaws that could contribute to unsatisfactory results. He also urged planners to reflect on their failures in order to draw lessons for the future rather than repress the experience in their disappointment.

Of Sork's four cases, probably the last two are most relevant to adult credit and degree programs, which often launch with initial success but then begin to have difficulty. These programs may have weaknesses that various positive factors obscured at the beginning, or the program environment and execution may change over time. In either circumstance, problems may appear unless program managers are vigilant.

In addition to Sork's factors, there are three other conditions that can influence program continuation. Two are outside programmers' control although the program may be able to adapt to them. In the third, the program itself can change the condition. The first is a change of policy or direction extrinsic to the program that affects its viability. Alverno College, which was created to provide degrees to members of its parent religious order, faced a crisis when the order decided to require new members to have degrees before admission. The college responded by recruiting new groups of learners for its competence-based program. More recently, the withdrawal of eligibility for Pell grants from prisoners has meant the death of a number of prison programs.

Second, a change in the environment in which a program is initially developed may alter its prospects. Some institutions have experienced positive or negative effects from economic changes in their region. Many programs currently speak of loss of enrollment as a result of corporate downsizing or reduced educational benefits for adults as corporations try to reduce costs. Some others, however, are reporting that enrollment drops during prosperity and high employment. In other cases, programs that started with a unique idea may find others emulating them and competing with them for students.

Third, over time, programs risk the problems of aging or of losing standing in their institutions. Faculty and staff may lose their initial energy, or alternatively, dedicated individuals who gave the program its early drive may move on and be replaced by persons who lack their enthusiasm. The values of the institution itself may change, so that the adult program is no longer highly regarded or adult oriented. This has happened in several programs considered during the preparation of this book. Or worst of all, the program may become complacent with its first, pathbreaking innovation and be unwilling to renew itself. The model, and sometimes the content, becomes outdated. Learning modes no longer appropriate to a changing population of students go unmodified. Technology outstrips the familiar pattern of delivery. I refer to this phenomenon as *the tradition of the nontradition,* and it affects more programs than presently recognize the symptoms.

The survey of institutional adult credit and degree programs conducted by the Commission for a Nation of Lifelong Learners' project illustrates these factors. One question addressed to the chief academic officers of all accredited higher education institutions asked, "Has your institution discontinued any credit program(s) primarily oriented to adult learners in the last 12 months?" If the officers responded yes, they were asked the name of the program and the reason for discontinuance.

Of the 1,271 chief academic officers who responded to the questionnaire, 990 indicated that adult learners were among the populations they served. And 36 reported that their institutions had discontinued programs during the preceding twelve months for a variety of reasons. The largest group (21) gave low enrollment or lack of interest as the reason for cancellation. Program names and other information provided suggest, however, that in many cases the low enrollment resulted from factors like the ones Sork suggested in his analysis, such as a misreading of the potential audience; competition from other, more credible providers; or choice of site. In some cases it was clear that a choice to reduce costs had been made and that some programs had been sacrificed to this choice. A few respondents mentioned withdrawal of student aid, like the loss of Pell grants for prisoners or the termination of government or military funding. In yet other cases, lack of personnel, due either to retirement or to shortage of faculty in the area, caused the discontinuance. In seven instances the host institution rejected the adult delivery model or the content as inappropriate. In another case the sequence was absorbed by a related program. It is interesting to speculate whether informed interventions might have changed these outcomes.

Of the many adult programs launched over the last two decades, many have failed, and others have shrunk from their original conceptions. The following sections allude to some of those casualties, but mainly they look at long-term programs that have adapted to their circumstances and, through change, have maintained their vitality. One of the original University Without Walls (UWW) programs was at Skidmore College. It separated from full participation in UWW fairly early but has maintained and grown that concept within the context of a distinctive institution. One of the earliest special adult degree programs, the Bachelor of Liberal Studies degree program at the University of Oklahoma, had adapted in many ways over several decades but eventually reached a critical point at which it needed to strike out in a different direction. Alfred North Whitehead College at the University of Redlands developed a flexible model in the early 1970s, and by maintaining that model's important central concept, the college has been able to adapt its program and respond successfully to a turbulent and changing environment. And finally, Georgetown University's Graduate Liberal Studies program, notwithstanding its current success, has decided to bank on the future by reinventing its model to appeal to a wider range of constituencies.

KEEPING A PROGRAM VITAL

The University Without Walls and Successors

Skidmore College—Saratoga Springs, New York

Individualized Bachelor's Degrees

The University Without Walls was among the several exciting experiments undertaken about 1970 to provide more individualized, flexible, and intellectually challenging higher education. Like Empire State College, with which it shared some concepts, it was open to students from adolescence to late in life, it encouraged learners to take the initiative in creating unique learning programs, and it reached beyond campus boundaries for learning resources wherever they could be found.

UWW was a consortium of cooperating institutions that shared a vision and opened their facilities to each other's participants. It grew out of explorations of ten innovative undergraduate institutions that in 1964 formed the Union for Research and Experimentation in Higher Education (UREHE). In 1969, at the suggestion of Royce Pitkin, president of Goddard College, it changed its name to the Union for Experimenting Colleges and Universities (UECU) (Kirkhorn, 1979; Benson & Adams, 1987). The original group, supported with funds from the

Charles F. Kettering Foundation, developed its ideas over several years and added new members, a process that eventually led to the formation of two programs within UECU, the undergraduate-level University Without Walls and the graduate-level Union Graduate School. In December 1970, UECU secured funding from the U.S. Department of Education and the Ford Foundation, and UWW began program operation in the fall of 1971. It initially projected twenty-five members, but it listed twenty in its first-year report. By 1974, the North Central Association of Colleges and Schools accepted UWW as a candidate for accreditation.

UWW declared itself an alternative form of education that "moves toward a new faith in the student and his capacity for learning on his own, while at the same time providing close and continuing contact between the student and teacher. It redefined the role of the teacher as a facilitator and coparticipant in the planning and design of the student's learning experience" (University Without Walls, 1972, p. 3; see this report for discussion of UWW's early experience). The educational design had many features now broadly adopted but revolutionary then. They included a facilitating, collaborative relationship between student and teacher; individually designed study plans; use of community faculty and resources; planned experiential learning; total freedom from traditional classes, terms, and credits; and at a program's completion, a review of the student's degree work by a committee of faculty, students and others with whom the student had worked.

The early experience of UWW appeared successful, and it received more grant funding as well as tuition income. As time passed, however, UECU encountered problems, due in part to withdrawal of some of its members and competition from other innovative programs but also to its own handling of management and finances. In 1979, it was forced into bankruptcy. The reorganization resulted in the formation of The Union Institute (TUI), which has grown to a major university offering both undergraduate and graduate programs but no longer in association with the broader member organization (Kirkhorn, 1979; Hall, 1991).

Although UECU and UWW are gone, The Union Institute's programs continue many concepts derived from UECU, as do the programs of a number of the former UECU partners. This review does not attempt to follow the course of all the original UWW programs. Instead it illustrates through several examples the different outcomes these programs had and, in some instances, the legacy of the original concept.

Some of the UWW programs, and even their initial host institutions, were absorbed by other institutions. Loretto Heights College in Denver participated in the first UWW group and for many years was a leading provider of adult learning opportunities in the Denver metropolitan area (Greenberg, 1980). When the college was forced to close in 1988, its adult programs, including UWW, were assumed by Regis University. The UWW designation persisted for a while, but as Regis developed its own guided independent study model, both the name and the separate program disappeared. In another case, the Union for Experimenting Colleges turned over control of UWW programs originally begun by Antioch College in Dayton, Columbus, and Cleveland to Capital University. Capital, in turn, built its own and different Adult Degree Program on the three sites and discontinued the UWW designation and model.

The title of University Without Walls persisted for a number of years at other institutions in programs that carried echoes of the earlier concepts. Increasingly, however, they adapted to the circumstances of their environments or took on characteristics of their parent institutions, relinquishing the UWW name for new titles that expressed their new situations. Through its School of Graduate and Continuing Education, Stephens College, an original UWW institution, now offers flexible graduate, undergraduate, and nondegree programs by various means of delivery, but all reference to UWW is gone. Similarly, the University of Minnesota's Program for Individualized Learning (PIL) is the descendant of a UWW program. PIL is located in University College, the outreach division of the university. It offers a highly individualized curriculum in which students design degree plans that fulfill *graduation criteria,* rather than credits, in breadth and depth areas. Along with university courses, independent study, direct learning from experience, and extensive assessment of prior learning can be used to fulfill degree plans.

UWW at Skidmore College

Skidmore College, in contrast to many other original UWW institutions, has retained the UWW title and character for its adult learning program. As a member of the initial consortium, Skidmore played an active role in development of its early concepts and participated in plans for UWW to award degrees. After a few years Skidmore left the Union for Experimenting Colleges, but it continued the program and awards its own degrees. Currently, the UWW program enrolls three hundred students annually, approximately 10 percent of the college's enrollment, and it is growing. It has had a thousand graduates since its beginning.

RECRUITMENT AND DEGREE PLANNING. The students Skidmore attracts are almost all adults, with an average age in the late thirties although the age range is from twenty to eighty-one. The majority—60 percent—are women. Forty percent live within driving distance of the Saratoga Springs campus. However, distance learning procedures and Internet promotion have led to some international enrollment. Applications require records of previous college work and writing samples but no standardized test scores. An interview at the campus is also required; staff and faculty look for strength of motivation, ability to work independently, ability to handle study at the level expected, and the applicant's prospects for persistence in the program. Once admitted, students pay an annual enrollment fee for program services, plus special fees for independent and self-directed study and final project assessments. They are responsible for enrollment charges at other institutions if they elect to take courses there.

A ROLLING CURRICULUM. Once admitted, students return for a second interview, a full-day degree planning session with two advisers, one from the program staff and one from the faculty. (With some advance arrangements, the application and degree planning interviews can be scheduled within the same seventy-two hour period.) Students, with adviser assistance, design individualized degree plans in terms of their interests, although they are required to include general education components.

Unlike many other student-designed programs, the Skidmore process sets an initial direction in the first interview, and planning continues in a rolling process that is not complete until the student presents a final degree plan for approval near the end of his or her study. This model is similar to the original UWW design with its final review. The apparent anomaly in this practice is resolved by the interaction of students and advisers as study proceeds. Working closely with the faculty adviser, students develop a focus area, often in a multidisciplinary concentration, and they select courses and experiences to fulfill it. The program also has some model curricula to suggest directions to students, and Skidmore has especially strong programs in the arts, which some UWW students pursue. Continuing interaction between students and their advisers is essential to ensure agreement between faculty and students when students return to the campus a final time for the last review of their degree work. Following approval, students submit a final undergraduate project.

Students fulfill their plans by various means. Many bring considerable credit for transfer, and they may qualify for further credit through a broad program of prior learning assessment. Those who live near the campus may take Skidmore courses or special adult seminars. Others take courses at institutions in their vicinity and transfer the credit. Students may also take correspondence and on-line courses, independent studies, and supervised internships and conduct projects with qualified community faculty. The program is self-paced, and students may complete it at any time. Most used to spend about three years in the program, but recently they have begun to finish sooner.

Summary

Skidmore's UWW program continues as a vigorous part of the college's offerings. Enrollment has grown in the recent past, and the college sees UWW as an integral part of its activity. The program's strengths include the close advising relationships, individual degree planning that develops throughout students' enrollment, access to distinctive faculty and programs throughout the college, and strong loyalty to the institution. The UWW director has college faculty status, and because UWW affects other aspects of the institution, the director and other UWW staff regularly participate in college planning groups. UWW has influenced other programs in the college by its experimental example and has led to innovations such as self-determined majors and interdisciplinary concentrations in women's studies, Asian studies, regional studies, and computer science.

In sum, it is fair to say that although UWW's original vision of experimentation and collaboration was not fulfilled, it has left a heritage of ideas and practice that remains valuable, whether in the overt continuation of the concept as at Skidmore or in the continuing activities of its former members and others they have influenced.

ADAPTING AN OLD PROGRAM FOR NEW AUDIENCES

University of Oklahoma—Norman, Oklahoma

College of Liberal Studies

Bachelor of Liberal Studies Program

Unlike UWW, which began as a networked system and foresaw extensive interaction among its members, the Bachelor of Liberal Studies (BLS) degree program at the University of Oklahoma developed in a single institution. It created a design in which persons could participate from any location so long as they could make occasional visits to the campus. It experimented with many other new concepts but over time found that it had to adapt as its audience changed.

The BLS program is one of the most venerable adult degree programs in the country. Planning by faculty began as early as 1957, and the program enrolled its first students in 1961. Syracuse University launched an adult degree program in the same year, and during the 1960s several other programs, similar in approach but sometimes differing in title, appeared at such institutions as Brooklyn College, Goddard College, the University of South Florida, Brigham Young University, Western Illinois University, and SUNY-College at Brockport. These were programs that Valley (1972) called *modes-of-learning* degrees, and that Houle (1973) labeled *special adult degrees* falling between early *extension* models and the emerging *external* degrees of the 1970s. In fact the BLS and similar programs combined periods of study at a distance with short residential sessions, and broke the way for the later external models.

The Oklahoma BLS program is well documented, and it continues to be acknowledged in accounts of the development of adult degree programs. A group of founding faculty and administrators have compiled an account of the initial formulation of the program (Burkett & Ruggiers, 1965). A doctoral dissertation has examined the equivalency of the BLS degree to traditional degrees (Adelman, 1973). Other notices have appeared in Troutt (1971), Medkser, Edelstein, Kreplin, Ruyle, and Shea (1975), White (1979), Gamson and Associates (1984), Langenbach (1988), Stubblefield and Keane (1994), and Knowles (1994a).

Over its nearly four decades the program has not remained static but has experienced evolution, experimentation, and development. It illustrates the challenges faced by long-term programs due to shifts in prospective learners' characteristics, changes in these learners' perception of the kind of education they need, and more competitive market conditions as a broader field of choices has emerged.

The Original Model

The BLS program grew out of an extended planning effort by faculty drawn from across the university. In 1957, the extension dean convened a yearlong seminar of about forty faculty members to consider guidelines for a new approach to providing degree study for adults. Their recommendations called for a liberal education program and provided direction for further planning. Ten faculty met over the next three years and produced the BLS degree proposal, which received university and state system approval. Planning proceeded contemporaneously with the construction of a W. K. Kellogg Foundation–funded residential education facility, the Oklahoma Center for Continuing Education, which provides housing for administrative offices and residential and classroom facilities for the program's residential seminars.

CURRICULUM AND THE LEARNERS. The resulting curriculum and learning model addressed three concerns of adult learners described by White (1979, pp. 40–41): to progress in areas that have meaning for them, to build on what they already know, and to study at convenient times and places. The interdisciplinary curriculum, which was strongly influenced by the University of Chicago College model of the Hutchins era, dealt with three knowledge areas—humanities, social sciences, and natural sciences—plus an integrating *inter-area*. It assumed that students brought with them varying degrees of acquaintance with these areas. The program asked students to approach the content in terms of a central theme (stated, naturally enough, in terms more resonant of the 1960s than of the present), "Man in the Twentieth Century." Employing a *central problems–central learnings* approach, students built on knowledge they already had, extending that knowledge through further study in the curriculum areas and applying their understanding to relevant problems of their own time. At the end, in the inter-area study segment, students sought to integrate their previous learning by completing an individual *study-in-depth,* dealing extensively with an issue or problem of their own selection. A guided independent study model enabled them to study at any location and at their own pace. They also attended annual three-week residential seminars at the campus to engage in group activities and to become acquainted with the university.

Access to the BLS program was open to any adult, twenty-five years old or older, with high school completion or its equivalent. New entrants took an initial battery of tests for placement and advisement purposes, but the tests were not used for admission screening.

The BLS program departed boldly from many traditional learning practices. It abandoned the model made up of varied three-credit courses, considering it fragmenting, and instead addressed content in broad interdisciplinary areas, each equivalent to a year of degree study. Tuition was priced in terms of independent study and seminar blocks, rather than credit hour fees. It measured achievement by completion of major written examinations in each study area, similar to those of the University of Chicago College at that time or of many European universities. It depended on self-paced and largely self-directed independent study in set readings and short on-campus seminars. Faculty, who were regular university faculty working on overload, served as advisers, or tutors, to guide students' efforts according to their individual backgrounds and interests. In the interdisciplinary seminars, faculty worked in teams of two or three to explore significant themes and to guide individual and team projects or research studies. The program departed from strict calendar patterns, so that student enrollment was schedule free, and students could complete work in either shorter or longer time periods than were customary.

The program began with assistance from a Carnegie Corporation grant that provided scholarships for an initial cadre of seventy-five students. Within three years enrollment grew to over four hundred, and it continued to increase. The comparatively light demands for physical attendance and the few nontraditional degree alternatives elsewhere attracted enrollment from considerable distances. For many years a majority of students came from outside the state of Oklahoma. An important number of students in the late 1960s and early 1970s were civilian employees of military services that supported expenses for degree study. At one time during this period the program enrolled over 1,500 students.

ADMINISTRATION AND EVOLUTION. The BLS program began as an administrative initiative in the university's Extension Division. With its foundation, the College of Continuing Education was created to serve as its host and sponsor. A twelve-member faculty *executive committee,* which still exists, governed the program, setting policy and arranging faculty assignments and seminars. The college also hoped to serve as a host for other interdisciplinary, adult-oriented degree programs, but, even though initiatives began in other content areas, none resulted in a fully developed degree program. Toward the end of the 1960s, demands for change and innovation led to an experiment with an on-campus adaptation of the BLS for traditional age students. The experiment was unsuccessful and ended after a couple of years, but it left a lasting effect on the administrative location of the College of Continuing Education. To reflect its broader constituency, the university renamed it the College of Liberal Studies and placed it under provost supervision, in parallel with the other degree colleges.

The BLS program evolved further over the next two decades. In 1968, the College of Liberal Studies extended its model to a Master of Liberal Studies (MLS) degree that alternated intensive seminars on campus with independent study based on more individualized plans than were used in the BLS program and that culminated in a research thesis. The University of Oklahoma MLS remains the only distance learning degree of its type. As the number of community colleges grew and more students brought considerable prior credit, the BLS program established an upper-division option in 1973 for persons with associate degrees or with sixty hours or more of completed credit. Under the influence of Malcolm Knowles's ideas, the program revised the independent study design, keeping some required content but enabling segments to be completed through individualized learning contracts. In the early 1980s, the MLS program acknowledged a connection between liberal education and professional goals by developing a *museum emphasis,* an option for persons in professional museum work.

The basis for BLS program funding also shifted during this time. Initially self-financed from tuition, with separate prices for the various program components, the program made a successful case for state support, which resulted in public funding and a distinction between in-state and out-of-state charges. BLS tuition remained distinct in terms of having several components, but a continuation, or *records maintenance,* fee was introduced that applied to second and subsequent years of enrollment in an independent study area. Also, to comply with state credit hour reporting requirements, credit hour values were assigned to the curriculum components that had originally shunned that practice.

ENROLLMENT. BLS enrollment levels became a problem after the early 1970s. During the Vietnam War, support for military employee degree education declined in favor of support for job-related courses. The floriation during the 1970s of alternative degree programs, especially those offering external degrees, deprived the handful of special adult degree programs of their distinctive role, and some even closed. Increasingly, undergraduate degree programs in professional fields arrived to challenge the general liberal education programs, and they attracted strongly career-oriented applicants. The Oklahoma BLS program sustained itself by its adaptations, but its student numbers declined significantly from their previous highs.

The problems became more acute in the early 1990s. The overall headcount remained stable, but credit hour production and degree completion declined. The numbers of active students masked the fact that many were extending their enrollments but not completing stages to the degree. New recruitment became difficult as potential students increasingly completed their first two college years in community colleges and became acclimated to classroom-based programs completed in defined academic terms. These learners found the BLS program unfamiliar in format and difficult to understand, and they resisted promotional efforts. They thought the three-week residential seminars would strain their ability to be away from work and families (an issue for earlier students also). And especially, many sought a study program that would increase their professional capability. Most important, more and more students expressed discomfort with and demonstrated incapacity for self-paced independent study, perhaps illustrating the adult difficulty with independent learning, or self-direction as adult educators conceive it, that Kegan (1994) mentions. College staff came to believe that only a small minority of adults were fully suited to the BLS independent study format. Yet there continued to be a population attracted to and satisfied by the personal enrichment goals of the original BLS concept.

Renewal—Two Tracks

These circumstances were serious enough to jeopardize the program and led the college to take major steps of renovation, adopting a two-track system within the original liberal studies program framework.

KEEPING THE TRADITION. Recognizing that a continuing constituency wanted to pursue a program similar in content and method to the original BLS, the college remodeled that degree into an explicitly lower- and upper-division program designated the BLS/Classic. It kept the original BLS elements of offering interdisciplinary content in broad knowledge areas, independent study, intensive seminars, and a concluding study-in-depth, but it packaged them in more convenient formats. All new enrollees, in either division, attend a common introductory orientation seminar scheduled over two weekends, which stresses skills for success in the program. Students with fewer than sixty previous credits enter the freshman-sophomore program, the BLS/Classic Lower Division. They complete three interdisciplinary independent area studies and two seminars selected from those areas. Students may be given advanced standing based on previous credit. Those who complete the lower division and those with associate degrees or sixty credits, proceed to the junior-senior program, or BLS/Classic Upper Division, in which they complete three more area independent studies, one area seminar, an inter-area independent study and seminar, and a study-in-depth. Credit hour values have been revised to total sixty credits for the first program and sixty-four for the second, plus two credits for the introductory seminar. As in the original BLS program, students pursue independent study with the guidance of a faculty adviser and study guides, follow a self-paced schedule, and receive satisfactory/unsatisfactory (S/U) grades for their work. However, study in each area is presented in shorter modules, and the learning contracts have been discontinued. Also, overall seminar duration has been shortened from fifteen to ten days and the daily meeting periods have been extended. There is now approximately a month-long interval between the first and second seminar sessions. The original "Man in the Twentieth Century" theme is now gone, and the program describes itself simply as a self-paced interdisciplinary liberal arts degree.

ADDRESSING NEW INTERESTS. For the second track, the college launched a parallel but more traditional, market-driven upper-division degree completion program in August 1996. It is titled the BLS/Administrative Leadership Concentration (BLS/ALC) and serves those seeking career-related content. Entrants must have associate degrees or sixty previous credits. The curriculum begins with an introductory seminar and proceeds through a series of classroom-based courses, totaling sixty-six credits. The courses include three elements: study in the three BLS knowledge areas and inter-area (in eight- or twelve-credit units), consideration of ethics in the three areas (totaling twelve credits), and a career-related leadership concentration in conflict resolution, leadership in organizations, quality initiatives in organizations, and cultural diversity in organizations (also totaling twelve credits). Study in the second and third elements is organized in two- or four-credit courses. Learners complete the degree with a four-credit study-in-depth. Unlike students in the BLS/Classic program, these students pursue study in the BLS areas through regularly scheduled classroom activity and out-of-class assignments. Development of teamwork is a program goal, so cohort members are divided into teams that work and report on course assignments together. Often students can draw upon job experience in class and immediately apply learning to work situations through class projects. Students who have sufficiently distributed previous upper-division credit may have already fulfilled some study requirements.

The cohort groups number about twenty-five. Cohorts attend one course at a time, always on weekends, and receive letter grades for their work. In a sixteen-week semester, cohorts will meet on nine or ten weekends. Cohorts may begin in the fall or spring semesters each year. If they maintain consistent participation, the fall groups complete in five terms, including one summer, and the spring groups complete in six terms, including two summers. Students who interrupt their cohort participation may rejoin later by entering other groups at the appropriate stage.

All curriculum components in both the Classic and ALC programs are now valued in credit hours, and enrollment is priced in terms of university-wide in-state and out-of-state fees. Classic seminars and ALC weekend classes are offered at the university main campus and at sites in metropolitan Oklahoma City and Tulsa.

LEARNER SERVICES. The principal service both BLS tracks provide students is faculty advising, which is integrated with the instructional process. College staff at the university campus also assist with student inquiries in person or at a distance and often serve as facilitators to solve student problems at the campus. Staff also travel regularly to off-campus sites. BLS student academic records are maintained in a special admission and records office that serves continuing education. University services relevant to distance learning students are available to BLS participants. These services include financial aid, and a financial aid office staff member has been designated to work with adult students. The College of Liberal Studies provides a limited number of scholarships for participants. Books for the BLS are available through a national book-ordering service frequently used by distance learning programs.

THE LEARNERS. The BLS/Classic has a current enrollment of about 325 and remains stable at that number. About one-third are lower division and two-thirds upper division. Student age averages between forty-two and forty-three. The program attracts about 40 percent men and 60 percent women, many of the latter single women with children. Many students of both genders are in clerical or low- to middle-management positions and are seeking to upgrade their qualifications. In contrast to the program's early enrollment history, 90 to 95 percent of the enrollment now is in state.

The BLS/ALC currently has about two hundred students in ten cohorts. At forty-two, the current average age of participants is similar to that of BLS/Classic students, but the program is now seeing interest from younger applicants. Gender proportions are the reverse of those in the Classic program: about 60 percent men and 40 percent women.

Participants are employed chiefly in professional roles and are seeking to improve their prospects through degree completion.

One cohort is sponsored by the Oklahoma City Police Department, which has dedicated funds to upgrade the educational level of police officers. The program offers these learners an upper-division degree completion opportunity that builds on an associate-level police science degree available in Oklahoma City. Because police have heavier call loads on weekends, this cohort meets in police facilities on a weeknight schedule.

Future

Clearly, the BLS program has come a long way from its beginnings and in the process has shed or mitigated many conceptions, such as broad blocks of study, largely self-guided independent study, learning contracts, and no assignment of credit hours. Yet it retains much of its early vision for those who are attracted to that model and content of learning. At the same time, it has responded to market demands by adjusting its options within its authorized format to appeal to a different audience. The new participants seem to respond well to the BLS/ALC offering. The first cohort completed in summer 1998 with an 81 percent graduation rate, and half the cohort members reported plans for further graduate or professional study.

Problems remain in that the guided independent study process presents difficulties for many. Both lower- and upper-division students have significant problems completing the BLS/Classic. The college has initiated a new guided independent study process that uses Web-based courses on the Internet, in the hope that this innovation may encourage completion at both levels.

The program anticipates growth in the ALC option, with the possibility that it may receive a majority of the college's enrollment. This in turn may lead college programs in a more professional direction, although the college has no specific plans for this yet. Adaptations, such as modules that extend the ALC emphasis or in-service internships, could also be tried.

EVOLUTION OF AN ADULT PROGRAM AND ITS COHORT MODEL

University of Redlands—Redlands, California

Alfred North Whitehead College for Lifelong Learning

Cohort Bachelor's and Master's Degrees

Alfred North Whitehead College (ANWC) is a leading southern California provider of bachelor's and master's degrees for adult learners. Early in its history it developed a cohort model that has enabled it to adapt to changing demands in its environment and within its parent institution. Through consistent adherence to its basic concept it has withstood challenges arising from economic conditions and policy direction, yet it has also developed new program responses for constituencies in its service area.

ANWC's host institution, the University of Redlands, was founded in 1907 by the American Baptist church, with which it maintains an informal association even though the university's educational goals have always been nonsectarian. Throughout that time it has sought to relate liberal education and professional preparation. The university is located in Redlands, California, a small city about sixty-five miles east of Los Angeles. Its surroundings have changed from citrus orchards and other agricultural crops to residential and robust business neighborhoods in a region that likes to refer to itself as the Inland Empire. It has easy access to the Los Angeles and San Diego metropolitan areas and the urban region between them. The emergence and development of ANWC illustrates the opportunities and challenges for an adult learning organization in the ebb and flow of a dynamic setting. The following account depends heavily on a senior faculty member's history of ANWC (Robertson, 1997).

Evolving an Organization for Adult Learning

Redlands began its commitment to adult degree programs in 1971 as the result of a grant from the Mott Foundation to Redlands, the University of San Francisco, and St. Mary's College, in association with John Sperling and Peter Ellis of San Jose State University. The emphasis of the grant was to develop community educational programs, largely directed to minority students. Each of the universities formed its own program, and in early 1974, Sperling and Ellis created the Institute for Professional Development (IPD) to market these programs (see the discussion of Thomas More College in Chapter Four for more information about IPD).

The grant stimulated Redlands to establish the Center for Special Programs, the precursor to the Alfred North Whitehead College, to develop adult offerings. Its first degree program was the Bachelor of Arts in Liberal Studies (BALS), begun in 1972, which was oriented chiefly to nurses and public service management employees. In many

ways the BALS program foreshadowed the basic cluster approach that
Redlands and ANWC would follow down to the present offerings, with
adjustments for different degrees, disciplines, and clientele. Redlands
also took the program out to communities in the San Francisco and
Sacramento areas and to locations in the southern California triangle
defined by Redlands and San Bernardino, Los Angeles, and San Diego.

The success of the BALS program led to development of other degree
options during the 1970s, including the Bachelor of Science in Public
Service Management (BSPSM), the Master of Arts in Education, and the
Master of Arts in Management (MAM). The new programs were conducted on an accelerated model and emphasized integration of classroom learning with workplace experience. Redlands contracted with
IPD to market the programs, to bill students and handle collections, to
engage faculty, and to provide facilities and logistical support in return
for a portion of tuition proceeds. The BSPSM attracted many public service employees, especially from regional police departments, and the
master's degrees drew students from school districts and businesses.

As these programs developed and found audiences, the university
trustees created a new home for them in the Alfred North Whitehead
College, approved in May 1976. Whitehead's name was adopted, with
permission from his family, in recognition of the mathematician and
philosopher's earlier work with adults at the University of London. The
college's mission was to provide new and flexible programs for adults
that would unite liberal with practical education at convenient times
and locations. At the time of its foundation, the adult programs already
had 1,600 students, mostly employed full time. The trustees took their
action in the face of resistance from faculty in the university's principal
traditional college and from some administrators, causing an institutional strain that took many years to reconcile. Nevertheless, ANWC in
cooperation with IPD, continued to grow during the 1970s.

Challenges and Development

Three developments in the late 1970s, two external and one internal,
affected the future direction of ANWC. First, in 1978, the adoption of
Proposition 13 in California restricted local tax revenues and therefore
the ability of local authorities to support employees in degree programs
such as the BSPSM and the master's in education. ANWC was forced to
adapt and to find new markets for its offerings. Then, in 1979, the university's regional accreditation association, the Western Association of
Schools and Colleges (WASC), strongly recommended that Redlands

discontinue its relationship with IPD, which it did by August 1979. Following this, ANWC retracted its service area to southern California, and it created an internal infrastructure to provide necessary services. Subsequently, ANWC established regional service centers in San Diego and Orange County to provide classrooms, offices, support services, and computer facilities at convenient sites. Others centers were added later in Los Angeles and the San Fernando Valley.

Meanwhile, in 1979, the university reorganized its structure in a way that seemed to threaten ANWC's standing. At this time, the university had three colleges: University College, its traditional core; Johnstone College, a special undergraduate college for individualized studies formed in 1969; and ANWC. Redlands now made ANWC and Johnstone into *centers* rather than colleges and discontinued the name University College. The action seemed prompted in part by lingering faculty resentment over the trustee-led foundation of ANWC. Yet, in the long run, the change began a process that left ANWC in a stronger position.

One outcome was that ANWC gradually gained a designated faculty. The university recognized that the 1979 reorganization made ANWC subject to faculty governance without any representation. To remedy this, several ANWC administrative appointments were declared to be faculty positions carrying the title of lecturer. Following a 1982 visit from WASC that focused on ANWC, the visiting WASC team recommended that ANWC have full-time faculty. The university responded by designating the former lecturers as full-time faculty on renewable term appointments. In 1989, a new faculty constitution gave an explicit voice in governance to ANWC faculty and made an ANWC faculty member president of the university-wide Academic Assembly in alternating years. The process was completed in 1990, when ANWC's term-contract faculty were designated as eligible for tenure. Since then ANWC has steadily increased its full-time, tenure-eligible faculty and the proportion of college courses that they teach. It is currently in a multiyear growth phase with a goal of 40 percent of courses taught by full-time faculty.

During this period three departments were formed in ANWC, each with distinct academic or service responsibilities. In 1984, the School of Education was moved to ANWC from the university's residential college, bringing with it faculty and programs. Education was constituted as a college department and through compromises and adjustments, it and ANWC's previous education programs were assimilated. In 1987, business and management programs were also brought together in the new Department of Management and Business. The Department of Liberal Studies followed in 1989, constituted as a service department to provide a centralized academic advising and assessment center, direction of optional weekend courses, and faculty direction for the introductory baccalaureate course Philosophical Foundations of Management. The college also undertook development of a new four-year program, Connections, in 1990.

This organizational evolution reached its latest stage in 1995 when the university trustees restored ANWC to collegiate status, naming it the Alfred North Whitehead College for Lifelong Learning.

The ANWC Cluster Model

Beginning with its first degree, the BALS in 1972, ANWC developed educational elements into a programmatic method that it has been able to apply through a series of iterations ever since. It took several years, but what emerged by the mid-1970s was one of the earliest cohort or, using ANWC's term, cluster models. By applying the cluster approach flexibly, ANWC has offered a series of degrees and other programs that have responded to emerging needs and changing conditions. The programs have evolved, disappeared, and sometimes been revived in altered design, but consistently they have followed a signature form that both ANWC and its audience find effective.

CALENDAR, CLUSTERS, AND CREDIT. The chief elements are the following, although not all appear in every case. The sequences are either degree completion programs, building on previous college learning, or complete master's programs. They require students to join continuing groups, or clusters, that provide pacing. In reflection of the university's mission to link liberal education and professional preparation, some coursework, usually at the beginning of a program, examines the philosophical background or ethics of the specialization. Clusters follow an accelerated model of required attendance once a week for four hours combined with approximately twenty hours of out-of-class assignments, often associated with work responsibilities. Two weeks of such effort are equivalent to one credit hour. Concurrently, over the duration of the program, some clusters pursue a project or practicum of at least 250 verified hours resulting in a final product. A well-developed program of prior learning assessment is available to undergraduate students. Students who require general education or elective courses may take them through a parallel weekend course offering. ANWC guarantees tuition rates for cluster members who stay with their groups.

Some variations occur in specific programs. In pre-ANWC days several programs were described as competence based, but that descriptive term has been dropped. Alternatives to the four-hour weekly meetings may be used to meet circumstances of specific groups. Not all sequences include the project-practicum requirement but may achieve a similar goal through other assignments.

PROGRAM ADAPTABILITY. The basic format has enabled ANWC to modify its offerings as conditions in its environment changed. It served public service employees well with the original BALS degree and the later Bachelor of Science in Public Service Management but has shifted to a health-oriented option now that Proposition 13 has eliminated most public service enrollees other than nurses. It has developed a number of business-related offerings, some in response to corporate requests, that give it a broad offering of programs in management and business. Its education programs serve a number of pressing current needs, from qualifying baccalaureate holders for teaching certificates to providing administrators with post-master's administrative credentials.

FACULTY. ANWC faculty fall into three groups, full-time, tenure-eligible core faculty, part-time core faculty who are usually practitioners and serve on long-term appointments, and adjunct faculty who are appointed from course to course. Full-time faculty are responsible for academic management, and each serves as a lead faculty member for part-timers in specific discipline areas. Core faculty with substantial experience carry the main load of teaching and are supplemented by adjuncts. ANWC identifies part-time faculty through a careful and extended recruitment and orientation process.

LEARNER SERVICES. The college provides ongoing support to students through services available at the campus and regional centers. Academic advising and assessment, as mentioned, are centralized services located in the Department of Liberal Studies. Representatives are accessible in person at the various centers and through telephone, fax, and e-mail. Staff teams orient new clusters to services at their initial meetings. Portfolio preparation for prior learning assessment at the undergraduate level and orientation to other advanced standing procedures occurs in various program introductory courses, and portfolios are evaluated by panels in the central office. ANWC students are eligible for various federal and state financial aid programs, and ANWC maintains its own financial aid office to assist them.

In an effort to give students direct experience of the main campus, ANWC holds semiannual orientation days in Redlands, and for one of their regular evening meetings, the clusters substitute a half-day session on campus, followed by various collegewide programs. In recent years ANWC has also established the Leadership Society, an organization composed of faculty and students selected for their academic achievement and professional leadership potential. The society meets twice a year for seminars with distinguished leaders and discussions of issues in members' professions. Members also provide one-on-one mentoring on professional opportunities to the younger undergraduate students in the university. Both Leadership Society members and ANWC graduates generally have become active alumni supporters of the university.

Three Program Examples

Three current programs will illustrate ANWC's responsiveness and adaptations to the changing conditions in its environment—the four-year undergraduate Connections program, the postbaccalaureate education certificate program, and the Master of Arts in Management program.

CONNECTIONS. Connections was initially developed with the cooperation and support of Pacific Bell to provide a full degree opportunity for company employees. It is now available to other selected corporations through ANWC's corporate partnership programs, and it is administered through the Liberal Studies Department. Participants, who have little or no previous college study, begin with a fourteen-week, credit-free seminar, Philosophical Foundations of Management, that reintroduces them to formal education and covers basic skills in reading, writing, and mathematics. They then enter a 120-credit sequence that fulfills general education and other foundational natural and social science courses, after which they proceed to business-related courses leading to the Bachelor of Science in Business and Management (BSBAM) degree. Students may transfer in equivalent courses they have taken previously. The program can be offered at work sites, as it is for Pacific Bell. ANWC presently is seeking to expand Connections to other employers.

BASIC TEACHING CERTIFICATE WITH CROSS-CULTURAL, LANGUAGE, AND ACADEMIC DEVELOPMENT. Recent California policy to reduce class size has led to an increased demand for teachers. ANWC's Department of Education has developed a program to enable persons who presently hold baccalaureate degrees to meet certification requirements for the Basic Teaching Credential with Cross-cultural, Language, and Academic Development (BTC/CLAD). The program totals twenty-seven credits and can be completed over a ten-month period, which includes fourteen weeks of student teaching. Sequences begin three times a year, in September, November, and March. Clusters meet two nights a week to complete the required courses.

Enrollment has not been concentrated enough to base clusters on single school districts, but the program has been able to bring students from neighboring districts together through flexibility in scheduling and course offerings. BTC/CLAD courses are applicable to master's degrees in education. Currently the program is encouraging paraprofessionals with associate degrees to complete bachelor's degrees with ANWC and then move into the certificate or master's programs.

MASTER OF ARTS IN MANAGEMENT. The Department of Management and Business had offered a Master of Arts in Management degree in the mid-1970s that later was merged with another program and eventually discontinued in the 1980s. In the early 1990s, corporate clients began to request in-house cluster programs that could serve managers who neither needed the MBA nor wanted to pursue its longer curriculum. The department revived MAM in 1993 in response.

The resuscitated program has been reconfigured to fill a special niche for currently employed, experienced managers who are not seeking entry positions or career change. Admission to the program requires five years experience in supervisory, management, or professional positions. The MAM students have capacity and skills but may benefit from a tune-up with additional formal background and the MAM degree qualification. Some of the first entrants were casualties of downsizing who were preparing for new employment. The curriculum requires sixteen courses and thirty-two credits, covering both technical and management content, including critical thinking, decision making, and ethics. Students take core courses in management and business; courses that fulfill an emphasis in geographical information systems, human resource management, international business, information systems, or Total Quality Management; and a practicum seminar. Learners can complete the sequence in sixteen months.

The MAM design drew clusters from single organizations, which later reported benefit from the simultaneous upgrading of cadres of managers who went through the program together. Corporate cluster members coalesced quickly into working groups and demonstrated high motivation. Enrollment was reduced by corporate downsizing, but improvement in the regional economy has revived interest in many companies. The program also sees the possibility of forming cross-business clusters among small to midsize organizations.

An unexpected audience for the program has been military personnel, especially in the San Diego area. Persons whose military service roles have been in management but who have not been at single stations long enough to complete an MBA are well served by MAM. Those approaching military retirement and second careers in civilian life also find the program attractive. Currently, military personnel make up half of the enrollment.

Through adaptations and innovations such as these and close cooperation with client groups, ANWC has maintained its leadership over nearly three decades. Its basic cluster model, used flexibly, has enabled it to attract and maintain strong support. The college has remained sensitive to emerging needs in its area, and it has been willing to adapt or create programs to serve them. It has developed a centralized system of student services and has linked them to the service centers that give it a presence over a broad area. The experience of Alfred North Whitehead College demonstrates both how deeply programs can be affected by circumstances over which they have no control and how programs can adapt successfully. Moreover, the revival of the southern California economy following the downturns of the late 1980s and early 1990s makes ANWC optimistic for the future.

EXPANDING OPTIONS FROM A SUCCESSFUL FOUNDATION

Georgetown University—Washington, District of Columbia

Liberal Studies Degree Program

Master of Arts in Liberal Studies

The Georgetown University Master of Arts in Liberal Studies (MALS) degree is one of the most established graduate liberal studies programs. Compared to its host institution, founded in 1789, the MALS program is not of great age, having begun only in 1974. Yet that places it among an early group of graduate liberal studies degrees. Since then, the MALS degree program has established itself as a strong offering of Georgetown's School for Summer and Continuing Education and has exercised national leadership in the graduate liberal studies (GLS) movement. It is a charter member of the Association of Graduate Liberal Studies Programs, and its director has served as president of that association as well as a frequent consultant to newly emerging programs.

It is because of this relatively long history and high regard that the Georgetown MALS degree presents an interesting example of a program that has reinvented itself. Enrollment for the program has been strong. Graduates praise the experience they had in the program. It is supported within its institution and seen as a leader elsewhere. Yet the MALS program made a choice to redesign itself to serve its audience better.

The Graduate Liberal Studies Concept

The concept of graduate liberal studies has served already well-educated mature adults for over four decades. The first program began at Wesleyan University in 1952, mainly to offer teachers a graduate degree option with strong liberal education content as an alternative to graduate study in the profession of education. Over the next two decades a handful more of these programs appeared, at institutions such as Johns Hopkins (1960), Reed (1966), SUNY-Stony Brook and St. John's (1967), the University of Oklahoma (1968), Hollins (1969), Dartmouth (1970), and Georgetown (1974). In 1975, Dartmouth convened a meeting of a dozen programs; they formed the Association of Graduate Liberal Studies Programs (AGLSP) to provide communication and exchange of experience among members. For several years AGLSP remained small, but with the growth of interest in the GLS approach and requests from institutions for help in starting GLS programs, AGLSP broadened its scope to foster and encourage new programs. Since the late 1970s, the association has grown to nearly 120 institutional members, two-thirds of whom have fully operating programs. Total national enrollment is about ten thousand, and liberal studies have become a recognized form of graduate study that has already generated a small bibliography (Hands, 1988; House, 1991; O'Callaghan, 1983, 1988, 1997) and a journal (*Journal of Graduate Liberal Studies*).

Except in one or two institutions, GLS programs are not an outgrowth of the adult liberal education models of the adult special degrees of the 1960s (Houle, 1973). The movement springs more from the dedication of liberal arts faculty who have undertaken interdisciplinary approaches and begun to work at the graduate level. Most early programs were in private institutions with strong liberal education traditions, and although more public institutions now have initiated programs, private college participation remains strong. Some AGLSP members believe the degrees may include explicit professional applications, but most members prefer these studies to be nonprofessional. GLS programs usually have these three characteristics in common: an interdisciplinary approach, core study designed specially for the program, and a capstone experience. They also often reflect the values or mission commitments of their host institutions, especially among private colleges. They progress mainly by study in familiar course formats scheduled at times convenient for adults. Most often they are administered by faculty or special offices in liberal arts departments rather than by continuing education units.

The Original Georgetown Program

Georgetown's MALS program has flourished in the highly educated, strongly professional, and cosmopolitan environment of Washington, D.C. It attracts mainly working adults from government service, military service, education, private business, health care, and social service. In recent years it has found an international audience among the staffs of diplomatic missions and of foreign businesses and trade associations for whom both the content and earning of a U.S. degree are desirable. It enrolls between 300 and 350 students each year, and approximately 75 to 80 complete degrees annually. Among the program's distinguished graduates is President Clinton's former press secretary Michael McCurry, who commented that the Georgetown MALS "approaches the interdisciplinary nature of this program in humanities by examining core values issues. And I think it has enormous implications for people who have got the public's trust" ("Advanced Study," 1995).

The program embodies Georgetown's value orientation, and program brochures state that "human life and human action have meaning and that human beings, throughout their lives, must seek it out and live by its implications." Courses therefore seek synthesis as well as analysis, and values, though not sectarian beliefs, pervade the curriculum.

Until recently, the curriculum has been a thirty-credit, ten-course sequence. Normally, students took all their courses from an interdisciplinary offering specially designed for the program, although with approval they could take two advanced departmental courses or transfer in up to six credits earned elsewhere. These courses included two liberal studies courses with core or human values content and a thesis course in which they did their final integrating project. Classes met one night a week or on Saturdays at the Georgetown campus.

Because the curriculum requirements were stated in general terms, students had considerable latitude in how they planned their degree content. They selected any one of five concentrations the program offered—American studies, humanities, international relations, social/public policy, and religious studies—or they created a unique integrated program by choosing courses across the concentrations. The possibilities appealed to the program's heterogeneous constituency.

To give shape and a sense of personal integration to this individualization, the program asked students to assess the direction and significance of their study by writing one reflective essay when they were a third of the way through their programs and a second essay at the two-thirds point. The essays and discussion of them with program faculty and staff could lead to changes in degree planning. Finally, in the thesis course, students wrote a thesis or completed a creative work that drew together their work over the program.

The New MALS Program

Although the original MALS model operated successfully and was in good health, the program decided early in 1998 to carry out major modifications, or *reinvention*. This decision was prompted by a regularly planned external review in late 1997. The outside reviewers complimented the program on its quality and recommended that it build on that base by expanding its offerings to new degree programs. Liberal studies planners considered that possibility but chose instead to add a greater range of concentrations to the basic MALS curriculum structure by using the more specified plan of the existing religious studies concentration. The changes preserve the same course-based delivery model and degree designation but offer potential students an array of curriculum tracks that may focus more directly on their interests. The changes were reviewed by related departments and approved by the Graduate Executive Committee.

The selection of twelve curricular fields was introduced in fall 1998. The original individualized concentration is one of these fields, and that is where entering students work until they choose a specialization or where they remain if they decide to create their own program.

The new curricular fields are American studies, art and culture, classical civilizations, English and American language and literature, ethics and the professions, humanities, international affairs, medieval and modern European studies, religious studies, social/public policy, and the theory and practice of American democracy. In spring 1999, two new fields—Islam and Muslim–Christian relations and Catholic studies—were added. New courses have been created in each field to supplement previous offerings, some of them designated as core or human values courses. Each field has a designated core faculty adviser, usually a regular Georgetown faculty member from a related department. These faculty are the main advisers and sources of guidance for students in each field, although students may also consult any other faculty members for assistance.

In addition to the new definition of fields, some changes have occurred in course content and requirements. All students still take ten courses, two of which are drawn from core or human values courses, but the courses must fall in students' concentration. Except for students following an individualized plan, students take four additional courses, either field-designated liberal studies courses or other relevant courses from Georgetown departments. They then complete their work with three electives and a three-credit thesis research and thesis writing course in their concentration field. Individualized field students take seven courses in their planned concentration and the three-credit thesis course. All students still may transfer six hours of approved courses from other institutions. Departments have agreed to accept the liberal studies enrollees in their courses, provided department majors are given priority in enrollment.

The reflective essays in the original program have been discontinued in the new model. Their function of planning and interrelating study choices in the individualized sequence is now served by the continuing advice of the core faculty and the structure of the field course offerings themselves. Either in the fall or spring semesters, students also take the new, credit-free, nontuition Thesis Preparation Workshop, which meets for four two-hour sessions. Students nearing completion plan their thesis proposals in this workshop and enroll subsequently in the three-credit thesis research and writing course.

The MALS program has been self-supporting from tuition income; MALS tuition is lower than the tuition for traditional residential students. Although the program is administered from the School for Summer and Continuing Education, it operates under the aegis of the Graduate School, which has strongly endorsed it. The MALS program also maintains close positive liaisons with academic departments whose faculty teach in the program on an overload basis.

Summary and Future

The Georgetown MALS has benefited from the high educational and professional level of many individuals in its area and from the high regard in which its parent institution is held. The program has built on this to offer strong academic content in newly conceived terms that participants find stimulating and meaningful. It provides the offering in formats that are convenient for adult learners, and it supports learners with accessible and personally responsive services. The new curriculum options indicate a willingness to examine older practices and assumptions to maintain the vitality of the program.

So far Georgetown has had limited experience with the new model, but early response is encouraging. It has required considerable effort on the part of program staff to recruit additional faculty and plan new courses designed for the curricular fields. However, this method of change has avoided the challenge and delay of securing approval for a new degree. The revisions also preserve the integrity of the GLS liberal education approach yet offer participants from fields such as government service, international business and relations, and public policy study that has professional application.

CONCLUSION

The four programs examined in this chapter represent long experience but very different situations. Together they reflect the ways external circumstances can affect a program's fate but also how a program can adapt, develop, and thrive through its own initiative. Faced with threat, an adult learning program can recover rather than succumb; having achieved success, it can ascend to greater achievement rather than lapse into comfortable complacency. Failure is not always avoidable, and success is not assured, but this group demonstrates the value of undertaking continual efforts at renewal.

Skidmore asserted its independence from the University Without Walls structure at an early stage, but it retained the model to an unusual degree. None of the present staff personally remember the program's origins, but they maintain the program's concepts and spirit. The program has enjoyed the asset of leadership tolerance at the least and active leadership support more recently and the further asset of Skidmore's reputation, especially in the arts, which has attracted a following over a wide area. Faculty and staff have kept the UWW program fresh with new content and individual adaptability. The program's future is reinforced by the regard it has from the rest of the institution and its integration with that institution.

After its initial success the University of Oklahoma's Bachelor of Liberal Studies degree maintained the tradition of the nontradition, even in the face of loss of its large-scale audience and its early favored position in the degree marketplace. Then it initiated innovations that attracted new interest and maintained its institutional support. Eventually, however, it found itself caught between a continuing audience for its basic model and a larger audience for whom that model was inappropriate. It chose to meet learner needs in both ways by developing two parallel models with elements of the original but addressing the new audiences with new content and new delivery.

Alfred North Whitehead College developed a model of adult learning delivery in the mid-1970s that was applicable to various content. It soon found itself in an economic, social, and political roller-coaster environment that affected its programming in ways it could not control. Internal changes that alienated some faculty made its situation even more difficult. By adapting its model to new content and new audiences and by maintaining core institutional values, it demonstrated its value to the institution and established itself as a major provider in its region.

Georgetown's Master of Liberal Arts program has built on existing success to differentiate its offerings for a broader audience. The new curriculum tracks it has developed are consistent with liberal studies values but offer concentrations that appeal to multiple motivations of learners. Its first year has started well and shows promise for the future.

These experiences suggest some lessons for adult learning programs:

- Avoid complacency.
- Maintain constant awareness of changes in learners' needs and the environment.
- Be willing to try new content and approaches within a context of core values.

10

CONCLUSION

Summary of Best Practices and
Future Trends in Adult Credit Programs

CLEARLY IN ADULT CREDIT and degree programs, one size does not fit all. Adult learning institutions and programs have multiple missions and purposes that lead them toward differing goals and objectives. Their divergent histories and traditions cause them to select varying tasks and to apply distinctive values as they undertake their work. Their past experience or immediate environment may suggest specific populations or educational needs for them to serve. Availability of resources such as underused physical facilities or surplus faculty in areas of declining enrollment may enable them to explore new activities; alternatively, shortage of facilities may limit how much they can do without external assistance. In some instances the stimulus for new programs may come from economic, social, and community sources who call upon the institutions for assistance. Further, some innovative programs and institutions that have been highly valuable to adults, such as the University Without Walls and Empire State College, were not initially conceived to serve adults solely even though persons over twenty-five years old have become their major patrons. The range and variety of programs offered therefore is extensive. Selecting programs that exemplify good practice, as I have done here, is not a contest in which there are winners and losers. Rather, the choice is a statement that, taken collectively, these programs and others like them constitute an excellent response to the needs of adult learners. My aim has been to discuss examples concretely and in depth to display characteristics that have made these and similar programs effective and viable, often for many years, so that others may benefit from the programs' experience.

Many excellent programs have not been included here, some dealing with populations and services beyond those discussed. However, my goal has been to deal with elements and systems that have proved successful in a broad enough set of circumstances that they can be illustrative of a range of possibilities. I hope practitioners will find these possibilities to be a bank of resources that they may adopt or reconfigure in new combinations.

Although these examples represent a broad variety of circumstances, they are unified by discussions in each case of most, if not all, of the domains, or characteristics, discussed at the end of Chapter Two. These domains arose from my review of the ideas of scholars, practitioners, and administrators with long experience in adult education. Eleven characteristics stand out:

- Clarity of mission and purpose
- A strong commitment, including funding, to undertake the program
- Appropriate match between learners and the program, as exhibited through recruitment, admission, entry, and continuing practices
- Provision of a favorable climate of learning, including advising and other services
- Provision of a learner-oriented curriculum and modes of learning
- Adaptability to learner circumstances, either individually or in context
- Recognition and involvement of learner experience.
- Commitment and development of faculty and staff
- Clearly identified administration and governance
- Ongoing program evaluation and documentation
- Positive program impact and future prospects

The programs described in this book participate in all these characteristics, although to varying degrees. In summarizing them here, I highlight some of the more prominent examples of each.

CLARITY OF MISSION AND PURPOSE

Clarity of mission and purpose is important for both the institution and the adult learner program. It can define what program creators will or will not attempt, and examination of mission can open new insights about appropriate program elements. Similarly, a distinct mission can set a program apart and provide learners with a basis for choosing one program over another. Often missions are normative, reflecting the institution's historical values, and these values in turn influence curriculum. Alverno College adopted competence-based learning after reexamining its educational mission to its students. The Prescott College adult master's degree is shaped by the college's regard for its multicultural setting and natural environment. Regents College is guided by a mission to acknowledge whatever learners know and can do, regardless of how learned. DePaul University and Harry S. Truman College, although having different origins, share a commitment to the people of Chicago and the disadvantaged. Rio Salado College's partnership programs seek to enhance the local economy and workforce capability through collaborative relations with local employers.

STRONG ORIGIN AND COMMITMENT

The origins of and commitment to adult learner programs are extremely varied, as are their means of funding during start-up and the subsequent continuation. The first steps toward an innovation reflect the mission and commitment of an institution, which in turn can bode well for the program's later success. A number of the early and large-scale innovations arose from a far-sighted system or from institutional leaders who recognized needs and envisioned new means of satisfying them. Such was the case with Empire State College, Regents College, and the University Without Walls. These programs were fortunate in their time, because major foundations were prepared to invest in the start-up costs, with public funds or program income providing additional support once the programs were under way. In other cases, presidents or other high-level leaders stimulated faculty and other administrators to explore new ideas that led to proposals. Some programs were fortunate enough to find external funding to assist at the beginning, as the University of Oklahoma Bachelor of Liberal Studies program, the Duke University Master of Arts in Liberal Studies program, and the Truman-DePaul Bridge program did. Others launched themselves, using internal institutional resources or extra commitment of faculty and staff. Examples are the Atlantic Union and Columbia Union degree completion programs, the University of Minnesota applied bachelor's degrees, and the University of Memphis individualized degrees. Some others, such as the Thomas More degree completion program and the Fielding Institute Master of Arts in Organization Design and Effectiveness, arose from initiatives of faculty members with the aid of internal resources. Most of these are expected to become self-sustaining from program income.

Finally, a group of diverse programs has been stimulated by the initiatives of potential clients, many of whom have assisted with start-up and continuation costs. The Central Maine individualized associate degrees were a response to specific learners. The Next Step program was created at the request of NYNEX and two of its unions. The Rensselaer Polytechnic Institute RSVP program emerged from the requests of long-time industry supporters for master's degrees for their personnel. Toyota convened a group of institutions to make education available to its workers.

APPROPRIATE MATCH BETWEEN LEARNERS AND PROGRAM

Many students of adult learning emphasize the importance of receptive and supportive climates for persons entering programs. This regard for students can begin with formal needs assessments, such as those conducted by the Alfred North Whitehead College at the University of Redlands, or with the less formal sensing of learner needs conducted by nearly all programs. Simplified admissions processes also facilitate new students' entry although this does not mean elimination of appropriate selectivity. Specific background or capability, such as evidence of motivation, writing ability, or foundation knowledge in a field, may be essential for success in a program and should be assessed. Flexibility in other admission requirements not as critical for adults as for younger students, such as standardized test scores or minimum grade averages, is usually helpful to adult learners. Most of the programs discussed here exercise such flexibility.

Persons entering programs with unfamiliar or individualized formats may also need assistance and support to understand the different system. Empire State mentors introduce new enrollees to the college's distinctive system, as do Regents College advising teams. Atlantic Union, Prescott College, Cambridge College, the University of Memphis, Capital University, St. Edward's University, Regis University, the Fielding Institute, and Nova Southeastern University all have extensive entry processes that acculturate adult learners to the new environment and continue support as they proceed in their special program.

PROVISION OF A FAVORABLE LEARNING CLIMATE WITH ADVISING AND OTHER SERVICES

Schlossberg, Lynch, and Chickering (1989) have argued vigorously for a comprehensive and continuing system of advisement and learner services throughout the adult learning experience. Such support is valuable not only at the outset, when many programs do make considerable investment in service, but also throughout the period of participation, including at the conclusion. Needs for advice and support change in the course of the program, but their significance is continuous.

The provision of advising and learner support services may be one of the strongest success factors of these programs as a group. Because so many of the programs have formats unfamiliar to learners and are individualized or offer major scope for learner choice, opportunities to discuss program planning, to identify learning resources, and to apply student experience are particularly important.

The methods of making advisory and other services available differ markedly from setting to setting, but nearly all the programs have made these services a central part of their design. In some programs with smaller numbers of students, such as the Duke MALS degree, the initial phases of the Truman-DePaul Bridge, and the Central Maine Technical College programs, the responsibility falls upon one or two individuals who make major personal commitment to this role. In other instances a new definition of faculty member has emerged. The Empire State faculty mentor engages with students much more broadly than a faculty member based in a single discipline elsewhere. At Regis, Capital, and St. Edward's, advisement interaction with students is intense, and major fractions of faculty assignments are devoted to that responsibility. At The McGregor School teacher preparation program, Cambridge College master's programs, and Fielding Institute Master's of Organization Design and Effectiveness degree program, significant peer advising supplements the work of advising faculty. Several programs, including those at RPI, Nova Southeastern, Redlands, University of Oklahoma, and Atlantic Union, use distance technology to supplement face-to-face advising. Some programs, as at Memphis and Redlands, hold recurring meetings at campus sites to establish an identification between the learners and the institution.

Other services vary considerably from one program to another. Where an adult program is conducted on the institution's campus, usually all student services are available to adult learners and at times scheduled for their convenience. Some programs working away from their campuses provide services at centers in the field, as Redlands, Dallas Baptist University, and the institutions participating in the Toyota Reach for the Stars! program do. Learner demand for particular services appears to vary considerably with different populations and the time and locations of program activities.

PROVISION OF A LEARNER-CENTERED CURRICULUM AND MODES OF LEARNING

Adaptation of curriculum and modes of learning to adult learner needs is one of the most pervasive characteristics of these programs. Repeatedly, innovative adult programs depart from assumptions made by traditional patterns of content and processes and ask instead, How best can our learning goals be achieved? Working from that question, they proceed to assemble elements of content, learning methods, flexibility, and integrated learning that accommodate adults' different learning styles and circumstances and accomplish their learning goals.

Some of the best examples of this adaptation and flexibility are found among the individualized and learner-centered programs discussed in Chapters Three and Four. These programs allow learners, working within fairly broad guidelines, to choose or negotiate unique content, to draw upon a variety of learning resources, to incorporate direct experience of what is being studied, and to proceed at their own pace and in their own locations. Empire State College, the University of Memphis, Atlantic Union College, Prescott College, and Regis University all are good examples of this approach. Other programs, such as Capital and St. Edward's Universities, Central Maine Technical College, and Cambridge College, give more structured guidance but still are highly responsive to individual differences and circumstances.

The same is true in many of the competence-based programs, such as Regents College, DePaul University, and The McGregor School. Even highly structured programs, such as the three cohort degree completion programs discussed in Chapter Five and the ANWC cohort programs, allow students to apply workplace experience or conduct projects related to circumstances in which they are involved.

Not all programs create totally new curricula for their sequences. They may enable adult participants to include preexisting courses in a program. Rensselaer's RSVP master's program is based on existing campus classes that are distributed by satellite. Many individualized or assessment of learning programs allow students to apply traditional courses to the degree plan. The University of Minnesota's applied bachelor's degrees include both existing departmental courses and specially created content, although the departmental courses may be presented in formats convenient for adults. The graduate liberal studies programs may include related departmental graduate-level courses as well as specially designed courses.

Many programs also emphasize continuing or summative elements that contribute to integration of the learning experience or yield a product that draws upon the whole program content and gives the learner an outcome that can be applied professionally in other useful circumstances. These summative elements may take the form of journals or portfolios of program experience, as at Cambridge College; periodic reflections in writing or seminars, as at The McGregor School; or final projects such as in programs at DePaul University, the University of Redlands, or the Fielding Institute.

ADAPTABILITY TO LEARNER CIRCUMSTANCES

A major adaptation in many programs is to alter meeting times and the academic calendar to provide greater flexibility or convenience. One of the oldest and most common changes is to offer courses in extended sessions on evenings or weekends, when participants are not otherwise engaged. Some programs have experimented with accelerated schedules that supplement class meetings with required study outside of class, as many cohort programs do. Dallas Baptist University courses offer nineteen different time formats. Atlantic Union and Prescott Colleges have arranged the academic calendar in longer blocks to fit program participants' needs. In the Next Step program, the employer sponsor gives participants a full day of release time with pay to attend classes, and New York City Technical College has adapted its teaching schedule to use this time. Programs with large elements of independent study or assessment allow learners to be self-paced, progressing as rapidly or as slowly as they need to fulfill learning segments.

The variety of curricula, methods of learning, and processes is very great. What it illustrates is how many creative alternatives to traditional classroom experiences are at the disposal of adult educators. These alternatives have the multiple benefits of encouraging more effective learning, relating that learning to other aspects of adults' lives, accommodating the different needs and circumstances of participants while they are in the programs, and leading to outcomes that have directly observable benefits for learners.

RECOGNITION AND INVOLVEMENT OF LEARNER EXPERIENCE

As we saw in Chapter Two, adult educators largely agree on the importance of experience to adults' self-concept and the significance of relating new learning to existing experience. Many adult programs have sought both to recognize the academically equivalent learning participants have gained from nonacademic experiences and to include planned experiences in the design of new learning. Many institutions throughout the country have been innovative in using prior learning assessment processes. The assessments may be based on institutional or standardized examinations, credit recommendations (by organizations such as the American Council for Education) for planned learning experiences, courses approved by licensing bodies, or portfolios that document individual learning achievements. Assessment processes are central to such assessment institutions as Regents College and Thomas Edison State College, and assessment programs are in place in most of the undergraduate institutions discussed here. Excellent examples are found in the programs at DePaul University, Empire State College, Dallas Baptist University, Regis University, and the University of Memphis. Graduate programs make less application of prior learning assessment, and some regional accreditation associations will not accept it at the graduate level.

In addition, many structured programs require or encourage direct application of course content to out-of-class activity, such as jobs or community involvement. Individualized program design often specifies application of content or observation and reflection on experience. A concluding program requirement may be a project grounded in experience. Such application is the case in the Bell Atlantic Next Step program and many cohort programs. The University of Minnesota applied bachelor's degrees, the University of Redlands BSIS degree, the Fielding Institute ODE program, and the Nova Southeastern University EdD degree all require experientially based applications for completion.

COMMITMENT AND DEVELOPMENT OF FACULTY AND STAFF

The programs examined in this book demonstrate many different modes of providing faculty and staff for adult programs. What unites the different cases is a deep commitment to the program by faculty and staff members, regular faculty and staff evaluation and feedback, and explicit efforts to provide initial and continuing faculty and staff development. When faculty and staff members are not physically proximate to each other, critical face-to-face contact is supplemented by other communication systems.

Most commonly, adult program faculty are drawn from the regular faculty of the institution and, if necessary, are supplemented by part-time or adjunct faculty. The graduate liberal studies programs at Duke and Georgetown depend almost entirely on regular, tenured faculty of the graduate college. The cohort programs at Columbia Union, Northwestern, and Thomas More Colleges all have approximately 50 percent regular and 50 percent adjunct faculty, although many adjuncts have participated over long periods. RPI depends on faculty who regularly teach departmental courses, some of whom may be adjuncts. Most regular faculty are employed on an overload basis, but occasionally some have adult assignments as part of their regular load.

A number of programs have specially designated, continuing faculty for the adult program. These faculty usually play roles different from those of traditional departmental faculty. Empire State mentors have responsibility for academic content in several fields but also perform several other functions. Faculty in such individualized or learner-centered programs as the DePaul School for New Learning, the Regis School for Professional Studies, and the adult programs at Capital and St. Edward's Universities have heavy advising or other assignments as part of their responsibilities.

Some individualized programs and those with considerable professional content purposely involve practitioner faculty, who are usually part time or ad hoc, in the individual student's learning plan. Individualized programs such as DePaul's or Prescott's adopt a team approach to advising in which one team member may represent field experience relevant to the student's degree plan. Others, such as those at Rio Salado or ANWC, have a small cadre of regularly appointed faculty who provide content leadership, but the majority of faculty are practice-based part-timers or adjuncts who often have taught in the programs for many years.

Some of the external or special programs or programs with unusual complexity have reconceived the faculty role completely. The Fielding Institute and Nova Southeastern University have small core groups of full-time faculty-administrators at headquarters sites who are joined by continuing but part-time faculty who reside throughout the country. Many of the latter are faculty at other universities, but some are in practice. They may lead clusters of learners or travel to various sites to conduct specialized instruction. Regents College has small groups of core faculty in specific content areas who describe and monitor content expectations in various fields, after which other specialized staff prepare learning guides, conduct advising, and develop assessment procedures. In the multistate Next Step program, most faculty are regular faculty at their home institutions, but procedures at annual faculty institutes and continuing electronic communication enable them to design and maintain curriculum content and exchange advice on aspects of the program. Several programs with dispersed sites, such as those at Empire State, Fielding, and Nova Southeastern, depend heavily on electronic communication for faculty cohesiveness.

Almost all programs have regular procedures for learner evaluation of faculty, and the faculty receive the results. Some programs, as at Atlantic Union, conduct mutual faculty and student evaluations.

All the programs have explicit processes for initial faculty orientation and later development. In a few smaller programs, this consists of individual discussion and counseling by the program director. However, in most, faculty attend recurring meetings to discuss the program and participate in special seminars on such topics as adult learning theory, new learning procedures, and use of computers and electronic communication. ANWC has an elaborate process for the identification and induction of new part-time faculty that includes several visits to the campus, demonstration of ability to lead an instructional group, observation of experienced faculty, and ultimately classroom monitoring of their own early teaching. Rio Salado, which has a very small cadre of full-time faculty, relies on its Adjunct Faculty Institute, which inducts practitioner faculty with an eight- to ten-hour initial orientation followed by faculty development seminars each semester.

Nonacademic staff are a critical element in the success of adult learner programs, to an extent even greater than in programs for younger students. For adult learners who do not spend extended periods at a campus and particularly in various distance learning programs, whether technology based or not, contact with staff may be their principal contact to the program. Staff may be able to supply information, solve problems, and take care of bureaucratic details that are inaccessible to the learner who does not regularly visit the program's home base. Friendly, informed, and concerned staff make a vital contribution to program morale. For these reasons, it is not surprising that many learners remember their programs as much in terms of a helpful staff member as in terms of faculty.

Many programs recognize this factor in their selection and preparation of staff. Through initial orientation, whether informal or formal, recurring feedback and advice, and explicit staff development activities, they acquaint staff with the special considerations of working with adult learners. Often this is undertaken in conjunction with faculty development activities, to develop a team relationship between faculty and staff. A good example is the School for New Learning at DePaul, where advising is central to the program design and both faculty and staff receive comprehensive orientation to its importance.

CLEARLY IDENTIFIED ADMINISTRATION AND GOVERNANCE

Adult degree programs reside both in organizations that offer many different educational opportunities, such as colleges and universities, and in institutions specially created to serve as hosts for them. Knowles (1962, 1977, 1994a), in his history of American adult education, articulated a set of "genetic" principles that made the point that adult education programs "tend to survive to the extent they became attached to agencies established for other purposes" (p. 258). It is a point he did not change in successive editions of the book, and it remains largely true, as many of the programs in this book demonstrate. Certainly, fledgling adult programs benefit from the initiative and support of a stronger host, but at the same time, the inertia and reluctance of a highly traditional institution can deter any effort on behalf of adults at all.

One of the developments of the last generation (which stands alongside Knowles's point) has been the emergence of numerous adult programs that reside in special-purpose organizations created especially to accommodate them. Often this occurred in the face of opposition from more conservative institutions and at considerable cost in energy and resources to the founders of the new entities. A few of these new bodies were creatures of public policy and benefited from that support.

Examples are Empire State, Regents, and Thomas Edison State Colleges. Other new programs have reflected private intellectual commitment, novel educational vision, and entrepreneurial skill. The Fielding Institute, Nova Southeastern University, Cambridge College, and Prescott College are examples, as are (among programs not discussed in this book) the Union and Saybrook Institutes, Walden University, and the University of Phoenix. As these more recently created entities mature, they risk taking on characteristics of older higher education institutions, but they demonstrate that new forms are possible.

Whether in general higher education institutions or special-purpose organizations, adult education programs benefit from a clearly identified administrative structure and visible status in the institution. Such designated offices can exercise sensitivity to adult clients and serve as advocates for the programs. It is desirable for the adult program to have considerable autonomy in decisions about academic content, faculty and staff, and regulations affecting the program, subject to the broad values and guidelines of the parent institution. The School for Professional Studies at Regis, the School for New Learning at DePaul, and University College at Memphis are examples of programs with such independence. In other cases, similar advocacy for adult programs can be achieved if program administration and faculty are included in decision making on a equivalent basis with other members of the institution. This is the case at ANWC, the accelerated degree program at Thomas More, and the College of Liberal Studies at Oklahoma.

Ongoing Evaluation and Documentation

All the programs represented here carry out continuing programs of evaluation, although the scope and extent vary. Evaluation by students of each segment of their experience, usually including comment on faculty performance, is universal. In most cases, evaluation information is also collected on staff and program administration. Evaluation results are communicated to those being assessed. A number of programs, but not all, have special means to recognize outstanding performance, varying from public notice of individuals at program or institutional social functions to specially designated awards and salary benefits.

End-of-program evaluations and postgraduation follow-up occur but are not as universal. One of the most extensive program completion evaluations is conducted by the Duke MALS program. Each year graduates receive a comprehensive survey questionnaire on all aspects of their experience in the program, and consistently about two-thirds respond. Most express strong satisfaction but also make useful suggestions for program development. Programs such as the University College at Memphis collect program completion information on students' experience in the program and their plans following graduation, including further education.

Fewer programs pursue postgraduation follow-up, although most have anecdotally based impressions of subsequent graduate experience, based on conversations and on requests for employment or graduate school admission references. Reports from these sources are positive and indicate considerable continuation in education. Most programs express a desire to undertake such follow-up study or have plans to do so. Yet many programs are small and have limited staff and find additional evaluation tasks difficult to carry out. It would be useful to undertake a comprehensive study of adult program evaluation and to offer support to those programs with meager evaluation resources.

The same is true of program documentation. A few documentation efforts—at the Oklahoma liberal studies program and Empire State College, for example—that attracted considerable attention at their outset or that made analysis of their innovation a priority, have yielded considerable publication. Other programs in technical or professional development areas—such as at Rio Salado and Fielding, for example—have attracted notice in human resource development publications. Some unpublished internal studies and reflection exist, but they are not easily available. One can only wish that more of such information would be collected and disseminated.

Positive Impact and Future Prospects

Many of the adult learner programs discussed here have had an important influence on the institutions of which they are part. At Columbia Union and Thomas More, adult learners have grown to nearly half the total enrollment of the colleges, and in many other cases adults constitute a significant proportion of the institution's total effort. At institutions such as Capital and St. Edward's Colleges and the Universities of Memphis and Oklahoma, curriculum elements developed for the adult program have been adopted or have influenced curriculum in the rest of the institution. Often reconceptualization of general education requirements for the adult program has proven attractive to the total institutional program. A less measurable impact, but one which many programs mention, is the effect on faculty members' teaching of younger students after their experience of working with adults. Many faculty are stimulated by their work with adult learners, finding approaches and applications of experience that are effective in both instances. The development of strong prior learning assessment programs for adult learners, as at Capital and St. Edward's, has led to the acceptance of assessment and a focus on learning outcomes throughout the entire faculty. And adult programs have brought idle facilities into use, as at Atlantic Union, and found mutually beneficial uses of faculty, as at Duke.

The external impact of programs is also very significant, whether it takes the form of service to important supporters or contribution to socially important goals. Nearly all programs achieve such influence. Some major examples are programs at RPI, Regis, Central Maine, Rio Salado, the University of Minnesota, Toyota and Bell Atlantic and their consortiums of colleges, Dallas Baptist, Empire State, and ANWC to enhance workforce and professional capability. Similarly, the Cambridge College and McGregor School programs to prepare teachers with a focus on those from minority backgrounds, the Truman-DePaul Bridge program to facilitate completion of four-year programs by disadvantaged learners, the University of Minnesota Child Abuse Prevention certificate program, and the Nova Southeastern doctorate in educational leadership all provide important social benefits.

All of the programs have given active consideration to their future development. Some foresee stability and moderate growth through continuation of their present activities. Many envision new areas of content they wish to address. Others are expanding their delivery options by adding facilities or new sites or applying electronic technology. Some of the most entrepreneurial activity is based on technology, and its proponents envision a new national and international scope for services they have offered locally in the past. Although some program leaders have commented in interviews about the strong competition among providers, all were optimistic about their prospects.

WHERE DO WE GO FROM HERE?

The main forecast of commentators on the future of postsecondary education is that more change is coming. Some, like the perennially optimistic Knowles (1994b), envision changes leading to a new Renaissance in which "colleges and universities will become essentially adult-education institutions," and, "our entire population will come to perceive learning as a lifelong process" (p. 23; see also Knowles, 1989, pp. 131–50). Others, such as Davis and Botkin (1994a, 1994b), Dolence and Norris

(1995), Noam (1995), and Rowley, Lujan, and Dolence (1998) anticipate turbulent times and major reconfiguration of the learning process. The times will be fraught with risk but also opportunity for those able to adapt. Above all, change will lead to new forms and mixes of accustomed organizations and activities.

No one can predict all the developments that will change the environment in which adults learn, but the following are a few that can be foreseen:

- Multiple opportunities for learning offered by diverse sources will replace the past monopoly of formal academic institutions.

- Learners will demand and find greater flexibility and fluidity in the learning process and the accrediting of learning.

- Technology not only will open up access to more learning but will conquer barriers of time, distance, and convenience that previously have been prohibitive.

- Learners will plan their own learning as they need it. They will demand just-in-time learning in segments or modules appropriate to their needs, and they will expect those modules to serve as building blocks to further credentials. They will seek out peers, knowledgeable persons, and other informal sources of learning wherever they are.

- Many learners will need guidance to and discrimination among the many sources of information and learning. Services along the lines of the Lifelong Learning Resource System (LLRS) that Knowles (1989) suggested may be necessary.

- Employers and consumers will have greater expectation that credentials accurately represent ability to apply learning and to perform roles based on that learning.

- Many persons will experience learning as a continual process intertwined with living that enhances their economic potential, enriches their lives, and engages them with their surrounding society.

- Disparity and inequality will continue among more and less educated people. Those who do not now recognize the value of lifelong learning will have to be actively engaged in developing their potential.

- Greater collaboration will be necessary among institutions to share resources and between institutions and client groups such as employers, unions, governmental agencies, and social agencies to achieve mutually sought learning goals.

What can the experience of adult learning innovation over the last generation bring to this rapidly changing environment? The answer is quite a lot.

First, innovation in adult programs and the new forms and processes with which adult educators have experimented have broken the constraints of older systems that prevented change. By asking questions such as, By what different means can we assist adults to reach the learning outcomes they seek? or, How can we reduce the barriers that prevent adult learners from participating in educational programs? adult education innovators have driven institutions to explore alternative processes to reach agreed-upon ends. The mold of old forms has been broken. The success of so many new forms establishes the precedent for further experimentation.

Second, the experience of programs such as those described in this book anticipates in many ways the adaptation and innovation that will soon be expected of postsecondary education generally. Examples of successful flexibility in time, place, and routine in nearly all these programs point the way for the greater flexibility that will be demanded in other programs. Adult learning program design indicates that numerous choices can serve students' varying goals. Highly individualized, or learner-centered, models can accommodate rich resources for learning and the self-determining initiative of many learners of the future. Faculty who serve as mentors or facilitators illustrate how personal attention can assist learners to select among learning resources, without compromising learners' autonomy as individuals. Simultaneously, more structured models that still show sensitivity and adaptability to individual learning styles can serve the more focused objectives of some groups of people. None of the programs remarked on here has solved the problem of how to reach persons who reject or are unaware of the possibility of learning, but a large number are marked by their inclusiveness and their involvement of persons who have been underrepresented in higher education in the past.

Competence-based programs demonstrate how their graduates will perform, whether in employment roles or in the humanist and socially beneficial application of broad-based learning. The recognition of previous learner experience in these programs and the incorporation of direct experience in learning plans is compatible with the circumstances of persons whose daily activities involve continual learning. These programs have broad experience in applying technology to learning. Many of their delivery systems are flexible enough to respond to urgent learner needs with modules that are appropriate and creditable. Numerous examples of collaboration among institutions or with learner sponsors to teach specific needed content demonstrate the benefits of that cooperation to the learners and the sponsors.

Much information and encouragement is available in the programs described here to help higher education institutions and other providers address future demands that can be seen only in outline at this time. These systems and their elements provide a base of information and experience that should encourage innovators of the future. A theme running through these programs that can give especial guidance is the consistency of each program with the mission and values of the host setting in which it resides, whether that setting has a history and tradition or is newly formed. If adult educators maintain that clarity of purpose and apply the experience of examples such as these to new challenges, postsecondary education can look forward to a bright future.

APPENDIX A

Members, Commission for a Nation of Lifelong Learners*

1995–1997

Morton Bahr, chair; president, Communication Workers of America

Eloise Anderson, director of social services, State of California

Bill Anoatubby, governor of the Chickasaw Nation

Evan Bayh, former governor, State of Indiana; U.S. Senator

Carolyn H. Becraft, deputy assistant secretary of defense (personnel support, families and education)

Anthony Carnevale, vice president for educational leadership, Educational Testing Service

Lawton Chiles, governor, State of Florida

Phyllis Eisen, executive director, Center for Workforce Success, National Association of Manufacturers

Melvin L. Gelade, commissioner of labor, State of New Jersey

Oliver W. Green, secretary-treasurer, Amalgamated Transit Union

Stanley O. Ikenberry, president, American Council on Education

Jeffrey H. Joseph, executive vice president, Center for Workforce Preparation, U. S. Chamber of Commerce

Deborah Kaplan, vice president, Issue Dynamics, Inc.

Augusta Souza Kappner, president, Bank Street College of Education

Sara E. Melendez, president, Independent Sector

*Titles at time of membership of Commission

Jules O. Pagano, executive director, Labor Advisory Board; vice president, American Income Life Insurance Company

Donald B. Reed, president and CEO, Cabletron Systems

Marilyn Schlack, president, Kalamazoo Valley Community College

FORMER COMMISSIONERS

Robert H. Atwell, former president, American Council on Education

Peter J. Calderone, former commissioner of labor, State of New Jersey

APPENDIX B

Programs and Contact Information

Antioch University
  The McGregor School
  800 Livermore Street
  Yellow Springs, OH 45387
  Tel.: 937–767–6321
  Fax: 937–767–6461
  Internet: www.mcgregor.edu

Master of Arts in Education with
Professional Preparation

Atlantic Union College
  Adult Degree Program
  South Lancaster, MA 01561
  Tel.: 978–368–2304
  Fax: 978–368–2514
  Internet: www.atlanticuc.edu

Baccalaureate degree program

Cambridge College
  Graduate Programs
  1000 Massachusetts Avenue
  Cambridge, MA 02138
  Tel.: 617–868–1000
  Fax: 617–349–3559
  Internet: www.cambridge.edu

Graduate programs, including
Master of Education

Capital University   Baccalaureate degree completion
  Adult Degree Program
  Renner Hall #139
  2199 East Main Street
  Columbus, OH 43209
  Tel.: 614–236–6374
  Fax: 614–236–6171
  Internet: www.capital.edu

Central Maine Technical College   Individualized Associate of
  Trade and Technical   Applied Science degree
  Occupations (TTO)
  General Technology (GET)
  1250 Turner Street
  Auburn, ME 04210
  Tel.: 207–784–2385
  Fax: 207–777–7386
  Internet: www.maine.com/cmtc

Columbia Union College   Baccalaureate degree completion
  Adult Evening Program
  7600 Flower Avenue
  Takoma Park, MD 20912
  Tel.: 301–891–4056
  Fax: 301–891–4023
  Internet: www.cuc.edu

Dallas Baptist University   Baccalaureate degree completion
  College of Adult Education
  3000 Mountain Creek Parkway
  Dallas, TX 75211–9299
  Tel.: 214–333–5337
  Fax: 214–333–5558
  Internet: www.dbu.edu

DePaul University
    School for New Learning
    243 South Wabash Avenue,
    7th Floor
    Chicago, IL 60604
    Tel.: 312–362–8001
    Fax: 312–362–8809
    Internet: www.depaul.edu

Competence-based baccalaureate
degree; Bridge Program

Duke University
    Master of Arts in Liberal
    Studies Program
    Box 90095
    Duke University
    Durham, NC 27708
    Tel.: 919–684–3222
    Fax: 919–681–8905
    Internet: www.duke.edu

Master of Arts in Liberal Studies

Fielding Institute
    Human and Organization
    Development
    2112 Santa Barbara Street
    Santa Barbara, CA 93105
    Tel.: 805–687–1099
    Fax: 805–687–4590
    Internet: www.fielding.edu

Master of Arts in Organization
Design and Effectiveness

Georgetown University
    Liberal Studies Program
    School of Summer and
    Continuing Education
    Box 571011
    Georgetown University

Increasing options in a Master of
Liberal Studies program

Washington, DC 20057–1011
Tel.: 202–687–5746
Fax: 202–687–8954
Internet: www.georgetown.edu

Harry S. Truman College   Bridge Program
1145 West Wilson Avenue
Chicago, IL 60640–5691
Tel.: 773–907–4067
Fax: 773–907–4464
Internet: www.ccc.edu/truman

Next Step   Associate of Arts Degree in
  Bell Atlantic/CWA/IBEW   Telecommunications Technology
Bell Atlantic Human
Resources
280 Locke Drive
Marlboro, MA 01752
Tel.: 508–460–4522
Fax: 508–460–4458

or

CUNY New York City
Technical College
Continuing Education and
External Partnerships
2 Metro Tech Center, Suite 4800
Brooklyn, NY 11201
Tel.: 718–260–4972
Fax: 718–260–4978
Internet: www.nyctc.cuny.edu

Northwestern College　　　　　　Baccalaureate degree completion
Focus 15
3003 Snelling Avenue North
St. Paul, MN 55113
Tel.: 651–631–5324
Fax: 651–628–3369
Internet: www.nwc.edu

Nova Southeastern University　　National Doctor of Education
Fischler Graduate Center for　　Program in Educational Leadership
the Advancement of Education
1750 NE 167th Street
North Miami Beach, FL 33162
Tel.: 800–986–3223, ext. 8530
Fax: 954–262–3903
Internet: www.edl.nova.edu

Prescott College　　　　　　　　Individualized master's degree
Adult Degree Programs　　　　　program
220 Grove Avenue
Prescott, AZ 86303
Tel.: 520–776–7116
Fax: 520–776–5151
Internet: www.prescott.edu

Regents College　　　　　　　　General competence model:
Assessment Program; Nursing　　associate and bachelor's degrees
Program　　　　　　　　　　　in nursing
7 Columbia Circle
Albany, NY 12203–5159
Tel.: 518–464–8757
Fax: 518–464–8777
Internet: www.regents.edu

Regis University   Baccalaureate degree programs

   School for Professional Studies

   3333 Regis Boulevard,

   ALC 313

   Mail Stop K-24

   Denver, CO 80221–1099

   Tel.: 303–458–1844

   Fax: 303–964–5532

   Internet: www.regis.edu

Rensselaer Polytechnic Institute   Satellite-delivered master's

   RSVP Program   degree programs

   Continuing and Distance
   Education

   110 8th Street

   Troy, NY 12180–3590

   Tel.: 518–276–8351

   Fax: 518–276–8026

   Internet: www.rpi.edu

Rio Salado College   Partnership Associate of Applied

   Division of Applied Programs   Science degree

   2323 West 14th Street

   Tempe, AZ 85281–6950

   Tel.: 602–517–8519

   Fax: 602–517–8519

   Internet: www.rio.maricopa.edu

St. Edward's University   Baccalaureate degree completion

   New College

   3001 South Congress

   Austin, TX 78704

   Tel.: 512–448–8700

Fax: 512–448–8767

Internet:
www.stedwards.edu/home.htm

Skidmore College   Individualized bachelor's degrees
University Without Walls
815 North Broadway
Saratoga Springs, NY
12866–1632
Tel.: 518–580–5459
Fax: 518)580–5449
Internet: www.skidmore.edu

SUNY-Empire State College   Individualized associate and
Corporate/College Program   bachelor's degrees
8 Metro Tech, Rm. 524
Brooklyn, NY 11201
Tel.: 718–260–1123
Fax: 718–260–1141
Internet: www.esc.edu

or

SUNY-Empire State College   Individualized baccalaureate degree
Office of Academic Affairs
One Union Avenue
Saratoga Springs, NY 12866
Tel.: 518–587–2100
Fax: 518–587–5448
Internet: www.esc.edu

Thomas Edison State College   Associate and baccalaureate degree
Military Degree Completion   completion
Program
101 West State Street

Trenton, NJ 08608
Tel.: 609–984–1132
Fax: 609–777–2956
Internet: www.tesc.edu

Thomas More College   Baccalaureate degree completion
  Accelerated Degree Program
  Graduate Studies and
  Continuing Education
  2670 Chancellor Drive
  Crestview Hills, KY 41701
  Tel.: 606–341–4554
  Fax: 606–578–3589
  Internet: www.thomasmore.edu

Toyota Motor Manufacturing,   Associate, bachelor's, and master's
  Kentucky   degree programs
  Reach for the Stars!
  Georgetown College and
  Consortium Colleges
  400 East College Street
  Georgetown, KY 40324
  Tel.: 502–863–8033
  Fax: 502–868–8891
  Internet:
  www.georgetowncollege.edu

University of Memphis   Bachelor of Professional Studies
  University College
  Memphis, TN 38152
  Tel.: 901–678–2716
  Fax: 901–678–4913
  Internet: www.utmem.edu

University of Minnesota/Twin Cities Higher Education Partnership University College Program Development and Management 200 Wesbrook Hall 77 Pleasant Street SE Minneapolis, MN 55455 Tel.: 612–625–8831 Fax: 612–625–5891 Internet: www.tc.umn.edu/tc	Bachelor of Applied Sciences

or

University of Minnesota University College Child Abuse Prevention Studies Program 200 Wesbrook Hall 77 Pleasant Street SE Minneapolis, MN 55455 Tel.: 612–625–3475 Fax: 612–624–5891 Internet: www.tc.umn.edu/tc	Graduate certificate program
University of Oklahoma College of Liberal Studies 1700 Asp Avenue, Suite 226 Norman, OK 73072–6400 Tel.: 405–325–1061 Fax: 405–325–7132 Internet: www.uoknor.edu	Redesign of Bachelor of Liberal Studies program

University of Redlands   Bachelor of Information Systems
Alfred North Whitehead
College
Department of Management
and Business
1200 East Colton Avenue
Redlands, CA 92374
Tel.: 909–335–4068
Fax: 909–335–5125
Internet: www.uor.edu

or

University of Redlands   Bachelor and master's degree
Alfred North Whitehead   programs
College
P.O. Box 3080
Redlands CA 92373–0999
Tel.: 909–335–4041
Fax: 909–335–3400
Internet: www.uor.edu

APPENDIX C

Survey of Innovative Adult Credit Programs

AS THE CNLL PROJECT progressed, staff realized they would not be able to gather sufficient information on large numbers of programs by informal means or professional networking, although those sources were helpful. The W. K. Kellogg Foundation agreed to support a national survey to identify and elicit detailed information. Project staff planned a three-step survey. The first step requested chief academic officers to provide institutional data and contacts to adult program staff. The second step requested the identified program staff to provide detailed information on their programs. A parallel survey requested detailed information on prior learning assessment. The third step involved individual interviews with a selection of the program staff who responded to Step 2. The Evaluation Consortium of SUNY-University at Albany cooperated with the project planning, the design of several instruments, and the administration of the survey. Third-step interviews were conducted by the author of this book through site visits to or telephone interviews with approximately ninety programs.

The Step 1 and Step 2 program information questionnaires are reproduced here, along with the protocol that guided the Step 3 interviews.

SURVEY STEP I

Survey of Innovative Adult Credit Programs

Institution Name: _____

To: _____ FICE # _____

From: Project for a Nation of Lifelong Learners

Subject: Survey of Innovative Adult Credit Programs

As the accompanying cover letter indicates, the Project for a Nation of Lifelong Learners is seeking to collect information on significant innovations in credit programs to serve the needs of adult learners. *By program, we mean an organized sequence of credit work leading to a degree, certificate, or other academic credential.* Your cooperation in providing information on your institution will be of great help to our effort.

We ask your help in the following:
  A. Supply of the brief information requested on this form, and
  B. Referral of the second enclosed form to your Registrar or other student records officer with a request for completion and return of that information.
Thank you very much for your assistance.

1. Please indicate the primary population that your institution serves.
   __ Adult learners (25+ years old) __ 18–22-year-old learners __ both

2. Has your institution taken any specific steps in your credit programs to serve adult learners, such as modifying of calendar or time schedules; designing of special curricula for adult learners; extending hours of administrative offices, libraries, and student services; providing of specially planned student learning services for adults, etc.?
   ____ Yes   ____ No

3. Does your institution offer students opportunities to receive credit through Prior Learning Assessment, e.g., institutional advanced standing tests, nationally standardized tests such as CLEP or ACT-PEP: Regents College Examinations, ACE recommendations for military or

nonmilitary education learning experiences, portfolio assessment, or other *demonstration of knowledge, skills, or competency?*

_____ Yes   _____ No

4. Has your institution adopted an explicit mission statement or other policy statement that is intended to include access and service to adult learners as part of the institution's commitment?

_____ Yes   _____ No

5. Does your institution make an explicit effort to disseminate information among, and to recruit, adult learners?

_____ Yes   _____ No

6. If your institution does undertake special credit-related activities for adult learners, which three programs/efforts/services do you regard as your most successful examples of assistance to adults? Please, also, give us a contact to a person who can provide more specific information on the program.

A. _____
   _____
   _____
   _____

   Contact information:
   Name: _____
   Address: _____
             _____
             _____

   Tel.:   _____ Fax: _____
   E-mail: _____

B. _____
   _____
   _____
   _____

   Contact information:
   Name: _____
   Address: _____
             _____
             _____

   Tel.:   _____ Fax: _____
   E-mail: _____

C. _____
   _____
   _____
   _____

   Contact information:
   Name: _____
   Address: _____
            _____
            _____
   Tel.:   _____ Fax: _____
   E-mail: _____

7. Has your institution discontinued any credit program(s) primarily oriented to adult learners in the last 12 months?
   ____ Yes   ____ No
   If Yes, please supply the following:
   A. Name of program(s): _____
      _____
      _____
      _____

   B. Reason(s) for discontinuance: _____
      _____
      _____
      _____

8. Does your institution plan to initiate any new credit program(s) primarily oriented to adult learners within the next 12 months?
   ____ Yes   ____ No
   If Yes, please supply the following:
   A. Name of program(s): _____
      _____
      _____
      _____

   B. Reason(s) for initiation: _____
      _____
      _____
      _____

Contact information: Please supply the name and address of the person(s) in your institution who have responsibility for the following functions and who may be able to provide further information. If there is more than one person in each category, please attach an additional sheet.

Central Administrator for Adult Learner Programs/Services (if appropriate):
    Contact person name: _____
    Title: _____
    Address: _____
    _____
    _____
    Tel.: _____ Fax: _____
    E-mail: _____

Administrator for Prior Learning Assessment:
    Contact person name: _____
    Title: _____
    Address: _____
    _____
    _____
    Tel.: _____ Fax: _____
    E-mail: _____

SURVEY STEP 2

Survey of Adult Learning Programs

1. **Institutional information and contacts**
   1. Name of the program: _____
   2. Name of the operating unit in the institution in which the program resides: _____
      _____
   3. Primary goals/objectives of the program: _____
      _____
   4. Brief description of the program: _____
      _____
      _____
   5. Beginning date of the program: ___ / ___
      $\quad\quad\quad\quad\quad\quad\quad\quad\quad\quad\quad\quad$ Month $\quad$ Year
   6. Name of faculty and staff who have primary responsibility working with adult learners: _____
   7. Program contact information:
      Name: _____ Title: _____
      Address: _____ Tel.: _____
      _____ Fax: _____
      _____ E-mail: _____

2. **Admission procedures and requirements**
   1. How frequently are admissions accepted? ___ Once a year
      ___ Each term ___ Rolling admission
   2. Is there a required application fee? ___ Yes ___ No If yes, how much? _____
   3. Is there a required evaluation fee? ___ Yes ___ No If yes, how much? _____
   4. Is there an age requirement for admissions? ___ Yes ___ No
      If yes, what is the minimum? _____
   5. Check all admission requirements that apply to your program:
      ___ Open admission   ___ Minimum GPA
      ___ Previous credential/degree   ___ Minimum class standing
      ___ Standardized test scores   ___ Interviews
      ___ Letters of recommendation   ___ Personal statement of goals

___ Portfolio   ___ Placement examinations

___ Other (please specify) _____

6. Check any alternative means that are available to satisfy adult
   learner admission requirements:
   ___ Deemphasis of poor   ___ Recognition of recent
       early academic work   employment
   ___ Recognition of civic achievement   ___ Assessment of motivation
   ___ Autobiographies or personal interviews
   ___ Other (please specify) _____

3. Curriculum

1. The curriculum is primarily designed for: ___ Career
   development ___ Personal enrichment ___ Both
2. The outcome goals of the curriculum are:
   ___ Cognitive mastery ___ Competency demonstration
   ___ Both
3. The program offers an organized course, workshop, etc., near
   the beginning of the program to facilitate reentry and overcome learner resistance, anxiety, or negative feelings about
   education: ___ Yes ___ No
4. The curriculum (check all that apply):
   ___ Leads to specialization in a particular discipline or field
   ___ Is oriented toward an interdisciplinary or multidisciplinary
       approach
   ___ Is problem centered
   ___ Relates program learning to application
   ___ Emphasizes integration of the learning experience
   ___ Develops participants as lifelong learners
5. The curriculum involves the individual learner in the:
   ___ Planning ___ Design ___ Evaluation of the learning
   experience (check all that apply)
6. Check all experiential learning opportunities that play a signifi-
   cant role in the curriculum:
   ___ Workplace learning   ___ Cooperative education
       opportunities   programs
   ___ Internships   ___ Field work placements
   ___ Individually planned experiences ___ Service learning
   ___ Other (please specify) _____

4. **Student population**
   1. Please describe the primary audience you serve: _____
   _____

   2. Check all the special populations you serve (if different from the above-described primary audience):
   ___ Reentry women   ___ Persons with disabilities
   ___ Incarcerated persons   ___ Rural learners
   ___ Specific minority populations (please specify) _____
   ___ Specific occupational groups (please specify, e.g., business, industry, labor organizations or trade groups) _____
   ___ Other (please specify) _____

   3. Number of students enrolled in the last twelve months: _____ Number of students completing the program in the last twelve months: _____

   4. Please indicate: ___ The percentage of adult learners, and/or: ___ The percentage of traditional students

5. **Program completion award and credit requirements**
   1. What credential is awarded to students who complete the program? ___ Degree ___ Certificate
   Other (please specify) _____

   2. Check all academic levels for which your program awards a degree or certificate:
   ___ Certificate ___ Associate ___ Bachelor ___ Master Doctorate ___ First Professional Degree ___ Certificate of Advanced Study (post-master's)
   ___ Other (please specify) _____

   3. Is academic progress measured in credit hours?
   ___ Yes ___ No
   If yes, total number of credits required (sem. hr. equiv.): _____
   If no, what alternative is used? _____

   4. How many credits of the total are required to be taken at your institution (sem. hr. equiv.)? _____

   5. Number of transfer credits allowed (sem. hr. equiv.): _____

   6. Number of prior learning assessment credits allowed (sem. hr. equiv.): _____

   7. Check the types of assessments used for awarding credits:
   ___ Guides to military training   ___ Institutional challenge
       experience   examinations
   ___ Standard tests   ___ Portfolio documentation

___ Faculty interview   ___ Credit-free certificates

___ License qualifications   ___ Guides to employer or
other noncollegiate
training

8. What's the minimum GPA for graduation? _____

6. Instructional modes and delivery system

1. Check the instructional formats that your program uses:

___ Organized courses   ___ Workshops

___ Self-paced independent study   ___ Intensive meeting schedule

___ Independent study   ___ External degree formats

___ Delivery by one or more media   ___ Combinations of the
above

___ Distance technologies (i.e., e-mail, fax, computer conferencing, and/or cable TV)

___ Other (please specify) _____

2. There is flexibility in the: ___ Calendar   ___ Class meeting schedule ___ Learning sites

7. Responsiveness to external constituencies and organizations

In what ways do you customize your programs/services to external constituencies and organizations? (e.g., employers, unions, military or other sponsoring organizations)

_____

_____

_____

8. Adult learner services

1. How are your services provided for adult learners?

___ One-stop service ___ Multiple offices

___ On campus   ___ Remote sites

2. Are services available to adult learner families?

___ Yes ___ No

If yes, please list the service(s): _____

_____

3. Does the program have comparable budget support to traditional students programs. ___ Yes ___ No

4. Does the program provide services to facilitate entry into the program for adult learners? ___ Yes ___ No

If yes, please check all that apply:

___ Remedial courses or   ___ English as a second
tutoring   language
___ Combinations of the above   ___ New entrant counseling
___ Other (please specify)   ___ Orientation or educational
                                         planning

5. Does the program provide continuing services to support adult learners while in the program? ___ Yes ___ No

   If yes, please check all that apply:

   ___ Convenient registration procedures   ___ Opportunities for self-assessment

   ___ Library/learning resources   ___ Developmental monitoring

   ___ Academic counseling   ___ Other (please specify)

6. Does the program provide services to assist adult learners nearing completion of the program? ___ Yes ___ No

   If yes, please check all that apply:

   ___ Program exit courses   ___ Transition support groups

   ___ Job placement services   ___ Opportunities for

   ___ Other (please specify)   developmental assessment

7. Which of the following nonacademic services are available at times convenient to adult learners (check all that apply)?

   ___ Financial aid counseling   ___ Career counseling

   ___ Mental health counseling   ___ Campus security

   ___ Convenient parking   ___ Shuttle transportation

   ___ Student government   ___ Recreational facilities

   ___ Adult learner newsletter   ___ Child care

   ___ Food service   ___ Others (please specify)

8. How does your program recruit new learners? _____

   _____

9. **Program faculty and staff**

   1. Please indicate the percentage (%) for each type of program faculty:

      ___ Full-time ___ Part-time ___ Adjunct ___ Practitioner or community-based faculty

   2. Have you provided orientation for faculty/staff working with adult learners? ___ Yes ___ No

      If yes, in what ways? _____

      _____

   3. Have you conducted any evaluations of faculty/staff working with adult learners? ___ Yes ___ No

4. Do you have strategies that recognize faculty/staff performance with adult learners (e.g., rewards, promotions, etc.)
___ Yes ___ No
If yes, please describe: _____

_____

10. Program evaluation

1. Does the institutional administrative structure periodically review its sensitivity to and provision of services to adult learners? ___ Yes ___ No
2. Has there been any cost-effectiveness assessment of adult learner programs? ___ Yes ___ No
3. What explicit evaluation procedures have been applied to this program? (Check all that apply.)
___ Student evaluation ___ Faculty evaluation ___ Program/cur-
___ External assessment ___ Other (please   riculum review
___ Accreditation review   specify)
4. Did these evaluation procedures demonstrate that learning objectives/outcomes were achieved? ___ Yes ___ No
5. Are there any feedback measures of the program besides those listed above? ___ Yes ___ No
If yes, what are they and from whom? _____

_____

6. Describe the contribution of the program to equity for adult learners (e.g., rural learners, incarcerated persons):_____

_____

7. Describe the contribution of the program to publicly deter-mined goals (e.g., welfare-to-work): _____

_____

11. Program impact and visibility

1. Has there been any recognition, influence, or acknowledgments of the program elsewhere in the home institution?
___ Yes ___ No
If yes, please describe: _____

_____

2. Have there been any unanticipated or unintended conse-quences, positive or negative, for the institution from the program? ___ Yes ___ No
If yes, please describe: _____

_____

3. What are the innovative features of the program that break previous patterns? _____

_____

4. Has there been any exposure, recognition, or acknowledgment of the program beyond the institution? ___ Yes ___ No
If yes, please complete the following questions:
By whom? _____
Describe the type of acknowledgment: _____

_____

Describe any resulting links to other institutions: _____

_____

12. Program documentation
1. Are there any internal reports or studies of the program which can be cited? ___ Yes ___ No

_____

2. Are there published descriptions, reports, comments, etc., on the program which can be cited? ___ Yes ___ No
If yes, please give citations: _____

_____

_____

Thank You for Your Cooperation in Completing This Survey!

SURVEY STEP 3

Protocol for CNLL Interview Follow-Up Topics

Institution: _____ FICE # _____

Program: _____ Interviewee: _____

I.   *Program administration:* How did the program originate?
   A. Sources of program funding?
     1. Start-up?
     2. Continuing?
     3. Philosophy of funding of adult programs compared to traditional?
   B. Are tuition rates for adults the same as or different from rates for traditional learners?
   C. What do you see the future direction or development of the program to be?

II. *Program clientele/recruitment*
   A. How does the program assess its potential market and reach out to prospective enrollees?
     1. Any attempt to motivate persons who have not considered participation?
     2. Any effort to evaluate ability of potential participants to benefit, or to provide diagnostic service?
     3. Educational broker role?
     4. Effort to reduce barriers to access?
   B. What do you consider critical threshold factors in considering admission?
   C. Have you identified any barriers to access that you would like to remove?

III. *Curriculum goals, process, and outcomes*
   A. Goals—What outcomes do you seek for the curriculum?
   B. Process—What elements or methods of the curriculum most contribute to the successful achievement of these outcomes?
     1. What opportunities are there for student involvement in curriculum?
     2. Any experiential learning opportunities?
     3. Any sensitivity to multiple roles of adults?
   C. Any responsiveness in program design to needs of external

interests: e.g., employers, sponsors, public policy such as welfare-to-work transition, etc.?

D. Outcomes—Any effort to track or facilitate graduates after
completion?

   1. Any information on what becomes of graduates?
   2. Any effort to facilitate transition to next stage of education or employment?
   3. Any effort at articulation between this program and either
   level preceding it or level to which graduates may
   proceed?

IV. *Adult learner services*

A. What learner services most contribute to success in the program? (Entry, continuing, exiting?) Why?

B. Is there anything more that you would like to provide in services?

V. *Faculty/staff*

A. What proportion is there among different categories of faculty: e.g., regular/adjunct, full-time/part-time, community or
clinical faculty, etc.?

B. Any orientation to working with adult learners for faculty?
For staff?

C. What criteria are used in evaluating work with adult learners
for faculty? For staff?

D. Any strategies for recognizing good performance in working
with adults?

VI. *Qualitative factors*

A. Is the administration of the program or institution evaluated
for its sensitivity to adult learner needs? If so, how?

B. Does the program seek to ameliorate any conditions of disad-
vantage for groups of adult learners: e.g., rural learners, wel-
fare recipients, incarcerated persons, disabled persons, etc.

C. Is the program planned to contribute to any specific public
policy goals: e.g., welfare-to-work transition, dislocated
workers, inner-city development, health maintenance, etc.?

VII. Is there anything we have overlooked or that you would like to
amplify?

VIII. What is the most important lesson or achievement that you have
experienced in the program?

REFERENCES

Adelman, F. J. (1973). *The bachelor of liberal studies program at the University of Oklahoma: An evaluation of a functional equivalent in adult education.* Unpublished doctoral dissertation, University of Minnesota, Minneapolis.

Advanced Study. (Fall 1995). *Georgetown Magazine,* pp. 29–30, 64.

American Association of Community Colleges. (1993). *The workforce training imperative: Meeting the training needs of the nation.* Washington, DC: Author.

American Association of State Colleges and Universities. (1986). *To secure the blessings of liberty.* Washington, DC: Author.

American Council on Education. (1991). *Focus on adults: A self-study guide for postsecondary education institutions.* Washington, DC: Author.

American Council on Education, Center for Adult Learning and Educational Credentials, & The Alliance: An Association for Alternative Degree Programs for Adults. (1990). *Principles of good practice for alternative and external degree programs for adults.* Washington, DC: American Council on Education.

Antioch University, McGregor School. (n.d.) Statement of program philosophy and goals in letter to prospective students.

Apps, J. W. (1985). *Improving practice in continuing education: Modern approaches for understanding the field and determining priorities.* San Francisco: Jossey-Bass.

Apps, J. W. (1988). *Higher education in a learning society: Meeting new demands for education and training.* San Francisco: Jossey-Bass.

Aslanian, C. B., & Brickell, H. M. (1980). *Americans in transition: Life changes as reasons for adult learning.* New York: College Entrance Examination Board.

Aslanian, C. B., & Brickell, H. M. (1988). *How Americans in transition study for college credit.* New York: College Entrance Examination Board.

Association for Continuing Higher Education. (1997). *Code of Ethics.* Author.

Association of American Colleges. (1990). *Integrity in the college curriculum: A report to the academic community.* Washington, DC: Author.

Association of Governing Boards of Universities and Colleges. (1992, June). Higher education must change. *AGB Reports.*

Association of Governing Boards of Universities and Colleges. (1994). *The public policy issues for higher education in 1994.* Washington, DC: Author.

Association of Graduate Liberal Studies Programs. (1994). *Program descriptions of full member institutions:* Author.

Bahr, M. (1999, January 12). Lifelong Learning as a National Priority. Remarks presented at the Vice President's National Summit on 21st Century Skills for 21st Century Jobs, Washington, DC.

Barnett, R. (1994). *The limits of competence: Knowledge, higher education and society.* Buckingham, England: Society for Research into Higher Education & Open University Press.

Bassi, L. J. (1992). *Smart workers, smart work: A survey of small businesses on workplace education and reorganization of work.* Washington, DC: Southport Institute for Policy Analysis.

Bear, J. (1994). *College degrees by mail: 100 good schools that offer bachelor's, master's and doctorates, and law degrees by home study.* Berkeley, CA: Ten Speed Press.

Bear, J., & Bear, M. (1995). *Bear's guide to earning degrees nontraditionally.* Benicia, CA: C&B.

Bear, J., & Bear, M. (1998). *College degrees by mail & modem.* Berkeley, CA: Ten Speed Press.

Beder, H. (1990). Purposes and philosophies of adult education. In S. B. Merriam & P. M. Cunningham (Eds.), *Handbook of adult and continuing education* (pp. 37–50). San Francisco: Jossey-Bass.

Belasen, A. T. (1995, January). Mentor role variability and mentor versatility: Some implications for selection and development. *All about mentoring* (newsletter of the SUNY-Empire State College Mentoring Institute), pp. 11–14.

Bennett, M. J. (1996). *When dreams came true: The GI bill and the making of modern America.* Washington, DC: Brassey's.

Benson, A. G., & Adams, F. (1987). *To know for real.* Adamant, VT: Adamant Press.

Blackburn, J. B. (1997, March 5). Testimony at the Commission for a Nation of Lifelong Learners Forum on Demographic Trends, Dallas, TX.

Bonnabeau, R. F. (1996). *The promise continues: Empire State College, the first twenty-five years.* Virginia Beach, VA: Donning.

Boornazian, S. (1997). *Learner guide to prior learning assessment at Cambridge College.* Cambridge, MA: Cambridge College.

Boulmetis, J. (1997, January–February). Helping adults through their career transitions. *Adult Learning, 8*(3), 11–12, 15.

Boyatzis, R. E., Cowen, S. S., Kolb, D. A., & Associates. (1994). *Innovation in professional education: Steps in a journey from teaching to learning.* San Francisco: Jossey-Bass.

Breneman, D. W. (1995). *A state of emergency? Higher education in California.* San Jose, CA: California Higher Education Policy Center.

Brockett, R. G., & Hiemstra, R. (1991). *Self-direction in adult learning: Perspectives on theory, research, and practice.* New York: Routledge.

Brody, W. R. (1998). The university in the twenty-first century. *Continuing Higher Education Review, 62,* 28–39.

Brookfield, S. (Ed.). (1985). *Self-directed learning: From theory to practice* (New Directions for Adult and Continuing Education, No. 25). San Francisco: Jossey-Bass.

Brookfield, S. (1986). *Understanding and facilitating adult learning: A comprehensive analysis of principles and effective practices.* San Francisco: Jossey-Bass.

Brookfield, S. (1988). *Training Educators of Adults.* London: Routledge.

Brookfield, S. (1993). Self-directed learning, political clarity, and the critical practice of adult education. *Adult Education Quarterly, 43*(4), 227–242.

Brown, D. K. (1995). *Degrees of control: A sociology of educational expansion and occupational credentialism.* New York: Teachers College Press.

Brundage, D. H., & MacKeracher, D. (1980). *Adult learning principles and their application to program planning.* Toronto: Ministry of Education, Ontario.

Burkett, J. E., & Ruggiers, P. G. (Eds.). (1965). *Bachelor of liberal studies: Development of a curriculum at the University of Oklahoma.* Boston: Center for the Study of Liberal Education for Adults.

Business-Higher Education Forum. (1988). *American potential: The human dimension.* Washington, DC: American Council on Education.

Business-Higher Education Forum. (1997). *Spanning the chasm: Corporate and academic cooperation to improve work-force preparation.* Washington, DC: American Council on Education.

Butler, J. (1994). *High-technology degree alternatives: Earning a high-tech degree while working full time.* Belmont, CA: Professional Publications.

Caffarella, R. S. (1993). Self-directed learning. In S. B. Merriam (Ed.), *An update on adult learning theory* (New Directions for Adult and Continuing Education, No. 57; pp. 25–35). San Francisco: Jossey-Bass.

Caffarella, R. S. (1994). *Planning programs for adult learners: A practical guide for educators, trainers, and staff developers.* San Francisco: Jossey-Bass.

Cambridge College. (1997). *Graduate course catalog and policies and procedures.* Cambridge, MA: Author.

Cambridge College. (1998). *National Institute for Teaching Excellence.* Cambridge, MA: Author.

Candy, P. C. (1991). *Self-direction for lifelong learning: A comprehensive guide to theory and practice.* San Francisco: Jossey-Bass.

The Carnegie Foundation for the Advancement of Teaching. (1994). *A classification of institutions of higher education.* Princeton, NJ: Author.

Carnevale, A. J. (1991). *America and the new economy.* Washington, DC:

American Society for Training and Development & U. S. Department of Labor.

Carnevale, A. P. (1998). *Education and training for America's future.* Washington, DC: Manufacturing Institute.

Carswell, B. (1997, February 6). Testimony at the Commission for a Nation of Lifelong Learners Forum on Citizenship and Community, Miami, FL.

Cervero, R. M. (1988). *Effective continuing education for professionals.* San Francisco: Jossey-Bass.

Cervero, R. M., & Wilson, A. L. (1994). *Planning responsibly for adult education: A guide for negotiating power and interests.* San Francisco: Jossey-Bass.

Cervero, R. M., & Wilson, A. L. (Eds.). (1996). *What really matters in adult education programming: Lessons in negotiating power and interests* (New Directions for Adult and Continuing Education, No. 69). San Francisco: Jossey-Bass.

Chisman, F. P. (1992). *The missing link: Workplace education in small business.* Washington, DC: Southport Institute for Policy Analysis.

Clark, B. W. (1992). *The distinctive college.* New Brunswick, NJ: Transaction.

Clinton, W. J. (1997, February 5). President Clinton's State of the Union address—text. *New York Times,* pp. A14–A15.

Coalition of Adult Education Organizations. (1991). *A bill of rights for the adult learner.* Washington, DC: Author.

Collins, M. (1983). A critical analysis of competency-based systems in adult education. *Adult Education Quarterly, 33*(3), 174–183.

Collins, M. (1984). Competency-based adult education and variations on a theme. *Adult Education Quarterly, 34*(4), 240–246.

Collins, M. (1991). *Adult education as vocation.* London: Routledge.

Commission for a Nation of Lifelong Learners. (1997). *A nation learning: Vision for the 21st century.* Albany, NY: Commission for a Nation of Lifelong Learners. Copies of the report are available from Regents College, 7 Columbia Circle, Albany, NY 12203–5159; tel.: 518–464–8524, Internet: www.regents.edu

Commission on Higher Education and the Adult Learner. (1984). *Adult learners: Key to the nation's future.* Washington, DC: Author.

Commission on Non-Traditional Study. (1973). *Diversity by design.* San Francisco: Jossey-Bass.

Commission on the Skills of the American Workforce. (1990). *America's choice: High skills or low wages.* Rochester, NY: National Center on Education and the Economy.

Conrad, C., Haworth, J. G., & Millar, S. B. (1993). *A silent success: Master's education in the United States.* Baltimore, MD: Johns Hopkins University Press.

Council for Adult and Experiential Learning. (1992). *Closing the skills gap: New solutions.* Chicago: Author.

Council for Adult and Experiential Learning & American Council on
    Education. (1993). *Adult degree programs: Quality issues, problem areas
    and action steps*. Chicago: Author.
Council of Graduate Schools. (1989). *Off-campus graduate education*.
    Washington, DC: Author.
Council of Graduate Schools. (1994). *Master's education: A guide for faculty
    and administrators*. Washington, DC: Author.
Council on the Continuing Education Unit. (1984). *Principles of good practice
    in continuing education*. Silver Spring, MD: Author.
Cronon, W. (1998). "Only connect . . .": The goals of a liberal education.
    American Scholar, 67(4), 73–80.
Cross, K. P. (1981). *Adults as learners: Increasing participation and facilitating
    learning*. San Francisco: Jossey-Bass.
CWA/NYNEX/IBEW. (1995). *Next Step Program Strategic Plan, 1995–1996*.
    Marlboro, MA: Bell Atlantic Human Resources.
Darkenwald, G. G., & Merriam, S. B. (1982). *Adult education: Foundations
    of practice*. New York: HarperCollins.
Dave, R. H. (1981). Characteristics of lifelong learning. In K. P. Cross (Ed.),
    Adults as learners: Increasing participation and facilitating learning
    (pp. 261–263). San Francisco: Jossey-Bass.
Davis, S., & Botkin, J. (1994a). The coming of knowledge-based business.
    Harvard Business Review, 72(5), 165–170.
Davis, S., & Botkin, J. (1994b). *The monster under the bed*. New York: Simon
    & Schuster.
Delors, J., & Associates. (1997). *Learning: The treasure within*. Paris:
    UNESCO, International Commission on Education for the Twenty-First
    Century.
Dillman, D. A., Christenson, J. A., Salant, P., & Warner, P. D. (1995). *What
    the public wants from higher education: Workforce implications from a
    1995 national survey* (Technical report 95–52). Pullman, WA:
    Washington State University, Social and Economic Sciences Research
    Center.
Dolence, M. G., & Norris, D. M. (1995). *Transforming higher education: A
    vision for learning in the 21st century*. Ann Arbor, MI: Society for
    College and University Planning.
Dorland, J. R. (1978, June 20). *A national focus on competency-based adult
    education*. Paper presented at the National Invitational Workshop on
    Competency-Based Adult Education, Austin, TX.
Drucker, P. F. (1993). *Post-Capitalist Society*. New York: Harper Business.
Duffy, J. P. (1994). *How to earn a college degree without going to college* (2nd
    ed.). New York: Wiley.
Duke University. (n.d.). Master of Arts in Liberal Studies program brochure.
    Chapel Hill, NC: Author.
Education Commission of the States Task Force on State Policy and

Independent Higher Education. (1990). *The preservation of excellence in American Higher Education: The essential role of private colleges and universities.* Denver, CO: Author.

Education and the wealth of nations. (1997, March 29). *The Economist,* pp. 15–16.

Elias, J. L., & Merriam, S. (1980). *Philosophical foundations of adult education.* Malabar, FL: Krieger.

Elias, J. L., & Merriam, S. B. (1995). *Philosophical foundations of adult education* (2nd ed.). Malabar, FL: Krieger.

Elsner, P. A. (1997). Becoming a learner-centered college system at Maricopa. In T. O'Banion (Ed.), *A learning college for the 21st century* (pp. 167–188). Phoenix, AZ: American Council on Education & Oryx Press.

Evangelauf, J. (1990, May 23). Business schools are urged to rethink MBA curriculum. *Chronicle of Higher Education,* p. A30.

Evers, F. T., Rush, J. C., & Berdrow, I. (1998). *The bases of competence: Skills for lifelong learning and employability.* San Francisco: Jossey-Bass.

Ewens, T. (1979). Transforming a liberal arts curriculum: Alverno College. In Grant, G., & Associates, *On competence: A critical analysis of competence-based reforms in higher education* (pp. 259–298). San Francisco: Jossey-Bass.

Faure, E., Herrera, F., Kaddoura, A., Lopes, H., Petrovsky, A. J., Rahnema, M., and Ward, F. C. (1972). *Learning to be: The world of education today and tomorrow.* Paris: UNESCO.

Fielding Institute. (n.d.). Master of Arts in Organizational Design and Effectiveness program brochure. Santa Barbara, CA: Author.

Flannery, D. D. (1993). [Review of the book *Self-direction in adult learning*]. *Adult Education Quarterly, 43*(2), 110–112.

Fujimoto, J. (1992). *Educational implications of mainstreaming new Americans.* Paper presented at the American Association of Higher Education annual meeting, Chicago.

Gamson, Z. F., & Associates. (1984). *Liberating education.* San Francisco: Jossey-Bass.

Gantz, J. (1997, February 6). Testimony at the Commission for a Nation of Lifelong Learners Forum on Citizenship and Community, Miami, FL.

Garrison, D. R. (1997–1998). Self-directed learning: Toward a comprehensive model. *Adult Education Quarterly, 48*(1), 18–33.

Gibb, J. R. (1960). Learning theory in adult education. In M. S. Knowles (Ed.), *Handbook of adult education in the United States* (pp. 54–64). Washington, DC: Adult Education Association.

Gilley, J. W., Fulmer, K. A., & Reithlingshoefer, S. J. (1986). *Searching for academic excellence: Twenty colleges and universities on the move and their leaders.* New York: American Council on Education & Macmillan.

Glazier, J. S. (1986). *The master's degree: Tradition, diversity, innovation.* Washington, DC: Association for the Study of Higher Education.

Grant, G., & Riesman, D. (1978). *The perpetual dream: Reform and experiment in the American college.* Chicago: University of Chicago Press.

Grant, G., & Associates. (1979). *On competence: A critical analysis of competence-based reforms in higher education.* San Francisco: Jossey-Bass.

Gray, M. J., Rolph, E., & Melamid, E. (1996). *Immigration and higher education: Institutional responses to changing demographics.* Santa Monica, CA: Rand.

Greenberg, E. (1980). The University Without Walls (UWW) program at Loretto Heights College: Individualization for adults. In E. Greenberg, K. M. O'Donnell, & W. Bergquist (Eds.), *Educating learners of all ages* (New Directions for Higher Education, No. 29, pp. 47–61). San Francisco: Jossey-Bass.

Grissom, B. M. (1996). Clearly, vision is powerful. *Adult Education, 7*(3), 4.

Grubb, W. N. (1996). *Working in the middle: Strengthening education and training for the mid-skilled labor force.* San Francisco: Jossey-Bass.

Hall, J. W. (1991). *Access through innovation: New colleges for new students.* New York: American Council on Education & Macmillan.

Hall, J. W., & Bonnabeau, R. F. (1993). Empire State College. In V. R. Cardozier (Ed.), *Important lessons from innovative colleges and universities* (New Directions for Higher Education, No. 82; pp. 55–66). San Francisco: Jossey-Bass.

Hands, C. B. (Ed.). (1988). *The tradition in modern times: Graduate liberal studies today.* Lanham, MD: University Press of America.

Hargis, J. L. (1996). *Changing the institutional culture: Focusing on incentives.* Paper presented at the annual meeting of the National Association of State Universities and Land Grant Colleges, San Diego, CA.

Harris, R., Guthrie, H., Hobart, B., & Lundberg, D. (1995). *Competency-based education and training: Between a rock and a whirlpool.* Melbourne: Macmillan Education Australia.

Healy, P. (1998, February 27). A two-year college in Arizona bills itself as a new model for public higher education. *Chronicle of Higher Education,* pp. A32–A33.

Henderson, C. (1995). *Undergraduate certificate programs of less than two years: 1991–92* (Research Brief, Vol. 6, No. 1). Washington, DC: American Council on Education.

Henschke, J. (1991). History of human resource developer competencies. In N. M. Dixon & J. Henkelman (Eds.), *Models for HRD practice: The academic guide* (pp. 9–29). Washington, DC: American Society for Training and Development.

Henschke, J. (1992). Practicing what we preach. *Adult Education, 4*(1), 9.

Herr, S. R. (1997). *Connected thoughts: A reinterpretation of the reorganization of Antioch College in the 1920s.* Lanham, MD: University Press of America.

Hertling, J. E. (1980). Competency-based education: Is it applicable to adult education programs? In J. T. Parker & P. G. Taylor (Eds.), *The CB Reader: A guide to understanding the competency-based adult education movement* (pp. 1–7). Upper Montclair, NJ: Montclair State College, National Adult Education Clearinghouse.

Hiemstra, R. (1993). Three underdeveloped models for adult learning. In S. Merriam (Ed.), *An update on adult learning theory* (New Directions for Adult and Continuing Education, No. 57; pp. 37–46). San Francisco: Jossey-Bass.

Hiemstra, R., & Brockett, R. G. (Eds.). (1994). *Overcoming resistance to self-direction in adult learning* (New Directions for Adult and Continuing Education, No. 64). San Francisco: Jossey-Bass.

Hiemstra, R., & Sisco, B. (1990). *Individualizing instruction: Making learning personal, empowering and successful.* San Francisco: Jossey-Bass.

Holton, D. W. (1997). *The state of the Bridge: SNL/Truman Bridge internal report.* Chicago: DePaul University, School for New Learning.

Houle, C. O. (1961). *The Inquiring Mind.* Madison: University of Wisconsin Press.

Houle, C. O. (1972). *The design of education.* San Francisco: Jossey-Bass.

Houle, C. O. (1973). *The external degree.* San Francisco: Jossey-Bass.

Houle, C. O. (1980). *Continuing learning in the professions.* San Francisco: Jossey-Bass.

Houle, C. O. (1992). *The literature of adult education: A bibliographic essay.* San Francisco: Jossey-Bass.

Houle, C. O. (1996). *The design of education* (2nd ed.). San Francisco: Jossey-Bass.

House, D. (1991). *Continuing liberal education.* New York: National University Continuing Education Association, American Council on Education, & Macmillan.

Hubler, E. (1999, January 3). The new faces of retirement. *New York Times,* sec. 3, pp. 1, 12.

Hughes, K. S., Frances, C., & Lombardo, B. J. (1991). *Years of challenge: The impact of demographic and workforce trends on higher education in the 1990s.* Washington, DC: National Association of College and University Business Officers.

Jacobs, F., & Allen, R. J. (Eds.). (1982). *Expanding the missions of graduate and professional education* (New Directions for Experiential Learning, No. 15). San Francisco: Jossey-Bass.

Jarvis, P. (1992). *Paradoxes of learning: On becoming an individual in society.* San Francisco: Jossey-Bass.

Jensen, G., Liveright, A. A., & Hallenbeck, W. (Eds.). (1964). *Adult education: Outlines of an emerging field of university study.* Washington, DC: Adult Education Association.

Johnson, L. (Ed.). (1996). *Common ground: Exemplary community college and corporate partnerships.* Mission Viejo, CA: League for Innovation in the Community College & National Association of Manufacturers.

Johnston, W., & Packer, A. (1987). *Workforce 2000: Work and workers for the 21st century.* Indianapolis, IN: Hudson Institute.

Johnstone, D. B. (1994). College at work: Partnerships and the rebuilding of American competence. *The Journal of Higher Education, 65*(2), 168–182.

Judy, R. W., & D'Amico, C. (1997). *Workforce 2020: Work and workers in the 21st century.* Indianapolis, IN: Hudson Institute.

K–12 reform? No, make that K–16 reform. (1997, April). *Work America,* pp. 4–5.

Keeton, M. T. (1997, March 5). Testimony at the Commission for a Nation of Lifelong Learners Forum on Demographic Trends, Dallas, TX.

Kegan, R. (1994). *In over our heads: The mental demands of modern life.* Cambridge, MA: Harvard University Press.

Kelley, L. Y., & Joel, L. A. (1996). *The nursing experience: Trends, challenges and transitions* (3rd ed.). New York: McGraw-Hill.

Kerschner, L. R. (1992). Immigration: Recognizing the benefit, meeting the challenges. In *A challenge of change: Public four-year higher education enrollment lessons from the 1980s for the 1990s* (pp. 51–62). Washington, DC: American Association of State Colleges and Universities & National Association of State Universities and Land Grant Colleges.

Kidd, J. R. (1973). *How adults learn* (Rev. ed.). New York: Association Press.

Kirkhorn, M. (1979, April). Union for experimenting colleges and universities: Back from the brink. *Change, 11,* 18–21.

Knowledge supply chain: Managing K–80 learning. (1998, May). *Work America,* pp. 4–6.

Knowles, M. S. (1950). *Informal adult education.* New York: Association Press.

Knowles, M. S. (1962). A history of the adult education movement in the United States. New York: Holt, Rinehart and Winston.

Knowles, M. S. (1975). *Self-directed learning: A guide for learners and teachers.* New York: Association Press.

Knowles, M. S. (1977). *A history of the adult education movement in the United States* (Rev. ed.). Malabar, FL: Krieger.

Knowles, M. S. (1980). *The modern practice of adult education: From pedagogy to andragogy* (2nd ed.). New York: Cambridge Books.

Knowles, M. S. (1989). *The making of an adult educator: An autobiographical journey.* San Francisco: Jossey-Bass.

Knowles, M. S. (1994a). *A history of the adult education movement in the United States* (Reissue with new preface and bibliography). Malabar, FL: Krieger.

Knowles, M. S. (1994b). Predicting the future of higher education. *The Network* (Union Institute), *12*(2), 23–25.

Knowles, M. S., & Associates. (1985). *Andragogy in action: Applying modern principles of adult learning.* San Francisco: Jossey-Bass.

Knox, A. B. (1977). *Adult development and learning: A handbook on individual growth and competence in the adult years for education and the helping professions.* San Francisco: Jossey-Bass.

Knox, A. B., & Associates. (1980). *Developing, administering, and evaluating adult education.* San Francisco: Jossey-Bass.

Kohl, K. J. (1998). An expanding demand for postbaccalaureate education. *Continuing Higher Education Review, 62*(3), 57–63.

Kolb, D. A. (1991). The challenges of advanced professional development. In L. Lamdin (Ed.), *Roads to the learning society* (pp. 111–121). Chicago: Council for Adult and Experiential Learning.

Kolb, D. A., & Wolfe, D. (1981). *Professional and career development: A cross-sectional study of adaptive competencies in experiential learning: Final report.* (NIE Grant No. NIE-G-77–0053). Unpublished report.

Labor-Higher Education Council. (1992). *Investing in people: Education and the workforce.* Washington, DC: American Council on Education.

Lancaster, H. (1997, March 11). Companies promise to help employees plot their careers. *Wall Street Journal,* sec. 2, p. 1.

Langenbach, M. (1988). *Curriculum models in adult education.* Malabar, FL: Krieger.

Lawson, K. H. (1982). *Analysis and ideology: Conceptual essays on the education of adults.* Nottingham, England: University of Nottingham.

Lawson, K. H. (1991). Philosophical foundations. In J. M. Peters, P. Jarvis, & Associates, *Adult education: Evolution and achievements in a developing field of study* (pp. 282—300). San Francisco: Jossey-Bass.

Lindeman, E. (1988). Preparing leaders in adult education. In S. Brookfield (Ed.), *Training educators of adults* (pp. 93–97). London: Routledge.

Lindeman, E. C. (1989). *The meaning of adult education* (4th ed.). Norman, OK: Oklahoma Center for Continuing Professional and Higher Education.

Linder, J. C., & Smith, H. J. (1992). The complex case of management education. *Harvard Business Review, 70*(5), 16–24.

London, J. (1960). Program development in adult education. In M. S. Knowles (Ed.), *Handbook of adult education in the United States* (pp. 65–81). Washington, DC: Adult Education Association.

Long, H. B. (1991). Evolution of a formal knowledge base. In J. M. Peters, P. Jarvis, & Associates, *Adult education: Evolution and achievements in a developing field of study* (pp. 66–96). San Francisco: Jossey-Bass.

Long, H. B., et al. (1988). *Self-directed learning: Emerging theory and practice.* Norman, OK: Oklahoma Research Center for Continuing Professional and Higher Education.

Long, H. B., et al. (1990). *Advances in research and practice in self-directed learning*. Norman, OK: Oklahoma Research Center for Continuing Professional and Higher Education.

Long, H. B., et al. (1991). *Self-directed learning: Consensus & conflict.* Norman, OK: Oklahoma Research Center for Continuing Professional and Higher Education.

Long, H. B., et al. (1992). *Self-directed learning: Application and research.* Norman, OK: Oklahoma Research Center for Continuing Professional and Higher Education.

Long, H. B., et al. (1993). *Emerging perspectives of self-directed learning.* Norman, OK: Oklahoma Research Center for Continuing Professional and Higher Education.

Long, H. B., et al. (1996). *Current developments in self-directed learning.* Norman, OK: Oklahoma Research Center for Continuing Professional and Higher Education.

Longworth, N., & Davies, W. K. (1996). *Lifelong learning: New vision, new implications, new roles for people, organizations, nations and communities in the 21st century.* London: Kogan Page.

Lynton, E. A. (1984). *The missing connection between business and the universities.* New York: Macmillan.

Lynton, E. A., & Elman, S. E. (1987). *New priorities for the university: Meeting society's needs for applied knowledge and competent individuals.* San Francisco: Jossey-Bass.

MacKeracher, D. (1996). *Making sense of adult learning.* Toronto: Culture Concepts.

Martin, W. B. (1978–1979, December–January). The limits to diversity. *Change, 10,* 41–45.

Martini, L. (1997, April). Thomas Edison State College institutes new military degree completion program. *Military Educator,* pp. 15.

McGregor, D. (1960). *The human side of enterprise.* New York: McGraw-Hill.

McMenamin, B. (1998, December 28). The tyranny of the diploma. *Forbes,* pp. 104–109.

Medsker, L., Edelstein, S., Kreplin, H., Ruyle, J., & Shea, J. (1975). *Extending opportunities for a college degree: Practices, problems, and potentials.* Berkeley: University of California-Berkeley, Center for Research and Development in Higher Education.

Meister, J. C. (1994). *Corporate quality universities: Lessons in building a world-class work force.* Burr Ridge, IL: Irwin.

Meister, R. J. (1998). *Thoughts on Vision 2006.* Unpublished manuscript, DePaul University.

Merriam, S. B., & Brockett, R. G. (1997). *The profession and practice of adult education: An introduction.* San Francisco: Jossey-Bass.

Merriam, S. B., & Caffarella, R. S. (1991). *Learning in adulthood: A comprehensive guide.* San Francisco: Jossey-Bass.

Merriam, S. B., & Caffarella, R. S. (1999). *Learning in adulthood: A compre-hensive guide* (2nd ed.). San Francisco: Jossey-Bass.

Mezirow, J. (1991). *Transformative dimensions of adult learning.* San Francisco: Jossey-Bass.

Millard, R. M. (1991). *Today's myths and tomorrow's realities: Overcoming obstacles to academic leadership in the twenty-first century.* San Francisco: Jossey-Bass.

Miller, H. L. (1964). *Teaching and learning in adult education.* New York: Macmillan.

Modernization Forum, Skills Commission. (1992). *Skills for industrial mod-ernization.* Dearborn, MI: Author.

The multifaceted returns to education. (1998, June). *Workforce Economic Trends,* pp. 1–12.

National Center for Education statistics. (1997a). *Non-traditional undergrad-uates: Trends in enrollment from 1986 to 1992 and persistence and attainment among 1989–90 beginning postsecondary students* (Statistical Analysis Report DEd, OERI Publication No. NCES 97–578). Washington, DC: U.S. Government Printing Office.

National Center for Education Statistics. (1997b). *Projections of education statistics to 2007* (DEd, OERI Publication No. 97–362). Washington, DC: U.S. Government Printing Office.

National Center for Education Statistics. (1998). *Digest of education statistics, 1997* (DEd, OERI Publication No. 98–015). Washington, DC: U.S. Government Printing Office.

National University Continuing Education Association. (1993a). *Human resource development: Continuing higher education's role.* Washington, DC: Author.

National University Continuing Education Association. (1993b). *Principles of good practice for continuing education.* Washington, DC: National University Continuing Education Association.

Nesler, M. S., Hanner, M. B., Lettus, M. K., & Melburg, V. (1995, August). *External degree graduates at work: Some empirical studies.* Paper pre-sented at the Proceedings of the National Council of State Boards of Nursing, St. Louis, MO.

Neumann, W. (1979). Educational responses to the concern for proficiency. In Grant, G., & Associates, *On competence: A critical analysis of compe-tence-based reforms in higher education* (pp. 66–94). San Francisco: Jossey-Bass.

New York City Technical College. (1996). *National Science Foundation annual report of advanced technological education grant DEU 9553738 for year 1, August 1996.* New York: Author.

New York City Technical College. (1997). *An industry/education collabora-tion model: The final report of advanced technological education grant DUE 9553738 for 1995–1997.* New York: Author.

Newman, D., Stahl, M., Pierce, C. E., & Borelli, C. C. (1995, August). *Regents College RN-ADN program: Perceptions of graduates and supervisors.* Paper presented at the National Council of State Boards of Nursing, St. Louis, MO.

Noam, E. M. (1995, October 13). Electronics and the dim future of the university. *Science, 270,* 247–249.

Nolan, D. J. (1998). *Regents college: The early years.* Virginia Beach, VA: Donning.

Norris, D. (1996, December 2). Testimony at the Commission for a Nation of Lifelong Learners Forum on Educational Technology, Davis, CA.

Nowlen, P. M. (1988). *A new approach to continuing education for business and the professions.* New York: Macmillan.

O'Banion, T. (Ed.). (1997). A learning college for the 21st century. Phoenix, AZ: American Council on Education & Oryx Press.

O'Brien, E. M. (1992). *Part-time enrollment: Trends and issues* (Research Brief, Vol. 3, No. 8). Washington, DC: American Council on Education.

O'Callaghan, P. (1983). Teaching values for adults: Graduate programs in liberal studies. In M. Collins (Ed.), *Teaching values and ethics in college.* (New Directions for Teaching and Learning, No. 13; pp. 45–52). San Francisco: Jossey-Bass.

O'Callaghan, P. (Ed.). (1988). *A clashing of symbols: Method and meaning in liberal studies.* Washington, DC: Georgetown University Press.

O'Callaghan, P. (Ed.). (1997). *Values in conflict: An interdisciplinary approach.* Lanham, MD: University Press of America.

Offerman, M. J. (1997). Collaborative degree programs: A facilitational model. *Continuing Higher Education Review, 61,* 28–55.

Parker, J. T., & Taylor, P. G. (Eds.). (1980). *The CB reader: A guide to understanding the competency-based adult education movement.* Upper Montclair, NJ: Montclair State College, National Adult Education Clearinghouse.

Pelczar, M. J., Jr., & Solmon, L. C. (Eds.). (1984). *Keeping graduate programs responsive to national needs* (New Directions for Higher Education, No. 46). San Francisco: Jossey-Bass.

Perkins, J. (1997, March 13). Testimony at the Commission for a Nation of Lifelong Learners Forum on the Economy, Chicago.

Peterson, R. E., & Associates. (1979). *Lifelong learning in America: An overview of current practices, available resources, and future prospects.* San Francisco: Jossey-Bass.

Phillips, V. (1998, July). Online universities teach knowledge beyond the books. *HR Magazine.*

Pope, L. (1995). *Looking beyond the Ivy League: Finding the college that's right for you* (Rev. ed.). New York: Penguin Books.

Pratt, D. D. (1993). Andragogy after twenty-five years. In S. B. Merriam (Ed.),

An update on adult learning theory (New Directions for Adult and
Continuing Education, No. 57; pp. 15–23). San Francisco: Jossey-Bass.

Presidents Focus Group. (1997, February 11). Discussion on the future of lifelong learning at the Commission for a Nation of Lifelong Learners Focus
Group of College and University Presidents, Washington, DC.

Prisuta, R. (1997, March 5). Testimony at the Commission for a Nation of
Lifelong Learners Forum on Demographic Trends, Dallas, TX.

Read, S. J., & Sharkey, S. R. (1985). Alverno college: Toward a community of
learning. In J. S. Green, A. Levine, & Associates, *Opportunity in adver-
sity: How colleges can succeed in hard times* (pp. 195–214). San
Francisco: Jossey-Bass.

Regents College. (1998). *Annual report, 1996–1997: Regents college,
America's first virtual university*. Albany, NY: Author.

Regents College Alumni Association. (n.d.). *List of external graduate programs*. Albany, NY: Author.

Reich singles out NYNEX pact with unions as model for high-tech employers.
(1994, April 4). *Telecommunications Reports*.

Robertson, C. A. (1997). *A brief history of the Alfred North Whitehead
College of the University of Redlands*. Redlands, CA: Alfred North
Whitehead College.

Rowley, D. J., Lujan, H. D., & Dolence, M. D. (1998). *Strategic choices for
the academy: How demand for lifelong learning will re-create higher
education*. San Francisco: Jossey-Bass.

Rubenstein, E. S. (1998, Fall). The college payoff illusion. *American Outlook*.

Salomon Smith Barney Research. (1997). *Innovations in education* (No.
SF11E239). New York: Salomon Smith Barney.

Saltiel, I. M., Sgroi, A., & Brockett, R. G. (Eds.). (1998). *The power and
potential of collaborative learning partnerships* (New Directions for
Adult and Continuing Education, No. 79). San Francisco: Jossey-Bass.

Scheibel, J. (1997, March 5). Testimony at the Commission for a Nation of
Lifelong Learners Forum on Demographic Trends, Dallas, TX.

Schlossberg, N. K., Lynch, A. Q., & Chickering, A. W. (1989). *Improving
higher education environments for adults: Responsive programs and services from entry to departure*. San Francisco: Jossey-Bass.

Schlossberg, N. K., Waters, E. B., & Goodman, J. (1995). *Counseling adults in
transition: Linking practice with theory* (2nd ed.). New York: Springer.

Sharp, L. M., & Sosdian, C. P. (1979). External degrees: How well do they
serve their holders? *Journal of higher education, 50*(5), 615–649.

Sheckley, B., Lamdin, L., & Keeton, M. T. (1993). *Employability in a high
performance economy*. Chicago: Council for Adult and Experiential
Learning.

Shelton, E. (1983, November 29). *Competency-based adult education: The
past, present and future*. Paper presented at the National Competency-
Based Adult Education Conference, New York.

Sisco, B., & Hiemstra, R. (1991). Individualizing the teaching and learning process. In M. W. Galbraith (Ed.), *Facilitating adult learning: A transactional process* (pp. 57–73). Malabar, FL: Krieger.

Smith, R. M. (1982). *Learning how to learn: Applied theory for adults.* Chicago: Follet.

Smith, V. C. (1995, July). Retraining the troops. *Human Resource Executive.*

Sork, T. J. (Ed.). (1991). *Mistakes made and lessons learned: Overcoming obstacles to successful program planning* (New Directions for Adult and Continuing Education, No. 49). San Francisco: Jossey-Bass.

Sork, T. J., & Buskey, J. H. (1986). A descriptive and evaluative analysis of program planning literature, 1950–1983. *Adult Education Quarterly, 32*(2), 86–96.

Sork, T. J., & Caffarella, R. S. (1989). Planning programs for adults. In S. B. Merriam & P. M. Cunningham (Eds.), *Handbook of adult and continuing education* (pp. 233–245). San Francisco: Jossey-Bass.

Spille, H. A., Stewart, D. A., & Sullivan, E. (1997). *External degrees in the information age: Legitimate choices.* Phoenix, AZ: Oryx Press.

Stern, M. R. (1983). *Power and conflict in continuing professional education.* Belmont, CA: Wadsworth.

Stewart, D. W. (1987). *Adult learning in America: Eduard Lindeman and his agenda for lifelong education.* Malabar, FL: Krieger.

Stewart, D. W., & Spille, H. A. (1988). *Diploma mills: Degrees of fraud.* New York: American Council on Education & Macmillan.

Strosnider, K. (1998, January 23). For-profit higher education sees booming enrollments and revenues. *Chronicle of Higher Education,* pp. A36–A38.

Stubblefield, H. W. (1988). *Toward a history of adult education in America: The search for a unifying principle.* London: Croom Helm.

Stubblefield, H. W., & Keane, P. (1994). *Adult education in the American experience: From the colonial period to the present.* San Francisco: Jossey-Bass.

Sullivan, E. (1993). *The adult learner's guide to alternative and external degree programs.* Phoenix, AZ: American Council of Education and Oryz Press

SUNY-Empire State College. (1992). *Innovative graduate programs directory '92* (6th ed.). Saratoga Springs, NY: SUNY-Empire State College.

Svetcov, D. (1995, December 15). Business schools tailor MBA programs to lure students. *Chronicle of Higher Education,* p. A17.

Tennant, M., & Pogson, P. (1995). *Learning and change in the adult years: A developmental perspective.* San Francisco: Jossey-Bass.

Theibert, P. R. (1995). Employers partner with colleges to offer on-the-job schooling. *HR Magazine, 40*(10), 63–66.

Theibert, P. R. (1996). Train them and degree them. *Personnel Journal, 75*(2), 26–37.

Thorson, M. K. (1994). *Campus-free college degrees: Thorson's guide to accredited off-campus degree programs* (6th ed.). Tulsa, OK: Thorson Guides.

Tough, A. (1971). *The adult's learning projects: A fresh approach to theory and practice in adult learning.* Toronto: Ontario Institute for Studies in Education.

Tough, A. (1979). *The adult's learning projects* (2nd ed.). Austin, TX: Learning Concepts.

Toyota Motor Manufacturing, Kentucky. (1997). *Reach for the Stars! The Toyota on-site college education program handbook.* Georgetown, KY: Toyota Motor Manufacturing, Kentucky.

Troutt, R. (1971). *Special degree programs for adults: Exploring non-traditional degrees in higher education.* Iowa City, IA: American College Testing Program.

Tyler, R. W. (1949). *Basic principles of curriculum and instruction.* Chicago: University of Chicago Press.

UNESCO, World Conference on Higher Education. (1998). *World declaration on higher education for the twenty-first century: Vision and action* [On-line]. Available: www.education.unesco.org/educprog/wche/declaration_eng.htm

University Continuing Education Association & Peterson's Guides. (1993). *The electronic university: A guide to distance learning programs.* Princeton, NJ: Peterson's Guides.

University Continuing Education Association & Peterson's Guides. (1997). *Distance learning: Guide to distance learning programs.* Princeton, NJ: Peterson's Guides.

University Continuing Education Association & Peterson's Guides. (1998). *The independent study catalog.* Princeton, NJ: Peterson's Guides.

University Without Walls. (1972). *University Without Walls first report.* Yellow Springs, OH: Union for Experimenting Colleges and Universities.

The U.S. labor market: Getting inside the numbers. (1998, October). *Workforce Economics, 4,* 3–7.

Vaill, P. B. (1996). *Learning as a way of being: Strategies for survival in a world of permanent white water.* San Francisco: Jossey-Bass.

Valley, J. R. (1972). External degree programs. In S. B. Gould & K. P. Cross (Eds.), *Explorations in nontraditional study* (pp. 95–128). San Francisco: Jossey-Bass.

Van Dyke, J. E. (1995). New directions in education and training partnerships for business and government agencies. Unpublished manuscript, Rio Salado College, Tempe, AZ.

Van Horn, C. E. (1996). *No one left behind: Report of the Task Force on Retraining America's Workforce.* New York: Twentieth Century Fund.

Vernez, G., & Abrahamse, A. (1996). *How immigrants fare in U. S. education.* Santa Monica, CA: Rand.

Verville, A.-L. (1995, Fall). What business needs from higher education. *Educational Record, 76*(4), 46–50.

Wang, W.K.S. (1975). The unbundling of higher education. *Duke Law Journal, 53,* 53–89.

Waterman, R. J., Jr., Waterman, J. A., & Collard, B. A. (1994, July–August). Toward a career resilient workforce. *Harvard Business Review, 72*(4), 87–95.

What business expects from education. (1996, February). *Work America,* p. 7.

White, T. J. (1979). The United States: A review of higher education degree programmes specially designed for adults. In *New structures, programmes and methods* (Vol. 2, pp. 38–60). Paris: Organization for Economic Cooperation and Development.

Wlodkowski, R. J., & Westover, T. (1998). *Report on accelerated learning research project: Phase II* (Research study report). Denver, CO: Regis University, School for Professional Studies.

Zemke, R., & Zemke, S. (1981). Thirty things we know for sure about learning. *Training, 18,* 45–49.

INDEX

Date Due

AG 27 '00			
AG 20 '03			
AP 8 04			
SE 01 04			
AP 11 05			
May 27			
OC 30 05			